De-monopolization and Competition Policy in Post-Communist Economies

De-monopolization and Competition Policy in Post-Communist Economies

EDITED BY

Ben Slay

WestviewPress

A Division of HarperCollins*Publishers*

Copyright © 1996 by Westview Press, Inc., A Division of HarperCollins Publishers, Inc.

Published in 1996 in the United States of America by Westview Press, Inc., 5500 Central Avenue, Boulder, Colorado 80301-2877, and in the United Kingdom by Westview Press, 12 Hid's Copse Road, Cumnor Hill, Oxford OX2 9JJ

Library of Congress Cataloging-in-Publication Data
De-monopolization and competition policy in post-communist economies /
    edited by Ben Slay.
      p. cm.
    Includes index.
    ISBN 0-8133-8864-3 (hardcover)
    1. Privatization—Europe, Eastern.   2. Privatization—Russia
(Federation)   3. Government monopolies—Europe, Eastern.
4. Government monopolies—Russia (Federation)   5. Post-communism.
I. Slay, Ben, 1958–   .
HD4140.7.D425   1996
338.947—dc20   95-49745
                                                                              CIP

The paper used in this publication meets the requirements of the American National Standard for Permanence of Paper for Printed Library Materials Z39.48-1984.

10   9   8   7   6   5   4   3   2   1

Contents

Tables

Tables

Acknowledgments

While the list of individuals and organizations that supported or contributed to the creative processes that led to the publication of this volume is too extensive to be justly recorded here, a number deserve special thanks. In addition to the contributors to this volume itself, thanks go to Cindy Alexander, Josef C. Brada, Timothy J. Brennan, Gregory Brock, Jon Cauley, Christopher Clague, Cynthia Clement, Jay Creswell, Paul T. Denis, Michael Einhorn, Mary E. Fitzpatrick, Barry Freeman, Clive Gray, Gary Hewitt, Ryszard Hoffman, Jim Hughes, Barry Ickes, Andrej Juris, Georges Korsun, Jim Leitzel, Michael Marrese, Peter Murrell, Richard P. O'Neill, Armando Rodriguez, Gerald Sazama, John Tedstrom, Peter van der Hoek, Ferenc Vissi, Michael Ward, Spencer Weber Waller, and Robert D. Willig, for commenting on this volume in its various previous incarnations. Gratitude is also expressed to the American Council of Learned Societies, the LICOS Institute of the Catholic University of Leuven, the Open Media and Radio Free Europe/Radio Liberty Research Institutes, the Social Science Research Council, the University of Maryland's Program for Institutional Reform of the Informal Sector, and the United States Agency for International Development for supporting the research on which this volume is based. Thanks also go to Fritz Burkhardt and Judy Olinick, for printing and organizational assistance.

On a more personal note, I would like to thank my father, Charles Slay, from whom I learned my first lessons about business and antitrust, and my wife and daughter, Liza and Amy, for putting up with my prolonged absences necessitated by this project. I would also like to thank Susan McEachern at Westview Press, for her early and unflagging support. Last but not least, a large debt of gratitude is owed to the men and women of the competition offices in Russia, Eastern Europe, Mongolia, and elsewhere, who took time out from their arduous and often thankless labors to share insights and information with the contributors to this volume.

Ben Slay

1

From Monopoly Socialism to Market Capitalism

Ben Slay

On "Monopoly Socialism"

With the exception of natural monopoly factors, where advantages of size and scope make production by a few large firms less costly to society than production by many smaller firms, there is little disagreement about the importance of competitive markets for well-functioning capitalist economies, or about the need for some sort of competition policy to promote and maintain those competitive markets. By contrast monopoly, understood as the absence of competitive market forces, has been the subject of near-unanimous condemnation by Western economists for more than two centuries. By producing less and charging a higher price than would be the case under competitive conditions, monopoly in a static sense is associated with allocative inefficiency. Monopoly may also be associated with technical and X-inefficiency, in that short-run disincentives to selecting cost-minimizing output levels and production methods, as well as long-run disincentives to innovate and promote technological progress, may be linked to monopoly. Finally, Marxian critics of markets have argued that undesirable concentrations of economic and political power are associated with "monopoly capitalism."[1]

Not only is the undesirability of monopoly one of the few issues on which Western economists find themselves in near-total agreement, it is also one of the few areas of Western economics that has been wholeheartedly accepted and applied in transitional economies. While policy makers in these economies may have reservations about adopting orthodox macroeconomic stabilization programs or privatizing thousands of state enterprises, the neoclassical condemnation of monopoly has been adopted–and often extended–almost universally throughout the post-communist world. De-monopolization has generally been viewed as a key element of any successful transition from socialism to capitalism, especially in industry. The passage of competition laws and the creation of competition agencies were often among the first tasks market-oriented governments set for themselves in the early 1990s, while advice from Western competition policy makers has been frequently proffered (and often accepted).

When viewed in historical perspective, however, these developments are something of a novelty. Monopoly under Soviet-type socialism was not widely perceived as a problem until the late 1980s, and was rarely investigated before then.[2] Socialist ideology traditionally ascribed the problems of monopoly to capitalism and imperialism, denying in the same breath the existence of a socialist monopoly problem.[3] Central planning was supposed to prevent enterprises from reallocating resources away from the "optimal" uses determined by central planners. By the late 1980s, however, the critics of this view were clearly carrying the day, so that monopoly was increasingly perceived as a critical feature of the Soviet-type economy. As a Russian observer put it as recently as 1994: "Monopoly in Russian conditions is not only a feature of the economic position of individual enterprises: it is a property of the economic system itself, inherited from the mechanisms of administrative-command regulation of the economy."[4] The entire state sector was increasingly viewed as a monopoly, since: (1) production agents had a common owner (the state) that was uninterested in market competition; and (2) these agents were organized in a hierarchical fashion in which the logic of administration generally precluded horizontal relations. Indeed, because this structure of organization and ownership was part and parcel of the centralized political control over the economy, some observers have emphasized the political dimension of monopoly socialism in a manner not dissimilar to Western Marxists' treatment of "monopoly capitalism."[5]

More concretely, it was frequently argued that the Soviet-type approach to industrial organization produced high degrees of structural concentration. Although the exact course of developments differed by country and time period, the general pattern behind this concentration began with an initial assault on the private sector that drove entrepreneurs underground or to the margins of economic life. The large-scale nationalization of private firms and property (or their forcible collectivization, accompanied by the *etatization* of cooperative movements) was followed by increased structural concentration within the state and cooperative sectors, often as a result of centrally-directed horizontal and vertical mergers among firms in these sectors.

Since data on structural concentration were rarely made available, comparisons of concentration levels across capitalist and socialist economies have generally used average enterprise (or plant) size (usually measured by production, sales, or employment data) as proxies for structural concentration. A typical comparison of enterprise size in the UK, Italy, Czechoslovakia, USSR, Yugoslavia, and Hungary in 1988 revealed that "enterprises in the Soviet-type economies are more than ten times the average size of those in the developed market economies."[6] The creation of these large, vertically-integrated enterprises often meant that the communities in which they were located became company towns, so that perceptions of monopoly socialism reflected large firms' monopsony power on local labor markets.[7]

As Brown, Ickes, and Ryterman have pointed out, however, the case for high levels of structural concentration in Russia is actually much weaker than was long thought, and is in fact poorly served by arguments about average enterprise size.[8] According to their study, industrial concentration levels in Russia during the second half of the 1980s were similar to US levels, while the average size of Russian enterprises was smaller (and frequently much smaller) than enterprises in developed capitalist economies. However, although international comparisons of concentration data are difficult to interpret, similar results are unlikely to be forthcoming for the other economies examined in this volume (i.e., Hungary, Mongolia, and Poland). The Russian economy's vast size implies the presence of many more enterprises (and therefore potential competitors) in any given industry or branch, while in the other, smaller economies considered here, such potential competition is more likely to be supplied via international trade than from domestic sources.

In any case, monopoly socialism was not simply a matter of structural concentration and company towns. Even if industrial structures had been more atomistic, the central planning of enterprise production, supply, investment, and pricing decisions precluded the independence necessary for firms to behave in a competitive manner. Administrative organs such as the intermediate-layer organizations supervising (and responsible for) enterprise performance, as well as the industrial ministries to which these organizations were subordinated, played a key role in circumscribing enterprise autonomy.[9] And because they were in many respects responsible for influencing managerial behavior, these organizations could also be classified as monopolies. Similar charges may be leveled against the state committees and offices charged with price setting, or the administrative allocation of materials and supplies.[10]

Monopoly socialism was not simply an organizational matter either, since reforms that abolished traditional central planning and increased enterprise autonomy vis-à-vis the central and local administration (in Hungary in 1968, or in Poland during the 1980s) revealed the continued existence of many barriers to market competition. These included:

- restrictions on private-sector activities;
- restrictions on state enterprise production profiles;
- the absence of an independent judiciary, to adjudicate commercial disputes and enforce contracts;
- the lack of decentralized capital allocation mechanisms; and
- shortage conditions, creating and perpetuating seller's market phenomena.[11] Shortages of convertible currencies (or currency inconvertibility) precluding import competition and integration into the international economy were particularly important barriers.

These factors interacted to create a final dimension of monopoly socialism–significant concentration at the *product* level (i.e., products produced by a single firm). According to 1988 Soviet data, 87 percent of the items produced by the Soviet machine building sector were manufactured by single firms. In Poland, some 72 percent of 2,380 industrial product groups in 1986 were produced by a single firm. In Hungary, some 89 industrial products in 1988 were produced by a single firm.[12] By the end of the 1980s, then, it was widely recognized that effectively addressing the problems of "monopoly socialism" required the resolution of all these issues. As it came into existence, then, competition policy was inextricably linked to the liberalization of prices, commercial activity, and foreign trade, privatization, and the development of capital markets.

Finally, monopoly socialism had a political dimension. Large state enterprises possessed considerable bargaining power due to their size and "importance to the national economy." The principal-agent problems inherent in this situation created informational and incentive pathologies (e.g., the ratchet syndrome) through which monopolistic agents were able to parlay control over information and resources into stronger bargaining positions vis-à-vis the central and local authorities. Representatives of large state enterprises held seats in the Parliament and the Central Committee of the ruling Communist Party, and thereby enjoyed an inside track in bureaucratic battles for resources. And, as mentioned earlier, even under strict central planning, the large size of many producers translated into monopsony power on local labor markets.

Four types of explanations for the creation and existence of such a system have been offered. The first, "benevolent design" answer, stresses efficiency arguments for concentrated industrial structures under central planning. Euken argued that the administrative costs of centrally planning and managing a small number of large units were likely to be lower than the administrative costs of planning a large number of small units.[13] Pryor offers some empirical support for this proposition in the Hungarian and Polish cases during the 1960s, although the support was strongest in the case of industrial establishments, rather than enterprises. Pryor also found that the size of industrial establishments varied much less in socialist countries than in capitalist countries.[14] More recently, Newbery and Kattuman have argued that "concentration can be defended as enabling the state to reap the economies of scale that justify planning in the first place, for the market is least likely to operate efficiently when economies of scale are dominant and firms behave monopolistically."[15] In this view, the captains of socialist industry created concentrated industrial structures as part of their benevolent construction of a better society.

Second, monopoly socialism can be understood as an aspect of what might be termed the "gigantomania" syndrome–the Stalinist predilection for large size. One observer writing in the 1960s described this predilection by noting: "There is something 'socialist' and 'progressive' about mere size, even if unaccompanied by lower costs. Gigantomania as such...reinforces the view that large capital expenditures are a good thing, even where smaller ones will do."[16] Various explanations can be offered for his "predilection," including: (1) the traditional practice (taken, perhaps erroneously, from Marx's labor theory of value, and not formally corrected in most socialist countries until the 1960s) of not using interest rates in investment decisions; or (2) political desires to build "monuments" to the achievements of socialism, in the form of massive industrial behemoths. While such explanations can not be justified on efficiency grounds, they do possess a certain intuitive appeal, and in any case seem to have been widely held in many socialist countries.

Third, monopoly socialism can be explained on the basis of a malevolent grand design. Newbery and Kattuman argue that, since "the pursuit of economic and more general power is fundamental, and the extraction of surplus provides the means of maintaining that power," legalized monopoly is an excellent method of extracting that surplus.[17] According to this view, monopoly socialism was not about socialism *per se*, but was instead a particularly pernicious variant of rapacious political economy in which the state was not subject to effective social control. To the extent that this view is correct, it implies that politicians and bureaucrats directing the post-communist transition also have strong incentives to maintain some legal monopolies, in order to maintain their hold on power and "extract surplus." Not surprisingly, political and administrative opposition to de-monopolization and market liberalization is one of the most important barriers faced by competition policy makers in the post-communist context.

Finally, monopoly socialism can be explained on the basis of grass-roots enterprise/institutional factors indigenous to Soviet-type economies. The supply pressures associated with the shortage economy promoted vertically-integrated monopolistic structures, since vertical integration could reduce supply uncertainty. Indeed, because all agents (not just enterprises) faced supply uncertainty and other ratchet-syndrome problems, monopoly socialism was not limited to enterprises. Intermediate-layer organizations supervising enterprise performance, the industrial ministries to which they were subordinated, and the state committees and offices charged with the administrative allocation of materials and supplies, all felt similar pressures.

Dissatisfaction with this state of affairs was a leading force behind attempts at reforming Soviet-type socialism, especially during the 1980s (in contrast to transforming it into capitalism in the 1990s). Ironically, however, these reforms brought out three new dimensions of monopoly socialism. First, as wielders of political and economic power, monopolistic organizations were often able to block decentralizing reforms. Many of the reforms introduced in the Soviet Union and Eastern Europe during the 1960s and 1970s therefore contained strong centralizing (or recentralizing) elements that would have precluded the establishment of effective market mechanisms, had this been the intention of the reform designers (and often it was not).[18] Opposition from large enterprises, intermediate-layer organizations, and industrial ministries to reforms attempting to introduce some sort of market socialist system (e.g., the Hungarian New Economic Mechanism of 1968, or the Polish "first stage" economic reform of 1981-1982) was a major cause of the difficulties these reforms encountered.[19] Second, when reforms actually did devolve price and output decisions to enterprises, firms with market power often reacted by restricting output and raising price. And third, reforms that tried to introduce hard budget constraints often foundered on the inefficiencies of large enterprises, and on the lack of an appropriate institutional infrastructure (i.e., the absence of viable bankruptcy procedures, economic courts, capital markets, and active labor-market policies) needed to close them down or restructure them.[20] This underscored the fact that the welfare losses associated with monopoly socialism were at least as likely to result from technical and X-inefficiency as from allocative inefficiency.

Thus, the willingness with which post-communist reformers have seized upon Western criticisms of monopoly should not obscure the differences between monopoly under capitalism and socialism–or post-socialism, for that matter.[21] While long-run above-normal profits may be associated with concentration and monopoly in the West, the greatest social cost of post-communist monopoly may lie in the ability of chronically-unprofitable firms with market and political power to resist restructuring or liquidation. Alternatively, while Western competition policy makers may reasonably expect that above-normal profits will sooner or later attract entry, even in concentrated industries, post-communist competition policy makers are less likely to have such expectations.

Perhaps most importantly, competition policy in Western economies is largely concerned with safeguarding competitive forces already in existence from the appearance of new monopolies. By contrast, post-communist competition policy faces a more demanding challenge. On the one hand, competition agencies must play an important role in *creating* those competitive forces, rather than simply *safeguarding* those market forces already in existence. On the other hand, competition agencies must avoid adopting excessively interventionist policies that prevent the development of the enterprise independence that is essential for a well-functioning market economy. In this sense, competition policy must avoid becoming an obstacle to the effective implementation of other policies associated with the transition, especially market liberalization and privatization. Competition agencies that administer the prices of firms that can be classified (all too easily) as monopolies, and prevent the ownership of such firms from passing in to private hands, may prevent, rather than promote, the development of market competition. Finding the appropriate balance between these two approaches is perhaps the most difficult of the challenges facing post-communist policy makers.

Data Issues

Western discussions of concentration and monopoly generally occur within the framework of a given industry or industries (or, better yet, market or markets), and emphasize conclusions suggested by the relevant data. Of the country chapters in this volume, however, only Chapters 2 (on Hungary) and 5 (on Poland) attempt to do more than pay lip service to the data provided by the official statistical authorities on concentration and monopoly. The treatment of the official data in chapters 3 (Russia) and 4 (Mongolia) is even less extensive. This is not a coincidence. While obtaining comparable data for different countries over time poses major difficulties for any comparison of industrial structures,[22] additional problems appear in the post-communist context. Consequently, even in countries like Poland and Hungary, which can with justification claim to be relatively "advanced" in the transition, the official data are extremely difficult to interpret. In other countries, official data on concentration and monopoly are often unavailable. Some of the most important data problems are the following.

Measuring and Interpreting Concentration Levels

Defining appropriate product and geographic boundaries is difficult in any economy.[23] In the post-communist context, these difficulties are magnified by the official methodologies employed in measuring concentration levels. The data published in the Polish statistical yearbooks, for example, are modified concentration ratios (showing the number of firms accounting for either 50 or 80 percent of total branch sales), and Gini coefficients. Both instruments have well-known weaknesses as measures of structural concentration. In the Polish case, concentration ratios reveal nothing about the distribution of sales among the firms responsible for the 50 or 80 percent of total branch sales; while Gini coefficients are really measures of inequality rather than concentration.

Despite their problems, however, the Polish concentration data would seem to be better than the official statistics produced by the other countries considered in this volume.[24] The data published in the Hungarian statistical yearbooks, for example, show only the number of firms whose annual gross production figures exceed certain levels.[25] Not only do these data reveal nothing about the distribution of sales within a certain group; because they are expressed in current forints, they are biased upwards over time by inflation. It is somewhat puzzling that Herfindahl-Hirschman indices are not released to the public, since they are both superior measures of concentration and appear to be widely used internally by the competition agencies.

Market Definition Issues

In any case, industrial concentration is generally measured as the share of gross sales within a given industrial branch concentrated in the sales of the branch's largest firms. Because this methodology measures concentration levels within industrial branches, rather than markets, it overestimates actual (market) concentration when a given market is supplied by firms from different branches.[26] It may either overestimate or underestimate actual concentration when firms in a given branch supply more than one market.[27] This methodology also equates industrial branches with national markets rather than local or regional markets, thus underestimating the actual concentration present at the local and regional levels.[28] Export and import data are not included, so that official data tend to overstate concentration in net importing branches, and understate it in net exporting branches. Finally, the statistical authorities frequently do not gather comprehensive sales data for small firms (and therefore most of the private sector), which tends to exaggerate official concentration levels.[29] And of course, such measures do not incorporate information about demand and supply elasticities, which are extremely relevant to considerations of market definition and contestability. Thus, even if the data showing high levels of structural concentration are correct, their implications for market structure and monopolization can hardly be viewed as unambiguous.

It should also be remembered that the concept of a "market" is only as useful as the definition of the "firms" competing on it. What constitutes a "firm" (as distinct from a "plant," "establishment," "undertaking," or even "entrepreneur") is of course one of the great question marks of microeconomics. As Ádám Török points out in Chapter 2, the ongoing redefinition and restructuring of enterprise management, governance, and physical plant in the post-communist transition makes this question even more urgent in our context. Until the Coasian boundaries between these firms come into sharper relief, the challenges of market definition will be all the greater.

De-monopolization and the
Post-Communist Transition

Much of the attention accorded to competition policy and de-monopolization in the post-communist transition has focused on their relationship with price liberalization, macroeconomic stabilization, and privatization.

De-monopolization, Liberalization, and Stabilization

When prices were liberalized and macroeconomic stabilization programs introduced in the early 1990s, they were often followed by inflation rates and declines in output that were well in excess of official forecasts. While the explanations for these developments have been many and varied, a number have emphasized unanticipated and pathological responses by state enterprises to the new situation in which they found themselves.[30] In particular, some observers laid the blame at the feet of monopolies who responded to declines in demand by reducing output and raising price.[31] These arguments helped create an intellectual climate supportive of competition policies that maintain traditional regulatory mechanisms for monopolistic firms, or break them up prior to the liberalization of the state enterprise sector.

Two types of specific propositions about monopoly can be found in this regard. According to the first, firms with market power generate sustained (as opposed to one-shot) cost-push inflationary pressures by increasing prices and reducing supply in response to liberalized output and input prices and inflationary expectations. This view was recently elaborated by Starodubrovskaya, who argued:

> the classical monopolistic reaction to demand constraints is not to lower prices but, on the contrary, to raise them while at the same time reducing the volume of production. In conditions where monopolistic relations overwhelmingly predominate, there is in practice no alternative to this tendency. Even if an enterprise preferred a different strategy its scope for choice is extremely narrow, owing to the continual increase in prices of raw materials, with a limited number of suppliers, and the necessity of raising wages. Consequently, attempts at macroeconomic stabilisation in such a system will never be able to deliver a lasting positive result.[32]

The proposition that firms with monopoly power can raise prices above competitive levels on individual markets is quite unobjectionable. However, the consequences of such one-shot price increases in the post-communist context are not unambiguous. Enterprise decisions to reduce output and raise prices after price liberalization may reflect a shift away from the output-maximizing behavior associated with the shortage economy towards profit-maximization.[33] The higher prices may eradicate shortage pressures, while the "lost" output may have been associated with activities that were revealed by market pressures to be value-subtracting and (arguably) welfare-reducing. But even if such monopoly-induced price increases are regarded as uniformly undesirable, other problems with this "monopoly causes inflation" argument appear. This is because the dynamic argument for monopoly power causing sustained (if not accelerating) price increases (i.e., rates of price change) in the absence of validating macroeconomic policies differs significantly from the static arguments against monopoly pricing.

Monopoly is generally understood to be a partial-equilibrium phenomenon, while inflation is a macroeconomic or general-equilibrium phenomenon. Simple aggregation of the problems of monopoly pricing may therefore run afoul of the fallacy of composition. Moreover, in a transitional economy with a reasonably effective stabilization program and some relatively competitive sectors, relative price increases in monopolized sectors must *ceteris paribus* reduce aggregate purchasing power and thus effective demand in competitive sectors which, presumably, are unable to raise prices commensurably by reducing supply. Although output would presumably fall in competitive sectors, so would prices. This would act as a deflationary counterweight to relative price increases in monopoly sectors. If, on the other hand, price increases are made to stick in the relatively competitive sectors as well as the monopolized sectors, stabilization efforts are ineffective, and the root of the problem is macroeconomic, not microeconomic.

Starodubrovskaya's argument refers, of course, to an economy in which "monopolistic relations overwhelmingly predominate"–in which, presumably, there are no "relatively competitive" sectors. The argument assumes both that competitive market forces are completely lacking at the start of the transition, and are unlikely to appear quickly once the transition begins–even if aggregate demand is stabilized. For relatively small, open economies (like Hungary or Poland or, for that matter, most of the European post-communist economies), imports can provide competition for the producers of tradable goods. While import competition must inevitably play a smaller role in more closed economies like Russia, other sources of potential competition can presumably be found, include newly-created private firms, as well as potential competitors within the state sector. For these reasons, it is difficult to accept *a priori* this form of the "monopoly causes inflation" proposition.

The second proposition linking the difficulties of liberalization and stabilization to monopoly can be seen as a defense of the first proposition, and may be paraphrased as follows. The introduction of decisive marketizing reforms ultimately will mean bankruptcy for many large, inefficient state firms employing significant amounts of (now redundant) capital and labor. Because their net worth is often negative, privatizing these firms is a difficult proposition. Instead, their economic and political power allows these firms to force subsidies (explicit and implicit) out of suppliers, banks, and the fiscal authorities. The well-known problems of inter-enterprise debt and credit allocation by negative selection are the results.[34] The absence of viable creditor-initiated bankruptcy procedures prevents creditors from laying binding claims to the large firms' assets, which further short-circuits the financial system. As debtors, then, such firms enjoy a form of system-specific reverse leverage over creditors that either weakens their supply response to stabilization efforts, or produces perverse effects. Rather than attempting to reduce costs through restructuring, these firms are able to pass on higher input costs via price increases or the extraction of informal credit from suppliers, banks, and fiscal authorities. Weak supply responses to market signals, and cost-push inflationary pressures, are the result. Activist competition policies that break up large firms could moderate the scale of these problems.

This proposition is certainly correct in that large, influential (and frequently value-subtracting) state enterprises able to avoid restructuring, privatization, and adaptation to market forces clearly pose a threat to the transition. However, closer inspection of this line of reasoning reveals two weaknesses. First, the property-rights problems associated with state ownership are an important cause of this "impossibility of exit," since the absence of credible bankruptcy mechanisms can mean that even firms with little or no market power can successfully extort credit from their suppliers. To the extent that this problem is one of ownership rather than market structure, it may be amenable to solution via reform of banking and bankruptcy systems.[35]

Second, while the problems of large, powerful state enterprises certainly predate the post-communist transition,[36] reliable information about the *specific* problems posed by *individual* firms is only likely to be forthcoming after prices have been liberalized and budget constraints hardened. Only then does it become clear which chronically-unprofitable enterprises are unprofitable because of bad management and distortions in the price system–problems that may be corrected easily (if not automatically) once the transition takes hold–and which enterprises are dinosaurs destined for extinction. Competition policies that break up large, chronically-insolvent state firms before hard budget constraints and viable bankruptcy regimes are in place thus run the risk of destroying firms that could emerge as winners under market conditions. Of course, creditors may prove to be no match for the political power of large-firm debtors, even in a reformed bankruptcy system. But why should the competition agencies be expected to have better luck? So while the difficulties posed for post-communist banking and financial systems by large state enterprises must be taken seriously, it is not clear that they offer a compelling *a priori* justification for activist competition policies.

De-monopolization and Privatization

Of the links between different elements of the transition, the relationship between de-monopolization and privatization has perhaps been the most controversial. Much of the controversy revolves around the following tension: governments are unlikely to be able to robustly privatize monopolistic firms if they also attempt, either simultaneously or subsequently, to pursue ambitious competition policies. This is because dissolution, divestiture, or close regulation of monopolistic firms prior to their privatization can be expected to reduce the monopoly rents that would otherwise allow the government to sell the firms at a premium. Indeed, even the threat of pursuing activist competition policies after regulation could be enough to reduce the firms' sale values. The privatization of monopolistic firms therefore has to yield to competition policy, or vice-versa. Alternatively, if privatization and de-monopolization are to take place together, the latter will have occur without the aid of dissolutions, divestitures, or close regulation by the competition authorities.

This tension seems to pose a number of stark choices. On the one hand, privatization without de-monopolization may simply reproduce the monopoly problem in its capitalist form, by creating large, privately-owned firms that misallocate resources and damage market competition via monopolistic practices. On the other hand, activist competition policies may perpetuate the administrative controls over enterprises that the transition is intended to eliminate. Should the privatization of monopolistic state enterprises be given priority over competition policies intended to promote de-monopolization, or should their privatization be subordinated to the strict dictates of competition policy? If the latter, under what conditions should monopolistic state firms be broken up first and privatized later? Under what conditions should these firms' price and output decisions be regulated, before and after privatization? Should such firms in fact be privatized at all?

"Privatization first" advocates point to the problems of administrative regulation, dissolution, and divestiture of post-communist monopolies. In the absence of capital markets, decision makers do not have independent information about the possible effects of dissolutions and divestitures. Competition policies based on such imperfect information are likely to be far from optimal, and have rarely been attempted in Western economies during the past 20 years. Moreover, the traditional central controls over state enterprises, the novelty of competition policy, and the large number of firms that could be classified as "monopolies" all imply that authorizing competition agencies to dissolve or closely regulate monopolistic firms could easily lead to regulatory abuse. Sachs and Lipton, for example, argue that:

> It is naive to think of the existing bureaucracy as equipped, professionally or temperamentally, to implement sophisticated policies based on Western-style theories of the welfare economics of the 'second-best.' The bureaucracy can not be relied upon for efficiency in regulating monopoly prices, promoting infant industries or implementing industrial policy.[37]

According to the "privatize first" view, de-monopolization naturally results from privatization and, more generally, from the transition itself. Privatization helps create the capital markets needed to provide the missing information about alternative forms of economic organization, as well as stronger incentives for firms to divest themselves of unnecessary activities. Trade liberalization and increased currency convertibility promote import competition. Liberalization of the domestic private sector, price reform, and the elimination of shortage conditions lower barriers to entry onto concentrated markets. These factors render activist competition policies unnecessary.[38] Competition policy in this view should be limited to merger supervision and the prevention of anti-competitive practices.

"De-monopolize first" advocates, by contrast, emphasize the dangers that monopoly socialism poses for the transformation.[39] Because of their market power, political connections, and the resources at their disposal, large state enterprises enjoy considerable power. Monopolistic structures that had sufficient influence to prevent the introduction of rational investment, industrial, and environmental policies under socialism may be able to thwart, or distort, the development of market capitalism. As Newbery and Kattuman put it:

> The major part of the case for dismantling the large enterprises is to reduce their relative bargaining power, particularly in persuading the state (or the still largely state-owned banks) to finance continued losses, and thereby harden the budget constraints.[40]

According to this view, their political power may allow large enterprises to capture the institutions meant to regulate them in the new market environment and use these institutions to prevent the development of effective competition. These firms may be able to exert an unhealthy influence over the privatization process as well. Levitas and Strzalkowski, for example, argue that:

> the nomenklatura as owners will see their self-interest not in a competitive market order but in a highly etatised, monopolized form of capitalism...it will be easier to make profits by manipulating state policy or forming cartels than by taking risks in the market place.[41]

According to this logic, then, de-monopolization via activist competition policies may be a precondition for effective privatization. Moreover, "de-monopolize first" advocates are unlikely to regard the argument that ambitious competition policies reduce monopolies' sale value as persuasive. While a monopoly may be able to command a higher selling price before it is broken up or closely regulated than afterwards, this premium is essentially a monopoly tax whose incidence is ultimately borne (after it is sold) by the firms' customers (and suppliers). The case for such a tax on either efficiency or equity grounds is somewhat ambiguous.

Dominant Firms and Natural Monopolies

The issues discussed in the theoretical debates of the early 1990s have since taken on more concrete forms in competition and privatization policies. In competition-policy practice, many of these issues have been dealt with within the context of regulating so-called "dominant" firms. That is, once it has been ascertained that a monopolistic enterprise possesses a market share that equals or exceeds some legally-defined critical threshold, these firms' pricing and output decisions are subject to regulation by the competition agencies. Conceptually, five different competition-policy regimes for dominant firms, emphasizing different forms and combinations of ownership and regulation, may be distinguished:

Divestiture and/or dissolution of these firms, before privatization (i.e., the maximalist "de-monopolize first" position). Such a regime has not been adopted in any of the countries examined in this volume.

Sanctions against the abuse of dominant position, irrespective of ownership. This regime, which has been extensively applied in all the countries examined in this volume, can amount to protection of competition by protection of smaller competitors. In this sense, it is similar to the logic of elements of the European Community's competition policy, or the Robinson-Patman Act in the United States. The hallmark of this approach is that activities that are not illegal when conducted by small firms may be illegal when conducted by firms judged to hold "dominant" market positions. The regulation of price and output decisions by these firms is therefore motivated by the need to prevent abuse of dominant position.

Retention of public ownership. In this regime, policy towards dominant firms ranges from the maintenance of tradition regulatory and managerial systems, to that of managing the US postal service, to that of managing Western European state holding companies. Competition policy in this regime is (ideally) a matter of: (1) determining the appropriate level of government in which to vest ownership rights; and (2) developing effective internal management structures and policies.[42] While it has not been an explicit goal of competition policy, this approach has also been widely applied in the countries examined in this volume, if only because significant numbers of large state enterprises in heavy industry and infrastructure sectors have not been privatized, and their privatization in the near future does not appear to be immanent.

Deregulation, in which potential and import competition provide market-generated limits to the abuse of dominant position. While competition policy in the countries examined here has not been inconsistent with the logic of this regime, in no country has it constituted the sole, or even the main, approach to dominant-firm question. It is hoped that the significance of deregulation will increase with the passage of time.

Private ownership with price and output regulation, as is the case (in the United States) with public utilities, local telephone service, and other sectors in which economies of scale or scope are judged to rule out competition. This regime is generally regarded as the most appropriate for regulating natural monopolies, both by Western and country specialists; and many firms that are treated (under post-communist competition law) as "dominant" are probably better understood as natural monopolies. However, the creation of such a regime implies the privatization of much of the infrastructure sector, as well as a new regulatory burden for the state. This burden may take the form of: (1) establishing new regulatory institutions independent of the competition agencies and other administrative bodies; or (2) the promulgation of new regulatory roles for the competition agencies. Perhaps for these reasons, this regime had not been adopted by 1995 on a significant scale in any of the countries examined in this volume.

Chapter Overviews: A Look Ahead

In the chapters that follow, the reader will find a great deal of information about, if not answers to, many of the questions and issues raised in this introduction. Many other issues are explored as well, both in standard chapter form, and via case studies that bring a concrete, real-world perspective to the problems of post-communist competition policy. These chapters do not attempt to provide a complete overview of de-monopolization and competition policy in all post-communist economies. Instead, four countries, at varying stages in this transition have been selected, and the different approaches to de-monopolization and competition policy they embody are analyzed in some detail. These four country chapters are followed by two chapters on natural monopoly regulation. The intent is to provide a picture of the problems and lessons of post-communist de-monopolization and competition policy that is simultaneously comparative, thorough, and fresh.

In Chapter 2, Ádám Török describes de-monopolization and the evolution of competition policy in Hungary. As Török points out, competition policy in Hungary is characterized by a greater degree of historical continuity than in most other post-communist countries. In addition to the introduction of the so-called "competitive pricing system" (which attempted to simulate the disciplinary effects of import competition on domestic prices) during the early 1980s, the Hungarian government promoted entrepreneurship in, and the deconcentration of, a number of industrial and agricultural branches during the 1980s. The liberalization of foreign trade, domestic prices, and commercial activities accelerated during the second half of the decade, even prior to the establishment of the Competition Office in 1990. Although, as Török points out, the Hungarian data on changes in structural concentration are quite problematic, a number of studies do indicate significant structural deconcentration trends in the 1990s which, combined with the effects of import competition, led to significant increases in market competition. Török also describes Hungary's path-breaking experience with post-communist natural monopoly regulation, especially in the natural gas industry.

The Russian experience with de-monopolization and competition policy is taken up by Vladimir Capelik and Ben Slay in Chapter 3. Following an overview of some of the data and issues commonly associated with monopoly and competition policy in Russia, a detailed analysis of Russian competition law is presented, both in terms of the original 1991 legislation and the amendments of May 1995. The activities of the State Committee on Antimonopoly Policy (SCAP) are then described and evaluated, at both the national and regional levels. Attention then turns to the Russian experience of regulating dominant firms via the so-called "Register of Monopolistic Enterprises," as well as the consequences and lessons of this policy regime. After discussing the legislation on natural monopoly regulation that, as of mid-1995, had been passed by the Duma and was awaiting presidential approval, the chapter concludes by noting that, while SCAP in its first years may not have been particularly effective as an agent of de-monopolization, other factors had contributed significantly to the development of competitive market forces in Russia.

Although advice has frequently been offered by Western competition policy agencies (and accepted by their post-communist counterparts) within the framework of technical-assistance programs, these programs have rarely (if ever) been subjected to scholarly analysis. The role of Western advisors in the development of Mongolian competition policy is therefore taken up by William E. Kovacic and Robert S. Thorpe in Chapter 4. In addition to describing the basic framework of Mongolian competition policy, Kovacic and Thorpe recount some of the lessons learned first-hand by a group of Western competition-policy makers advising the Mongolian government during the drafting of that country's basic competition law between November 1992 and July 1993. According to Kovacic and Thorpe, this experience supports three conclusions. First, competition policy does have an important role to play in the post-communist context, even for economies like Mongolia, which (prior to 1992) had almost no previous experience with market reforms. Second, technical assistance provided by Western specialists can have an important positive impact on the development of post-communist competition policy. Third, in order to be truly effective, such assistance must be rendered on a continuous basis by Western specialists located in the country itself.

The Polish experience with de-monopolization and competition policy is examined by Ben Slay in Chapter 5. Poland is similar to Hungary in that policies designed to promote market competition preceded the collapse of communist rule in the late 1980s; the first competition office in what was then the Eastern bloc was in fact established in Poland in 1987. Although the official data on structural concentration are full of problems, they are more extensive than many other countries' data, and do indicate that industrial structures became much less concentrated during the 1987-1992 period. Combined with increased import competition, the deregulation of commercial activity, and the rapid growth of the private sector, declining structural concentration played an important role in the rapid expansion of competitive-market forces after 1990. The Antimonopoly Office played a relatively small role in these developments, although the Office has been an important general advocate for the adoption of pro-competitive economic policies. The Antimonopoly Office did encounter some difficulties in dominant-firm regulation that were similar to the problems experienced by the Russian competition agencies, however; and other problems for competition policy have been posed since late 1993 by the governments formed on the basis of parties descended from the communist political system. These governments have taken a more interventionist, anti-competitive approach to economic policy, one which has frustrated repeated attempts at securing approval for much-needed legislation that would regulate natural monopolies.

General issues of natural monopoly regulation in post-communist economies are addressed in Chapter 6 by Janusz A. Ordover, Russell W. Pittman, and Paul Clyde. In claiming that "there are few microeconomic issues of greater importance now in the post-socialist countries than those surrounding the privatization and the design of competition policies for infrastructure sectors," the authors argue that "antitrust scrutiny may in some circumstances offer an effective and reasonably low-cost method of restraining undue exercise of market power" by natural monopolies. This view reflects the scarcity of competition-policy expertise in post-communist economies, which mitigates against the establishment of additional competition agencies beyond those already in existence. It also reflects prevailing legal frameworks which, by classifying natural monopolies as dominant firms, can be used to regulate natural monopoly price and output decisions. Finally, since the existing agencies are responsible for competition policies in a variety of settings, they are unlikely to be captured by a single industry. Where possible, the authors argue for setting prices for natural monopolies according to world market levels, as incentive regulation would help minimize the problems of asymmetric information and regulatory capture–provided the regulatory agencies can give credible commitments. For non-tradables, however, the authors argue that such incentive-regulation regimes are much less viable, so that traditional cost-of-service regulation is the only option. The question of whether this regulation should be performed by the existing competition agencies, or whether new regulatory institutions should be established, should be determined by the complexity and specificity of the industry in question, and by the anticipated duration of the regulation.

Chapter 7, in which Erik Whitlock compares the deregulation and privatization of the Russian and Hungarian telecommunications industries, provides a concrete counterpoint to Chapter 6's general treatment of natural monopoly issues. Following a description of the formation and evolution of the telecom monopolies, Whitlock contrasts the gradual, planned transition of Hungarian telecom with the more chaotic deregulation of the Russian telecommunications sector. The author goes so far as to argue that, as of 1995, the rights and responsibilities of state ownership "had been foregone entirely" in Russia, without creating a viable competitive or regulatory regime to take its place. Whitlock's comparison is then followed by Chapter 8, which sets forth some of this volume's most important conclusions.

Notes

1. Baran and Sweezy 1966.

2. Among the most important early Western works were Euken 1949, Nove 1969, and Pryor 1973. Economic reform proposals developed in Poland and Hungary during the early 1980s produced some important discussion of this issue in Eastern Europe; see Szalai 1981, Csillag and Szalai 1985, Jakóbik 1988, and Fornalczyk and Kasperkiewicz 1988.

3. See, for example, *Politicheskaya Ekonomiya: Slovar'* 1979:217.

4. Starodubrovskaya 1994:4.

5. See, for example, Ageev 1991.

6. Newbery and Kattuman 1992:315,334.

7. Leitzel 1994:47.

8. Brown, Ickes, and Ryterman 1993.

9. Organizations such as the Russian *ob"yedinyeniye*, the Polish *zjednoczenia*, *wielkie organizacje gospodarcze, wspólnoty*, and *gwarectwa*, the Hungarian trösztök and (to some extent) *nagyvállalatok*, or the East German *kombinate* serve as good examples.

10. Organizations such as *Gossnab* in the USSR, the *Urząd Gospodarki Materiałowej* in Poland, and their regional- and local-government equivalents, serve as good examples.

11. Kornai 1980.

12. See Capelik and Slay, Chapter 3, Parkot 1989:8-9, and Berta-Forgács *et al.* 1990:110.

13. Euken 1949.

14. Pryor 1973:162, 166, 190.

15. Newbery and Kattuman 1992:317.

16. Wiles 1962:304, as cited in Brown, Ickes, and Ryterman 1993:3.

17. Newbery and Kattuman 1992:319.

18. Examples here would be the Kosygin reforms of 1965-1968 in the USSR that created the branch industrial ministries (Hewett 1988), or the 1973-1975 WOG reforms in Poland that grouped hundreds of enterprises into large industrial groupings (Wanless 1980, Wojciechowska 1978).

19. Soós 1987, Fallenbuchl 1988.

20. Kúti and Móra 1991, Mizsei 1994.

21. See, for example, Leitzel 1994.

22. See, for example, Caves *et al.* 1992.

23. See, for example, Peterson 1993:109-17.

24. Brown, Ickes, and Ryterman do report Western-type four- and eight-firm concentration ratios for Russian industry, however (1993:55-59).

25. More specifically, the *Statistical Yearbook 1989-1991* categorizes firms within a given industrial branch according to whether their annual gross output exceeds 10 billion current forints, falls between 5 and 10 billion current forints, falls between 1 and 5 billion current forints, or is less than 1 billion gross forints (*Statistical Yearbook 1989-1991* 1991:146-47).

26. This is a particularly important in Russia, where "civilian" production from military plants is frequently not included in the official statistics (Leitzel 1994:46-47).

27. The extent of overestimation depends upon the degree to which extra-branch sales are concentrated in the branch's largest firms. If a above-average share of the largest firms' total sales occurs outside of the branch, this methodology will overstate actual market concentration. Likewise, if a below-average share of the largest firms' total sales occurs outside of the branch, this methodology will understate market concentration.

28. According to the Polish statistics, for example, national concentration levels in electrical energy production are relatively low. Since, however, suppliers of electricity are frequently natural monopolies in a given locality, this measure of concentration is quite misleading.

29. Moreover, while all firms regardless of size have an incentive to under-report sales data in order to reduce their tax liabilities, small private firms that are used to living at the margins of the law are more likely to successfully engage in such practices.

30. See, for example, Winiecki 1992.

31. Such arguments can be found, for example, in Capelik 1992, Modzelewski 1991, and Starodubrovskaya 1994.

32. Starodubrovskaya 1994:6.

33. That is, enterprises under traditional central planning faced a variety of incentives to maximize output, even when the costs of supplying the additional output exceeded the revenues received from selling it.

34. See, for example, Ickes and Ryterman 1992.

35. Mizsei 1994.

36. See, for example, Szalai 1989, 1981.

37. Sachs and Lipton 1990b:88.

38. See Sachs and Lipton (1990a:301, 1990b:100-101) for an elaboration of this view.

39. Those on record as having favored, at one time or another, the "de-monopolize first" approach include Grosfeld (1990:142), Newbery and Kattuman (1992:325), Nuti (1991:60), and Schaffer (1990:199).

40. Newbery and Kattuman 1992:325.

41. Levitas and Strzalkowski 1990:415-16.

42. For more on this, see Aharoni 1986.

References

Ageev, A. 1991. "Antimonopol'naya politika i razvitiye konkurentsii v SSSR" (Antimonopoly Policy and the Development of Competition in the USSR). Mimeo. Moscow: Economic Strategy Institute.

Aharoni, Y. 1986. *The Evolution and Management of State Owned Enterprises*. Cambridge, Massachusetts: Ballinger Publishing Company.

Baran, P.A., and P.M. Sweezy. 1966. *Monopoly Capital*. New York: Modern Reader Paperbacks.

Berta-Forgács, A., Bód, P.A., and Z. Nagy. 1990. "Between Monopoly and Competition on the Market: Market Patterns of the Manufacturing Industry 1980-1988." *Acta Oeconomica* 1-2: 105-20.

Brown, A.N., B.W. Ickes, and R. Ryterman. 1994. "The Myth of Monopoly: A New View of Industrial Structure in Russia." Policy Research Working Paper No. 1331. Washington D.C.: World Bank.

Capelik, V. 1992. "Yeltsin's Economic Reform: A Pessimistic Appraisal." *Radio Free Europe/Radio Liberty Research Report* 4: 26-32.

Caves, R.E., *et al.*, eds. 1992. *Industrial Efficiency in Six Nations*. Cambridge: MIT Press.

Csillag, I., and E. Szalai. 1985. "Basic Elements of an Anti-Monopoly Policy." *Acta Oeconomica* 1-2: 65-77.

Euken, W. 1948. "On the Theory of the Centrally Administered Economy: An Analysis of the German Experience." *Economica* (May): 79-100.

Fallenbuchl, Z.M. 1991. "Poland: The New Government and Privatization." *Radio Free Europe Report on Eastern Europe* 12: 11-16.

———. 1988. "Present State of the Economic Reform," in P. Marer and W. Siwiński, eds., *Creditworthiness and Reform in Poland*. Bloomington: Indiana University Press.

Fornalczyk, A. and W. Kasperkiewicz. 1988. "Demonopolizacja polskiej gospodarki: Założenia i praktyki lat 1981-84" (The De-monopolization of the Polish Economy: Principles and Practice during 1981-84) in W. Caban, ed., *System ekonomiczny w procesie przemian* (The Economic System in the Process of Change). Warsaw: Państwowe Wydawnictwo Ekonomiczne.

Grosfeld, I. 1991. "Privatization of State Enterprises in Eastern Europe: The Search for a Market Environment." *East European Politics and Society* 1: 142-61.

———. 1990. "Prospects for Privatization in Poland." *European Economy* (March): 139-51.

Hewett, E.A. 1988. *Reforming the Soviet Economy: Equality versus Efficiency*. Washington DC: Brookings.

Ickes, B.W., and R. Ryterman. 1992. "Credit for Small Firms, Not Dinosaurs." *Orbis* (Summer): 333-48.

Jakóbik, W. 1988. *Monopol na rynku polskim* (Monopoly on the Polish Market). Warsaw: Państwowe Wydawnictwo Ekonomiczne.

Kornai, J. 1980. *Economics of Shortage*. New York: North Holland.

Kúti, A., and M. Móra. 1991. "Reorganization and Liquidation Proceedings Since 1986." *Eastern European Economics* 4: 5-33.

Leitzel, J. 1994. "A Note on Monopoly and Russian Economic Reform." *Communist Economies and Economic Transition* 1: 45-53.

Levitas, A., and P. Strzalkowski. 1990. "What Does 'uwlaszczenie nomenklatury' ('Propertisation of the nomenklatura') Really Mean?" *Communist Economies* 3: 413-16.

Mizsei, K. 1994. "Bankruptcy and the Post-Communist Economies of East Central Europe." *Russian and East European Finance and Trade* 2: 34-70.

Modzelewski, W. 1991. "Nowelizacja ustawy antymonopolowej: niektóre wątpliwości" (Amending the Antimonopoly Law: Some Doubts). *Rzeczpospolita* (September 16).

Newbery, D.M., and P. Kattuman. 1992. "Market Concentration and Competition in Eastern Europe." *The World Today* 2: 315-34.

Nove, A. 1969. "Internal Economies." *Economic Journal* (December)" 847-61.

Nuti, D.M. 1991. "Privatisation in Socialist Economies: General Issues and the Polish Case," in H.J. Blommestein and M. Marrese, eds., *Transformation of Planned Economies: Property Rights Reform and Macroeconomic Stability*. Pp. 51-68. Paris: Organization for Economic Co-operation and Development.

Parkot, M. 1989. *Raport na temat stanu koncentracji i zmonopolizowania struktur w gospodarce polskiej* (Report on the State of Structural Concentration and Monopolization in the Polish Economy.) Warsaw: Ministry of Finance (April).

Peterson, H.C. 1993. *Business and Government*. New York: HarperCollins College Publishers.

Pittman, R. 1992. "Some Critical Provisions in the Antimonopoly Laws of Central and Eastern Europe." *International Lawyer* 2: 485-503.

Politicheskaya Ekonomiya: Slovar' (A Dictionary of Political Economy). 1979. Moscow: Izdatel'stvo Politicheskoi Literatury.

Pryor, F.L. 1973. *Property and Industrial Organization in Communist and Capitalist Nations*. Bloomington: Indiana University Press.

Sachs, J., and D. Lipton. 1990a. "Privatization in Eastern Europe: The Case of Poland." *Brooking Papers on Economic Activity* 2: 293-333.

_____. 1990b. "Creating A Market Economy in Eastern Europe: The Case of Poland." *Brooking Papers on Economic Activity* 1: 75-148.

Sah, R.K., and J.E. Stiglitz, 1986. "The Architecture of Economic Systems: Hierarchies and Polyarchies." *American Economic Review* (September): 716-27.

Schaffer, M.E. 1990. "State-Owned Enterprises in Poland: Taxation, Subsidization and Competition Policies". *European Economy* (March): 183-201.

Scherer, F.M. 1980. *Industrial Market Structure and Economic Performance*. Boston: Houghton Mifflin.

Soós, K.A. 1987. "Wage Bargaining and the 'Policy of Grievances': A Contribution to the Explanation of the First Halt of the Hungarian New Economic Mechanism in 1969." *Soviet Studies* 3: 434-451.

Starodubrovskaya, I. 1994. "The Nature of Monopoly and Barriers to Entry in Russia." *Communist Economies and Economic Transition* 1: 3-18.

Statistical Yearbook 1989-1991. 1991. Budapest: Central Statistical Office.

Szalai, E. 1989. *Gazdasági mechanizmus, reformtörekvések és nagyvállalati érdekek* (The Economic Mechanism, Reform Attempts, and Large-Enterprise Interests). Budapest: Közgazdasági és Jogi Könyvkiadó.

_____. 1981. *Kiemelt Vállalat—Beruházás—Érdek*. Budapest: Akadémia Kiadó.

Tirole, J. 1991. "Privatization in Eastern Europe: Incentives and the Economics of Transition," in Blanchard, O.J., and S. Fisher, eds., *NBER Macroeconomics Annual*. Pp. 221-59. Cambridge, Massachusetts and London: The MIT Press.

Wanless, P.T. 1980. "Economic Reform in Poland: 1973-79." *Soviet Studies* 1: 28-57.

Wiles, P.J.D. 1962. *The Political Economy of Communism*. Oxford: Basil Blackwell.

Winiecki, J. 1992. "The Polish Transition Programme: Stabilisation Under Threat." *Communist Economies and Economic Transformation* 2: 191-213.

Wojciechowska, U. 1978. *Studia nad systemem wielkich organizacji gospodarczych 1973-75* (Studies of the Large Economic Organization System, 1973-75). Warsaw: Państwowe Wydawnictwo Ekonomiczne.

2

Competition Policy and De-monopolization in Hungary After 1990

Ádám Török

Competition Policy Before the Transition

This chapter gives an assessment of Hungarian competition policy during the transition process. A few introductory remarks seem necessary to show the more or less organic character of the evolution of this policy after 1990 in Hungary. In fact, reform efforts in the 1980s included several original measures intended to stimulate competition or, at least, to simulate it. If we want to understand Hungarian competition policy in the 1990s, it is necessary to see how certain elements of "Western" type systems of price formation and market organization were introduced in Hungary from 1980 on. It is also necessary to understand why these initiatives failed.

The first such attempt was the so-called "competitive pricing system" introduced in 1980.[1] This initiative, which was really an "export-dependent" pricing system, was based on the assumption that domestic demand and exports to socialist countries would be constrained by general economic policy. Therefore the only scope for enterprise growth would be convertible currency exports. Firm performance in this area would then determine the extent to which enterprises could increase profits on domestic and CMEA markets.

This pricing system was built on a nominal anchor. In stabilization programs of the 1980s, in such places as Argentina and Israel, the nominal anchor was the exchange rate. Hungary chose the price of a product fundamental to the world economy and having an exact equivalent on the domestic market: Saudi light petrol FOB Ras Tanura. The pricing of most raw materials was based on convertible currency import prices. Most manufactured goods were priced according to this export-dependent pricing principle.

This principle was meant to simulate the effects of economic integration on the not-quite-open Hungarian market for manufactured goods. Within the branches where the principle was applied, every enterprise with convertible-currency exports exceeding five percent of sales had to use the prices and profitability obtaining in convertible-currency exports as a benchmark for other sales as well. So, in a sense, convertible-currency export prices became one of the exogenous variables of the enterprise price function. Many firms that underpriced their hard-currency exports in order to gain market share either had to give up a part of these exports or cut prices on the domestic market, in order to adjust profitability levels to those on exports. This system could, in theory, have had a certain de-monopolizing effect, since firms should have been unable to cross-subsidize underpriced exports from artificially high profits earned on the domestic market.

This original emulation of the world market was not really effective or successful, largely because it was not accompanied by any import liberalization. Furthermore, the system was softened already in the first year of its implementation. A number of sectoral and enterprise-level exceptions were made at the outset in order to avoid reductions in exports, since firms near the five percent limit were interested in getting below it, thus exempting themselves from the connection between their domestic and export prices. As a result, an overall trend of turning towards softer markets was observable at the enterprise level. This was a serious blow to the export-dependent pricing system, which in any case gradually lost importance. The system was finally abolished in 1987, because firms with substantial exports to the West threatened the government with increasing the efficiency of these sales by dropping their least profitable exports. In order to persuade these firms to keep their least profitable exports, the government had to exempt them from the system or give them special export subsidies.

The Hungarian experience with this simulative pricing system showed that the opening of the domestic market cannot be replaced by initiatives aimed at simulating competitive markets. As such, it was one of the most important examples of why economic reforms in East European countries cannot be successful without well-defined policies for market opening, market regulation, and competition. On the one hand, the Hungarian government did not really have the freedom necessary to introduce such policies before the political and economic transition. On the other hand, it is likely that experts in or linked to the government were aware of the urgency of increasing competitive pressure on domestic firms together with the necessity of de-monopolization. The failure of this export-dependent pricing system showed that such a system cannot be forced upon the firms if markets are not opened.

Therefore the government tried to cooperate with certain firms (mostly large hard-currency exporters) in increasing the scope of competitive behavioral patterns in the economy. One result of this effort was the creation of the so-called Price Club in 1984. Potential members included enterprises belonging to the export-dependent pricing system but interested in gaining more freedom in determining their domestic prices. Enterprises had to apply for membership in this quite grotesque club. Application for membership had to include a detailed description of R&D, production, pricing, and marketing practices together with a serious promise not to allow the prices charged on domestic markets to exceed the prices of competitive imports. Firms belonging to this club obtained a certain degree of freedom in determining domestic prices, as long as they were able to convince the authorities of the conformity of their pricing behavior to the rules of the club.

The softening up of the export-dependent pricing system also resulted, in some cases, from the autonomous efforts of Hungarian firms suffering from certain pro-cartel effects of this system. For example, a group of engineering firms wanted to break the pricing cartel of domestic steel producers in 1986.[2] These firms had frequently suffered from the abuse of the export-dependent pricing system by domestic metallurgical firms. While metallurgical firms generally used their own (usually quite depressed) export prices in determining prices for sales to the domestic engineering industry, occasional imports of iron and steel could nonetheless be obtained for 10 to 40 percent less than these official prices. These price reductions resulted from informal price cutting among exporters, due to the very depressed international steel market.

Some engineering firms realized that the export-dependent pricing system effectively served as an umbrella protecting their domestic suppliers from following the informal price cuts then prevailing on international markets. The government and the Chamber of Commerce in principle supported the engineering firms' initiative, admitting that artificially high domestic iron and steel prices negatively affected the competitiveness of engineering exports. In spite of government support, steel prices were not reduced, since the metallurgical firms could defend their prices by producing exact documentation only for the high official world market prices. The engineering firms did not at that time have access to the alternative imports, so they had to accept the domestic steel producers' price cartel.

The story of the export-dependent pricing system gives two important reasons why the transition had to bring about a completely new and much more active competition policy in Hungary. First, there was no reasonable alternative to the full liberalization of entry to the domestic market, because no solution could be found to force the discipline of competitive pricing behavior on domestic firms supplying the domestic market. Second, there were no viable substitutes to well-functioning markets and effective competition laws and policies.

The Monopoly Problem at the Start of the Transition

The scale of Hungary's monopoly problem was quite considerable in 1989-1990, although some product markets had displayed quite a high degree of competition since the 1960s or 1970s. The existence of such markets was not, of course, a result of active competition policies, since Hungary did not have such policies prior to the adoption of the Competition Act in 1990. This competition was instead one of the most visible results of the liberalization of private entrepreneurship that began in 1982. This was apparent in agricultural policy, which supported private farming, in the toleration of local produce markets that were not under state control, and also in structural development patterns of several branches after their nationalization. This was a marked difference between Hungary and, say, East Germany, where practically all industries were organized in nationwide monopolies (*kombinate*).[3]

There were practically no analyses of the functioning of product markets in the Hungarian literature before the transition. An isolated (and much more methodology- than policy-oriented) attempt was performed in 1980 by Salgó and Török.[4] This study used a comprehensive analysis of goods tests from the then "monopolistic" consumer protection monthly *Nagyító*. The tests used in the research had been published between 1972 and 1980. The study demonstrated that there was real import competition in more than 30 different Hungarian goods markets, though this was competition in a quite special sense on a market not really open to imports. There was domestic production in all product groups, and imports from CMEA countries in practically all product groups analyzed. "Western" imports were also present in most of these markets, but only some of these goods were produced by leading multinational firms. Most "Western" imports in fact came from Yugoslavia or Third World countries (e.g., India or Malaysia) where they were manufactured under older licenses from West European, American, or Japanese manufacturers.

The study showed a surprisingly clear segmentation of the markets reviewed. The highest segment (high quality, high price) of these product markets consisted of West European or Japanese products. Hungarian, East German, and Czechoslovak products constituted the "middle" segment of these markets, while Yugoslav, Third World, and Soviet products were at the bottom. For the "bottom category," this ranking reflects only quality, because most Yugoslav and Third World engineering products were quite high priced. This segmentation also pointed to the existence of quite strong intra-segmental competition (except for the highest segment, where normally only one company was present on the Hungarian market, like Akai in consumer electronics), and to limited inter-segmental competition. The analysis also showed that competition was present in practically all the product markets reviewed. The authors were unable to show, of course, whether this was true for the markets of investment goods as well; most likely, this was not the case.

The scale of the monopoly problem immediately before 1990 as compared to the transition period can be assessed on the basis of an analysis comparing the structure of Hungarian manufacturing in 1988 and in 1991.[5] This period of only three years bridges a very wide gap between a reformed socialist economy at the half-hearted beginning of privatization,[6] and an almost full-fledged market economy (at least in the legal sense of the term).[7] Petz calculated Herfindahl indexes for 68 Hungarian manufacturing branches, and equated individual branches with individual product markets. This assumption does not conform with reality of course, especially for branches with differentiated products (e.g., electronics components). However, refusing to adopt this assumption would make the analysis of market structures practically impossible. On the other hand, the study is based on the assumption that the territory of Hungary constitutes a "geographic market" which is probably not far from reality.

Petz distinguished five types of market structures: (1) full or almost full monopoly; (2) high concentration; (3) moderate concentration; (4) low concentration; and (5) fully or almost fully competitive markets. This approach is markedly different from what is used in several more policy- than structure-oriented analyses, where the number of players on the market and their *de facto* market power count.[8] For example, the concentration-oriented approach used by Petz does not differentiate between oligopoly and monopolistic competition, both of which can exist on markets with apparently moderate levels of concentration. Putting the methodological problems aside, it is still quite interesting to see the extent of changes in structural concentration recorded in Hungarian industry between 1988 and 1991 (see Table 2.1).

TABLE 2.1   Changes in Hungarian Market Structure, 1988-1991

	Number of Branches in:	
Type of Market Structure	1988	1991
Full (or almost full) monopoly	8 (4.75%)	3 (4.29%)
High concentration	10 (9.94%)	7 (5.03%)
Moderate concentration	14 (25.16%)	11 (15.62%)
Low concentration	15 (28.68%)	17 (27.45%)
Full (or almost full) competition	21 (31.47%)	31 (47.61%)

Source: Petz 1993:57-58.

While the number of fully or almost fully monopolistic branches decreased from eight to three in three years, Petz found that their combined share of aggregate manufacturing sales remained essentially unchanged. (It should be added that the remaining three monopolistic branches, like oil and gas refining, are in the energy sector, and may be supposed to be eventually close to natural monopolies, at least in Hungary.) The number of branches in the high concentration category fell from ten to seven, and their combined share of manufacturing sales declined from 10 to 5 percent. While the number of branches falling into the moderate concentration group also declined from fourteen to eleven, this modest decrease was accompanied by a more significant decline in the percentage of these branches in aggregate manufacturing sales, from 25 percent in 1988 to 16 percent in 1991. Although the number and share of branches in the low concentration category remained almost the same during these three years, dramatic changes occurred in the "fully or almost fully competitive markets" category. Here, the number of branches grew from 21 to 31, while their share in aggregate manufacturing sales grew from 31 to 48 percent.

While the overall picture is one of a quite far-reaching de-monopolization in Hungarian manufacturing, a few footnotes are required. First, analyses at the branch level are still too aggregated to really capture the course of de-monopolization. Second, concentration levels are a one-sided measure of monopolization, because they do not reflect the relative positions of market players. For example, a market can be misleadingly characterized by a low level of concentration where one firm has a dominant position with only 15 percent of the market, because of that firm's indirect ownership control over other market participants (through, for example, shareholding subsidiaries). Third, the propensity for tacit collusion is probably not very reliably measured by this indicator.

An indirect indicator of the de-monopolization process is the overall increase of the number of enterprises in the Hungarian economy. Our figures for this trend cover the December 31, 1989—December 31, 1993 period, so they are not comparable with the data used by Petz.[9] At the end of 1989 there were 15,235 incorporated firms (joint stock and limited liability companies) in Hungary, including approximately 2800 state enterprises that had not been transformed. The number of non-incorporated firms (mainly partnerships) was 17,882, and there were 320,619 individual entrepreneurs (non-incorporated family businesses and freelance intellectuals). Four years later, most of these numbers had grown quite impressively. The number of incorporated firms reached 83,645, of which only about 50 were non-transformed state enterprises. Non-incorporated firms showed parallel growth (to 84,183), and the number of individual entrepreneurs more than doubled (to 686,242). Moreover, the number of firms per 1000 inhabitants in Hungary stood at 85 the end of 1993, which was very high in comparison with the EU average (45), or with the highest figure in the EU (Greece, 67).

This is a somewhat misleading indicator of de-monopolization, however, since these figures have a strong upward bias. An estimated one fourth of the firms registered in Hungary are thought to be "phantom" companies existing only for fiscal reasons; and some 60 percent of family businesses do not provide full-time jobs, because their owners are fully employed elsewhere. There is, finally, a far-reaching problem linked to the "boundaries" of firms.[10] A great number of state enterprises were split up into several successor firms during privatization.[11] Many of these successor companies are only nominally independent of one another, or of their common asset-management center or holding. A great number of these firms therefore do not have strong or clear boundaries, and are not really competitors.

These analyses suggest that the monopoly problem in Hungary was very serious before 1990, but that some "spontaneous" de-monopolization processes had already taken hold. There were several product markets with at least three players, especially in consumer goods industries, and the demand side of the market had a real choice. On the other hand, imports were not liberalized, there were no legal guarantees of the freedom of entry and competition, and there was state control even over "free" prices. Therefore it had to be expected that de-monopolization, and the creation of a modern legal framework for competition, would be declared policy goals of the transition.

Structural Concentration: Measurement and Problems

The previous section has already touched upon the measurement problem. Our review of the Hungarian literature on monopoly and concentration before and after 1990 indicates a great number of gaps in methodology and in statistics. These are now elaborated in more detail.

Access to and Validity of Data[12]

Sectoral, branch and sub-branch data for production and sales are available from the Central Statistical Office. In addition to being too-highly aggregated, these data cover only firms with less than twenty employees on a sample basis. Moreover, these data do not reflect import competition at all. While import data can be obtained from foreign trade statistics, these are not compatible with industrial statistics.

This compatibility problem is twofold. First, the ISIC (International Standard of Industry Classification) and SITC (Standard of International Trade Classification) standards are not compatible with one another. While the ISIC code numbers indicate sectors, branches, or sub-branches, the SITC code numbers refer to commodity classes, groups, sub-groups, and the like. Second, the Hungarian system of industrial statistics uses data obtained from firms and aggregated only among firms. Each firm therefore has a sectoral plus branch plus sub-branch code number in the system, and its sales and output figures appear under the total figure of these headings in the system. This causes no problem for firms with more or less homogenous products (e.g., oil or gas, steel, petrochemicals, beer, construction materials). Serious statistical difficulties arise, though, in the case of firms with non-homogeneous products (i.e., diversified firms). Take an engineering firm producing mainly household and industrial refrigerators and classified as such. This firm's output will enter the Hungarian industrial statistics system under Code 31 ("Production and repair of electrical machinery and equipment"). This firm's output and sales therefore will be treated as the output and sales of the "Electrical engineering" branch. If, however, this company also produces and exports metal goods (Code 28) such as fittings, these will be attributed to the sales of "Electrical machinery and equipment" in the industrial statistics, but to the export of "Metal goods" (SITC Code 69) in trade statistics.

Unregistered Sales

The size of "black market" trade in Hungary is not known, and reliable estimates are not available (the existing unofficial estimates put the size of the "second economy" at 20 to 40 per cent of GDP). However, high consumption and value added taxes, as well as the prolonged existence of the "global quota" system for some consumer goods imports (a special licensing system in which the annual value of imports is fixed in advance for a number of product groups)[13] and the inadequacies of the monitoring foreign trade flows, imply that black market trade is sizeable, amounting to at least $1 billion a year. Serious loopholes in import regulation encourage some trading firms to change their import labelling (which is equivalent to tax fraud). For example, imports of second-hand clothing items are exempt from customs and VAT duties. Therefore, the simple reclassification of new clothing into second-hand items gives the importer a 20—35 percent cost advantage over the imports of the same goods declared as "new" at customs.

Measurement Problems

The measures of concentration most widely used in Hungary are the Gini-Hirschman coefficient and the Herfindahl index. Both of these tools are based on the assumption that greater inequalities in market shares and lower numbers of market players generally indicate a higher degree of market concentration and a greater likelihood of monopolization. Apart from the data problems referred to above, the relevance of these indicators in the Hungarian case is questionable for other reasons as well. The main problem lies in identifying the participants on a given market. This can be a real threat to both competition policy and research if (as in the Hungarian paper industry) subsidiaries of a given holding (which remains in the background) acquire several competitors on the same market. Such a situation is not usual in international competition policy, because it is very rare that more than one player on the same market becomes available for acquisition at the same time. However, privatization creates exceptional situations in which it is extremely difficult to ascertain whether takeovers actually increase or decrease market concentration. Because apparent and actual levels of market concentration may strongly differ in such situations, the utility of the standard measures of concentration becomes even more dubious.

There is an additional problem with any technique of measuring concentration which assumes that a given number of firms provides a good proxy for the number of players on a given set of markets. This problem is again a result of privatization, and is related to the phenomenon of "cross-ownership." This is not unheard of in market economies, especially in such cases when partners in strategic alliances need additional guarantees from each other.[14] These examples from the leading industrial countries mainly exist (at least in their visible forms) between big multinational firms.

There are many more such cases in Hungary, partly owing to special enterprise transformation deals during the period of "spontaneous" privatization. In such cases a holding became the successor of the former state enterprise, while several subsidiaries were transformed into joint stock or limited liability companies. Although the holding usually had most if not all of the subsidiaries' assets in its portfolio, some of the holding's shares were sometimes held by the subsidiaries. The cross-ownership between Videoton Holding and its biggest subsidiary, Videoton Industrial Ltd. (VIRT) during 1989-1991 was an example of this pattern.[15] Cross-ownership is quite frequent among newly created small private firms organized in groups, although not necessarily around a holding. In such cases cross-ownership may be very helpful for parking or reallocating profits among firms, for obvious fiscal purposes.

These data and informational problems imply that most competition-related research will of necessity have an institutional and/or legal focus during the coming years. The root of the problem lies not so much in the statistical system, but rather in the transition itself, due to its speed and the new behavioral patterns it creates.

The Evolution of Antitrust Legislation, Policies, and Institutions[16]

The main role in competition policy belongs to the Office of Competition.[17] Although the topic of this section, antitrust policy, is only one (albeit perhaps the most important) aspect of competition policy, it shall be presented in the broader context of competition policy, in order to illuminate the legal and institutional constraints on Hungarian antitrust policy.

The Legal Framework

Competition policy in Hungary is based on the Competition Act (LXXXVI/1990) or, by its legally correct name, the Law on Prohibiting Unfair Market Behavior. The Competition Office's main task is the protection of competition under this act. The introduction of other important elements of competition regulation actually preceded the adoption of the Competition Act, however. The regulation of minority participation appeared in the chapter on joint stock companies in the Act on Economic Associations (Art. 321-330, 1988/6).[18] The framework for merger control was included in the Enterprise Transformation Act (Art. 59-70, XIII/1989.[19] Enterprise decentralization and the dissolution of big, often monopolistic state firms was made legally possible by the Decentralization Act of 1990.[20]

In accordance with the Competition Act, the main areas of Hungarian competition policy are the following:[21]

Protection of Freedom and Fairness of Competition. These include cases where disturbances to competition cannot be sanctioned on the basis of specific paragraphs in the Competition Act. These issues are covered by the so-called "General Clause" of the Competition Act (paragraph 3). This clause has been widely criticized because its scope is essentially supplemental to all the other clauses of the Act. "Nevertheless, this general clause cannot be waived since the transformation process very often produces abrupt situations which cannot be dealt with by legislation but which can appropriately be treated juridically."[22]

Unfair Competition. Most such cases also constitute violations of civil law. As such, they can be taken either to court or to the Competition Office.

Consumer Deception. These mostly concern misleading advertising or withholding information about negative properties of the product by the producer and/or seller. This field of Competition Office activity is regulated by the Competition Act and by the Act on Product Liability (X/1993).[23]

Prohibition of Agreements Restricting Competition.[24] Our analysis focuses here on this part of the Competition Office's activities. There seems to be a certain danger of excessive and/or increasing market concentration in some sectors of the Hungarian economy owing to the shrinkage of most domestic markets and to some perverse effects of privatization. According to the Competition Office, however, this danger seems to be somewhat exaggerated.[25]

Abuse of Market Dominance.[26] This has been the area in which the Competition Office has been most involved. Experience from a number of such cases indicates that market players are frequently quite passive in their bargaining with larger business partners.[27] This may be because the smaller firms hope that their passivity will put their partners in the legally uncomfortable "dominant position." This passivity may also reflect the belief that their partners' dominant position cannot be challenged in simple business dealings, and that intervention by the Competitive Office would improve their bargaining position.

Merger Control. Several merger cases ended with the Competition Office's authorization of the merger, due to its belief that the merger in question would bring more benefits (e.g., lower transport costs, increased competitiveness of Hungarian products abroad) than costs for competition. In most other cases, mergers did not increase market concentration beyond levels that have to be reported to the Competition Office. These levels are exceeded when (1) joint market shares are above 30 percent; or (2) joint annual sales exceeding 10 billion forints (approximately $100 million). Mergers ordered by the government are covered by the Competition Act regardless the degree of concentration they create. For acquisition control, the threshold is a joint market share above 30 percent.

Registration and Examination of Declarations of Price Increases for Products in Strongly Concentrated Markets. This function can be seen as a legacy of the Office for Prices and Materials, which was abolished in 1990. The Office for Prices and Materials was not the predecessor of the Competition Office in any sense, but the latter now uses the former's premises and employs a part of its staff.[28]

Other Fields. These include consultation with other state agencies or courts on competition-related issues. Such work could be termed the para-legislative (or pre-legislative) function of the Competition Office.

A large number of cases brought before the Competition Office are concerned with market concentration. This would seem to suggest that the market creation process in the Hungarian economy is far from over. The relative importance of such cases is decreasing, however. The figures show that the diminishing importance of concentration-related cases is matched by the growth of umbrella "general clause" related cases, and by increasing numbers of consumer deception cases. In 1991, antitrust, merger, and market domination cases comprised 41 of 77 decisions (53 percent) taken up by the Competition Council (the ultimate decision-making body to which the Competition Office is subordinated.)[29] In 1992, the corresponding share was 44 percent (45/102).[30] By 1993, however, out of 101 decisions, there were only 3 antitrust, 3 merger, and 26 market domination cases (32 percent).[31]

These developments suggest two partly contradictory hypotheses: (1) the functioning of markets seems to be not completely smooth yet, since almost one third of the cases brought to the Competition Council are related to market concentration problems (even if it is a fact that American and West European competition authorities have to deal with new market concentration cases all the time); or (2) market concentration is decreasing, and so that product and service markets are becoming increasingly competitive. Verifying these hypotheses requires an assessment of the degree of competition present on different product markets in Hungary. Such an assessment is provided by Vissi.[32] Six types of market models are considered: monopoly, dominant firms, tight oligopoly, loose oligopoly, monopolistic competition, and pure competition. According to Vissi, the final three structures are "clearly workable competitive structures" with low or no entry barriers, so that intervention by competition policy makers is only necessary in the case of monopolies, dominant firms, and tight oligopolies (so-called "endangered markets").[33]

Reflections on Types of Markets

Monopolistic market structures "endanger" competition in the sense that "the precondition for a working market is the regulation of monopolies and prevention of the abuse of dominant position through antitrust policy." For markets with dominant firms or tight oligopolies "the prerequisite for a workable competitive structure is on the one hand a commercial policy entailing relatively low transaction costs for entry, and on the other hand the prevention of abuse of dominant position and of restrictive practices through antitrust policy".[34] In Vissi's approach, a market is "endangered" by a monopolist. On the other hand, markets can be "contestable" only if there is a danger of entry from outside when there are low entry barriers. Entry would result from the monopolist's price increasing or supply withholding practices.

The concept of "contestability" is itself contested in the literature, of course, and is not entirely clear. Two different interpretations of the theory could shed some light on this problem. According to one: "contestability theory (which describes the circumstances under which potential competition could be just as effective as actual competition in disciplining market power) is admittedly of somewhat doubtful relevance to actual markets, not least because it is incredible that firms' pricing responses to entry by competitors are as slow as the theory requires for the mere threat of entry to constrain monopoly pricing. Nevertheless, McGowan and Seabright find evidence that "the presence of potential competitors can act to reduce the costs of incumbent firms, thereby reducing their prices even if they do not directly practice limit pricing to deter entry."[35] Doubts about the actual validity of the theory were expressed earlier by Schwartz and Reynolds as well.[36] A different explanation of contestability is given by Williamson: "Markets are thoroughly contestable...if asset specificity is presumed to be absent. In this sense contestability theory and transaction cost economics are looking at the very same phenomenon-the condition of asset specificity—through opposite ends of the telescope."[37]

Contestability theory seems to have a certain degree validity for actual markets. Its relevance can be summarized along the following lines (the explanation below is based on a comment by Russell Pittman):

1. Pure contestability is unlikely.
2. Under some circumstances, the presence of potential competition may constrain the behavior of incumbent firms.
3. This constraint is most likely to operate when few sunk costs are necessary for firms to enter the market (for example, firms currently selling in related geographic or product markets).

The opposing approaches to contestability have different implications for its practical relevance. The Kühn-Seabright-Smith interpretation questions the validity of contestability on the grounds of rapid price responses by incumbents to entry. While this is certainly true, it remains to be seen how incumbents react to threats of immediate entry at the low end of the market. If the incumbents do not cut prices before entry, they could lose market share even if their post-entry price response is rapid. If they cut prices before entry, and that entry does not take place, they have made the market contestable without wishing to do so. The asset specificity approach (represented here by Williamson) is based on the assumption that assets are, in most cases, not specific enough to deter entry. Therefore incumbents should either increase asset specificity to transform it into a really high strategic barrier to entry, or—as is more practical and probably less costly—respond to low asset specificity by being ready to face entry at any time. Williamson's approach to contestability seems to have some relevance for transitional economies, largely due to the rapid liberalization of imports. Because of this, most monopolies on goods markets were effectively downgraded into dominant positions with a suddenly high degree of market contestability.

Vissi lists the Hungarian goods markets belonging to the three "endangered" categories.[38] For dominant firms and tight oligopolies, he also specifies the main barriers to entry, listed in brackets (the entire list is not reproduced here):[39]

Monopolies: electricity, gas, oil products. In all three cases, the monopoly of the state firm is based on its ownership of distribution or transportation networks.

Dominant Firms: oil refining (2); vegetable oil (1, 4); aluminum industry (2, 4); light bulb manufacturing (3); refrigerators (3); bus manufacturing (1, 2, 4); oil extraction equipment (3); tobacco fermentation (1); yeast production (3).

Tight Oligopolies: ferrous metals (1, 2); elevator manufacturing (3); cable production (2); cement industry (1, 2, 4); paper industry (1, 2, 4); sheet glass production (3, 4); sugar processing (1, 4).

This list reflects the competitive conditions on Hungarian industrial product markets at the end of 1994 very well. As such, it offers a good starting point for the analysis of possible cooperation or conflict between competition policy (including antitrust policy) and other policy components of the role of government in the transition,

Competition Policy and Other
Elements of the Transition

To be effective, competition policy has to influence the market behavior of economic agents. The latter normally have to adapt first of all to their changing market environment. In the transition, however, the transformation of the legal, institutional, and ownership environment also confronts economic agents (especially firms) with major behavioral challenges. The next sections examine some important components of the transition process and identify how they interact with de-monopolization, as a policy effort and as a trend.

Competition Policy versus Privatization

Vissi's research indicates that a number of goods markets with a high degree of market concentration and multiple barriers to entry were quickly privatized by single foreign firms, or by subsidiaries of the same foreign holding. Industries whose markets are protected by multiple barriers to entry include the paper industry, the cement industry, the sugar industry, the vegetable oil industry, and the manufacturing of motor vehicles (buses). Most of these are evident cases of policy conflict. The motive of nearly or completely hostile takeovers could be identified in a few such privatizations.

Hostile takeovers usually block or at least slow down the de-monopolization process. This can happen through "predatory behavior," when the acquisition of an incumbent firm by a possible entrant leads to the involuntary exit of the incumbent from the market. The other case is "foreclosure," when the incumbent is not formally forced to exit but is instead increasingly cut off from inputs and markets. It will therefore end up as a simple retailing arm of its new owner on the domestic market, and thus lose its manufacturing capability. Some privatizations in the above mentioned industries were counter-productive in terms of de-monopolization, because they led to the *de facto* acquisition of dominant positions by potential foreign entrants. Several examples of more or less hostile takeovers via privatization speak of a very serious lack of coordination between competition policy and privatization policy in Hungary.

For example, Hungarian paper production during 1992-1993 was substantially reduced (and output at the big Szolnok Paper Mill stopped) by new foreign owners (members of the Austrian Prinzhorn Group, the Brigl and Bergmeister AG) in response to the government's refusal to increase duties on paper imports. (Of course, some absurd distortions in the Hungarian tariff structure gave the Austrian investors a good pretext for this decision).[40] The other side of the coin, however, was that the Austrians requested governmental help in the range of $10 million in order to overcome "technical difficulties" when restarting the Szolnok plant. Not surprisingly, the supply of the discontinued paper mill was replaced by largely by Austrian imports. The domestic vegetable oil industry turned to imported inputs after privatization (by the Ferruzzi Group of Italy), contributing to a great crisis for domestic oil seed producers. This privatization could be considered a takeover hostile to the upstream Hungarian firms, or a form of vertical foreclosure. These examples show that, in some cases, direct foreign investment was counterproductive in terms of de-monopolization, and shows that competition policy considerations were sometimes not afforded the significance they deserve during the course of privatization. This resulted mainly from the lack of effective cooperation between the Competition Office and the State Property Agency.

Trade Policy and Domestic Competition

While several branches seemingly do not have entry barriers according to Vissi, some of these do in fact have quite original strategic barriers specific to the branch or even to one dominant company:

Tungsram: The light bulb manufacturer (acquired by General Electric in 1989) had built up excellent goodwill on the domestic market as the only truly worldwide exporter (the "flagship" firm) of the Hungarian engineering industry. Tungsram had a monopolistic position on the domestic market prior to import liberalization, and even afterwards, it was able to retain a dominant position.

Lehel: The refrigerator manufacturer (acquired by Electrolux in 1991) has a very strong and entry-deterring competitive edge on the domestic market, due to its national sales and servicing system.

DKG: The oil and gas equipment manufacturer (51 percent of which was acquired by GAZPROM of Russia in 1994) had been the monopolistic supplier of the monopolistic oil and gas producer MOL, as a part of the latter conglomerate. It became independent in 1991, but the very close technological links between the two firms remained basically intact. Now MOL relies much more on imports than before but, at least in the field of wellhead equipment, DKG remained its only domestic supplier.

Trade policy barriers to entry have been quite low in several industries, even if in some cases they have been complemented by other, mostly "natural" barriers (e.g., high transportation costs for potential competitors). This was the case in ferrous metallurgy, the cement industry, and the paper industry. Iron and steel as well as cement exporters from Slovakia and Romania benefitted from low energy prices in those countries, which distorted the development of competition on Hungarian markets. Anti-dumping legislation was therefore used against these imports. These developments raised the following theoretical dilemma: should de-monopolization be welcomed if it takes place through dumping?

The entry barriers in Vissi's list have, for the most part, been inherited from Hungary's "semi-market economy" or "modified planned economy" of the past. Most of them still reflect the crisis situation after several years of industrial recession in many industries.[41] This crisis and the shrinking of domestic markets could eventually force incumbents or the government to make certain entry barriers higher.

Excess capacity as a strategic entry barrier becomes more important as capacity utilization decreases. Asset specificity as a natural entry barrier has a greater entry-deterring effect if the investment climate is depressed due to the crisis. The privatization of an incumbent by a major multinational firm could, on the other hand, replace some of these entry barriers with others, such as strategic "goodwill" factors.

Therefore, the role of competition policy in the policy package of the transition has to be clarified. There are several situations of policy conflict in which privatization or trade policy considerations (both of these policies belong to the sectorally-biased industrial policy, while competition policy is sector neutral) can easily dominate competition policy-based convictions, policy tools, or objectives.

Competition Policy in Conflict Situations

There have been several cases of more or less open conflict of interest between the Hungarian Office of Competition, the Ministry of Industry and Trade, and the governmental institutions responsible for privatization. The main reason behind these problems is the lack of coordination between the strategic targets of different policies.[42] The three policies in question are competition policy, import (trade) policy, and privatization policy. Conflicts inevitably arise between them when all the three policies are aimed at "mainstream" targets usual in transition economies. These "mainstream" targets include far-reaching de-monopolization for competition policy, almost complete import liberalization for trade policy, and substantial reductions in the state's ownership share of the capital stock for privatization policy.

Competition policy faces a serious challenge when a foreign investor acquires a domestic manufacturer in a monopolistic position. This could be the case also if several subsidiaries of the same foreign holding (seemingly different firms) acquire different Hungarian competitors on the same market. In these circumstances, a *de facto* monopoly will be created on a hitherto competitive market. The foreign investor(s) will then be interested in maintaining its (their) monopolistic position by bargaining for exceptions from import liberalization for its products. The result of an apparently successful privatization transaction could therefore be increasing pressure on competition and trade policies. While the Hungarian Competition Office is entitled to comment on privatization transactions with respect to their impact on market structures, it is not legally allowed to intervene in the privatization process.

To be sure, import liberalization has contributed significantly to the de-monopolization process in Hungary through "the establishing and expanding of import competition."[43] However, trade policy could be in conflict with privatization and de-monopolization in the following way. Foreign investors have entered the Hungarian food, clothing, and consumer electronics markets by acquiring sales channels rather than production capacities. In such cases, liberalized imports can provide an avenue for foreign firms to use their market power to drive domestic production from the market, even if the imports are not necessarily more competitive.[44] The combined effects of privatization and import liberalization could be harmful for the de-monopolization efforts of competition policy. The objectives of privatization policy would be easier to achieve if competition policy permitted the sale of domestic monopolies to foreign investors, and trade policy provided protection from import competition. In such cases it may well happen that a domestic monopoly cannot be privatized, and liberalized imports might gradually erode the privatization value of the monopolistic firm.[45]

The three cases can be summarized in the following way. A foreign firm exporting to Hungary is interested in weak trade policy protection of the Hungarian market (low barriers to entry) and a strong antimonopoly policy, especially if there is already at least one incumbent and strong competitor on the market. If this foreign firm intends to participate in privatization, it might well try to acquire its strong incumbent competitor. After privatization, its interests will change dramatically: the foreign company will probably lobby for strong protection of the domestic market and weaker antitrust regulation. In other words, the policy triangle between privatization (based on DFI), trade, and competition policies can not simultaneously serve the goals of "marketization" and liberalization. Two of these goals will inevitably be in conflict with the third one: the government can not lower trade barriers, pursue de-monopolization, and hope to increase direct foreign investment at the same time. Moreover, if the government wants to attract more direct foreign investment, this is likely to preclude both the maintenance of an open trade regime and, more generally, an aggressive competition policy.

In Hungary, it is likely that this triangle will be weakest at its competition policy edge. This is due to a quite specific feature of the Hungarian competition legislation. Contrary to the Polish or German legal systems, the Hungarian Competition Office has no right to block privatization deals creating or strengthening monopolies, although it can subsequently use the abuse-of-dominance provisions of the Competition Law. But prior to the privatization, it can only give its opinion on proposed sales of state firms.

One explanation for this apparent anomaly is linked to the small size of the domestic market.[46] The Hungarian market for most products is deemed "contestable" because virtually none of the non-natural monopolies can feel safe behind the exceedingly low entry barriers. Also, because the Competition Office is not part of the Hungarian government, it is not and cannot be held responsible for policy issues or for eventual policy conflicts. Ultimately, policy decisions, also in the field of privatization, belong to the government.

In Hungary, then, this "policy triangle" is not a real one. While competition policy is quite independent of other economic policy centers, its legal and administrative grounds for action are quite limited.

Natural Monopoly Regulation

Natural monopolies are a very special testing ground for the efficiency of competition policy. Competition policy in general pursues two fundamental goals: protecting competition, and promoting economic efficiency. These two fundamental goals are, to a large extent, in conflict in the case of natural monopolies.[47] The Competition Office can also serve as a regulator of otherwise unregulated natural monopolies using its capacity to enforce abuse-of-dominance provisions of the Competition Law (see Chapters 6 and 7).

The below quotation is from an American textbook of business law, but the principle is equally valid in most other countries, and also in Hungary. "It is illegal to seek a monopoly or to attempt to keep a monopoly once one is attained, but it is not illegal to have a monopoly."[48] This means antitrust policy cannot attack monopolies just because they exist.

The wording of the U.S. Supreme Court (in *U.S. versus Grinnell Corporation*) is also very telling in this respect:

> The offense of monopoly under Art. 2 of the Sherman Act has two elements: (1) the possession of monopoly power in the relevant market; and (2) the willful acquisition or maintenance of that power as distinguished from growth or development as a consequence of a superior product, business acumen, or historic accident.[49]

Natural monopolies can be regarded as a special case of monopolies already existing. Natural monopolies are only a limitedly antitrust policy-related issue at the outset, as far as the protection of the consumer is concerned.

The regulation of natural monopolies is closely linked to tax policy, but this link can generate serious policy conflict. This was the case with the rate structure for telephone services to which the Competition Office objected in 1993.[50] The obviously monopolistic character of the structure was not, however, changed by the Minister of Transport and Telecommunications. This rate structure proved lucrative for foreign investors who were willing to pay more for Hungarian Telecom shares; but while the investors' revenues were quite well protected by this structure, it was not very favorable for the consumer.

In the Hungarian legal system, the state is the primary owner of natural monopolies. This means double ownership: of the monopolies themselves (concessions), and of the monopolistic firms. This double ownership leads to a pattern of contradictory interests of the state with respect to regulation.[51] On the one hand, the state's fiscal policy interest is linked to the maximization of concession and service-related revenue, which is ultimately served by increased consumer expenditures. On the other hand, its competition policy interest includes the protection of the consumer. The government can sell both kinds of properties and ownership rights, either by deregulating natural monopoly markets and selling concessions; or by privatizing the service companies previously built up on the basis of the natural monopolies. The two kinds of sales took place simultaneously in the case of the partial privatization of Matáv (Hungarian Telecom) in late 1993 (see Chapter 7).

The Hungarian policy vis-à-vis natural monopoly regulation is discussed below in the natural gas industry. In this sub-section, we use data from O'Neill and Brown,[52] as well as information collected through interviews with managers of regional natural gas firms in Hungary.[53]

The Hungarian Natural Gas Industry

The natural gas industry belonged to OKGT (the Hungarian Oil and Gas Trust) until mid-1991 when the Trust was broken up into eleven independent firms.[54] Its biggest successor is MOL Rt covering the oil industry and a small part of gas transportation (pipelines linking the border to regional distribution centers). Other successors include companies manufacturing oil and gas production and transportation equipment, pipeline operators, and research and exploration firms. Six successor firms of the former OKGT were created in the natural gas industry on July 1, 1991. These firms are organized on a regional basis and are, in fact, regional monopolies dealing with transportation and distribution. The five that operate outside of Budapest are, at the moment, 100 percent state owned, and are under the control of SAMCO (the State Assets Management Corporation, a state holding company).[55] The sixth firm, Fővárosi Gázmüvek, serves the capital city, and it is owned by the Municipality of Budapest.

The regulation of this industry is to be gradually liberalized, with several steps of privatization. Municipalities whose populations are served by the regional gas firms will acquire altogether 10 to 25 percent ownership in the regional gas companies. The equity stake of each municipality will correspond to the share of those pipelines in the assets of the gas firms which are in the territory of the given municipality. It is expected that 51 percent of the shares of each regional gas firm will be open for privatization by strategic investors, and the Hungarian state will retain only one "golden share."

Major West European gas firms such as British Gas, Gaz de France, Ruhrgas and Italgas seem to have an interest in these privatizations, but as of January 1995, tenders had not yet been announced. There had been a sales tender for the regional gas firms in 1992, but it was withdrawn shortly thereafter. The probable reason of this was the lack of a modern natural gas act; the old one was adopted in 1911, and amended in 1969 (VII/1969).

The new Natural Gas Act (XLI/1994) came into effect on July 25, 1994. This legislation breaks up the state monopoly on the distribution and sale of natural gas. It defines the rights and obligations of gas companies, the consumers, and the new regulatory authority, the Hungarian Energy Office. This body has the right to authorize the functioning of gas companies if they comply with all the technical, safety-related, and commercial standards of the industry set by the law.

The law also regulates the commercial relationship between gas companies and industrial, commercial, and household gas consumers. It does not create an absolutely comprehensive regulatory framework, however. This problem may be unavoidable in cases where the state gives up the ownership of natural monopolies, but the loopholes in this framework still seem quite considerable. To a great extent, this is because the detailed directives for implementing the law had not been made public at the time this chapter was being written, so that it was not clear which loopholes will be filled.

Some of the evident loopholes left after and linked to the de-monopolization of gas distribution are the following:

1. It is not clear where municipal gas pipelines end and household pipelines begin in those cases where there is one pipeline tap for more than one household consumer. This point could perhaps be the border of the real estate owned or rented by the individual consumer.

2. The Gas Act does not give a priority list of the types of consumers to be cut from the system in the case of gas supply problems.

3. The Gas Act maintains the scheme of "network development contributions" to be paid by each new consumer linked to the gas pipeline system.[56] It specifies a flat price (unit of development contribution calculated by the length of new pipeline) based on a national average. This pricing principle has the effect of putting consumers in well-developed and densely-populated areas at a relative disadvantage. This hidden cross-subsidization is meant to replace state subsidies, but it could make pipeline development relatively lucrative in those areas which are less suited for pipeline extension for natural reasons.

The "minimal cost principle" is a fundamental element of the Gas Act. According to this principle, the least expensive technological option has to be chosen for new pipeline investment from the options that meet technological and minimum safety standards. Because this principle is not adequately explained, it seems to suggest a strongly short-term approach that does not consider, for example, the life expectancy or suitability for the consumer of different technological options.

The above list offers a picture of the extent to which the dissolution of a natural monopoly creates problems that must be tackled by subsequent regulation. Similar problems are likely to arise in all fields (especially in public utilities) where the owner of the natural monopoly is linked to millions of consumers. For these and other reasons, reform in the natural monopoly area is likely to be an extremely sensitive sphere of de-monopolization.

De-monopolization in Hungary: An Assessment

A comprehensive analysis of the development of Hungarian market structures is provided by the Competition Office's *Annual Report*.[57] Some industries are still suffering from parallel decreases in demand and supply. These industries include textiles, shoes, fertilizers, plastic materials, poultry and meat processing, and dairy products. Capacity utilization rates in these industries were much below the Hungarian industrial average (70 percent in 1993). The continuing crisis in these industries led to a growing number to exits from the market. Since this was not compensated by new entries, these exits tended to increase the degree of market concentration. Coal mining was perhaps the best example for this kind of adverse development.

Adjustment in many other industries was quite successful, however. Adjustment to new patterns of demand took place in several industries through new entry. This happened, for example, in the restaurant industry: despite declines in overall sales, new entrants were able to get substantial market shares by exploring the fast food market. Small new entrants into the furniture, construction, and tourism markets in many cases acquired significant market shares from much larger traditional incumbents. In general, de-monopolization occurred in most successfully adjusting industries thanks to aggressive, small new entrants.

Of course, the lack of reliable data and measures of market concentration makes an overall judgment of the Hungarian de-monopolization process very difficult. Still, it seems reasonable to share the moderate optimism of the Competition Office in this matter. This limitedly positive assessment of the de-monopolization process is based on conclusions from three fields:

Cartels

There was only one negative (out of three total) cartel decision made by the Competition Council in 1993. This negative decision was taken against the sugar cartel, which had been under the Competition Office's scrutiny since 1990. This cartel was created by the privatization of the Hungarian sugar firms, rather than through any concentration of ownership control. The Hungarian firms were sold to several West European sugar firms whose tacit collusion transferred, in fact, the sugar cartel already functioning in Western Europe to Hungary. The emergence of the sugar cartel in Hungary was promoted by the not altogether smoothly functioning price and market regulation system for agricultural products introduced starting in 1993. In any event, cartelization currently does not seem to be a major threat to the de-monopolization process in Hungary.

Abuse of Market Dominance

The Competition Council examined 26 complaints of this kind in 1993. The fact that only seven of these complaints were found to be justified can also be seen as a good sign with respect to de-monopolization. Most of these cases had a regional or local character, with local monopolies attempting to enforce price increases by threatening to reduce supply. This happened with the steam supply system in the small industrial town of Inota, and the electricity works of another "smokestack city," Borsodnádasd.

While he relatively small importance of the complaints that met with negative decisions also speaks of progress in de-monopolization, this progress must not be exaggerated. It remains to be seen—as in the case of the gas industry—how effective the regulation of former natural monopolies will be. If these new regulations will not be not efficient enough, a significant rise in the number of complaints against abuse of market dominance is to be expected.

Merger Regulation

The Competition Council issued three decisions in this field in 1993. In all of these (including the acquisition of 35 percent of the equity of MALÉV Hungarian Airlines by Alitalia [see the accompanying case study], and the privatization-related increase in market concentration in the detergent industry) no harm to the development of competition could be established.

Conclusions

Our review of the de-monopolization process in Hungary demonstrates that competition is less and less distorted in the economy. This does not mean, however, that the functioning of markets is already as smooth as in most developed market economies. There are two main reasons why the de-monopolization process cannot be considered to have run its course in Hungary.

First, "post-deregulation regulation" of most natural monopolies is still an open issue. There is a danger that currently existing natural monopolies will be transformed into legally protected "new" monopolies. This danger could become serious if fiscal- and privatization-policy considerations dominate competition-policy decision in the development of the new regulatory systems. This can be seen in the pre-privatization regulation of tariffs in the telephone market. Second, the Hungarian Competition Act has a quite unbalanced structure. It is open in several important fields, while others are quite comprehensively covered by the General Clause. While the Act's open structure makes it flexible and well suited for adjustment to European Union regulations, this openness could allow well-prepared actual or potential monopolists to adapt to the loopholes of the law. This is not a threat to the de-monopolization process *per se*, as long as the Competition Office and the Competition Council take a precedent-based approach to decision making and arbitration. Such an approach would help fill the gaps of the law more or less automatically, and make it unnecessary to amend the Competition Act which has proved to be absolutely viable in its four years of existence.[58]

APPENDIX: CASE STUDY

Collusion or Collision? Competition Policy and the Hungarian National Airline: MALÉV-Alitalia[59]

Ádám Török

Several national airlines of the former East European socialist countries were partly or entirely absorbed by West European airlines. These takeovers were undoubtedly beneficial for the East European carriers, who were facing serious financial problems as well as obsolescence in their fleets. The first such case was that of the former East German carrier Interflug, which was entirely absorbed by Lufthansa during 1991. CSA of Czechoslovakia was partly acquired by Air France during 1992. 35 percent of the equity in MALÉV, the Hungarian national airline, was offered for privatization. Out of the two serious competitors, Alitalia and Lufthansa, the Italian state airline came out the winner in 1993.

While an official explanation for Alitalia's selection was not provided, it was widely believed that Lufthansa wanted to integrate MALÉV a little bit too strongly into its global network as just one of several regional carriers. In addition to the quite favorable financial conditions of the Alitalia offer, a decisive factor could have been that the Italian airline agreed to allow MALÉV to maintain its autonomy as the Hungarian national carrier. This autonomy was to be guaranteed by the composition of MALÉV's corporate governance structure.

The Italian state company Alitalia, in cooperation with SIMEST S.p.A., an investment firm owned by the Italian government, sought to acquire a 35 percent equity stake in MALÉV. It offered a price of $77 million in cash. MALÉV was a joint stock company, 99 percent of which was owned by the State Assets Management Co (SAMCo). The partial acquisition was to take place through a corresponding increase in MALÉV's equity capital.

Before concluding the deal, MALÉV and Alitalia applied to the Hungarian Competition Council for preliminary authorization for the acquisition. At issue was whether this partial acquisition would give Alitalia a decisive influence over MALÉV and the Hungarian commercial air transport market, as well as limit potential competition on this market.

MALÉV and Alitalia sought preliminary authorization from the Competition Council for two reasons. First, it was evident that a MALÉV co-owned by Alitalia would dominate the Hungarian air transport market in such a way that this dominant position would be shared by Alitalia; it would not belong solely to the national carrier. Second, MALÉV's planned new corporate governance framework would have given exclusive voting rights to Alitalia on certain issues. Therefore, the Competition Council in this case had to an important, if somewhat rare, merger control problem. It had to decide whether the merger would create a new Alitalia-dominated airline that would then dominate the Hungarian air transport market. The Competition Council also had to decide whether Alitalia's influence on MALÉV decisions concerning market strategy and behavior would be crucial or not.

This example illustrates the importance of corporate governance issues in large firms undergoing even partial acquisition, in terms of merger supervision. This merger supervision case was extremely delicate for political reasons. If it had been shown that Alitalia would have acquired decisive influence over MALÉV, this would have meant that Hungary would have *de facto* lost her flagship carrier to foreigners. While it was evident that Alitalia would gain *some* influence over MALÉV, it was unclear whether this influence would reach a critical level. Establishing this "critical level" of influence of one company over another when the voting rights of shares depend on the topic of the vote turned out to be extremely difficult.

The core of the acquisition deal, and a decisive issue in the Competition Council's ruling, was the distinction between the four types of shares used to represent ownership in the new joint venture. "A" shares could be owned only by Hungarian natural or legal persons (currently SAMCo and six Hungarian municipalities, whose joint shares comprised less than one percent of the total). "B" shares could be owned only by legal persons (currently SAMCo) so authorized by the Hungarian government. "C" shares could be owned only by Alitalia and SIMEST. "D" shares would be issued later in an ESOP scheme to a maximum 9.99 percent of MALÉV Ltd.'s equity capital.

While voting rights at stockholders' meetings reflected the face value of the shares, special voting rights are linked to "B" and "C" shares. "B" shares carry voting rights equal to three million times their face value for "B-type" decisions, which pertained to MALÉV's "national airline" status. "C" shares carry voting rights equal to one thousand times their face value for "C-type" decisions, which concern the appointment or dismissal of Board and Supervisory Board members appointed by the owners of "C" shares.

Voting rights were thereafter distributed as follows:

- For normal decisions: "A" shares—65 percent; "B" shares—practically 0 percent; and "C" shares—35 percent.
- For "B-type" decisions: "A" shares—0.2 percent; "B" shares—99.7 percent; and "C" shares—0.1 percent.
- For "C-type" decisions: "A" shares—0.2 percent; "B" shares—practically 0 percent; "C" shares—99.8 percent.

This structure meant that Alitalia could exercise a decisive influence on MALÉV's strategy only for "C" type decisions. The Competition Council therefore ruled that this influence was far from decisive, since the Italian partners can nominate or appoint at most 35 percent of the Board and Supervisory Board members.

The Competition Council's ruling showed a certain sophistication. It declared that Alitalia and MALÉV were not obligated to apply for preliminary authorization because, due to the maximum 35 percent voting share in all key strategic decisions, there was no legal possibility for Alitalia to acquire decisive influence over MALÉV. For this reason, the merger was permitted.

The two companies' application to the Competition Council followed the initiation of similar proceedings in the Italian courts. While the ultimately favorable (for Alitalia) outcome of the Italian proceedings might have been influenced by the Hungarian monitoring of the acquisition, this cannot be proven.

Notes

1. This brief description of this system is based on Brada, Singh, and Török 1994:5-7.

2. This case comes from Brada, Singh, and Török 1994:6-7.

3. Examples of non-monopolized industries in pre-transition Hungary included food retail trade, where two state-owned retail chains coexisted on a national scale. KÖZÉRT was organized as a countrywide retailing chain composed of nationalized local shops belonging to different owners, while Csemege was a successor to the Austrian-owned Julius Meinl retailing chain. In consumer electronics, Videoton and Orion constituted a duopoly. Videoton was created in the early 1960s from an armaments company, while Orion had been a privately owned electronics firm (under the same name) before 1948. The pharmaceutical industry maintained the appearance of its pre-war market structure: pre-war private firms like Chinoin, Gedeon Richter, EGIS, Alkaloida, and Reanal existed within their former "boundaries" and partly under their old names in the period between their nationalization in the late 1940s and privatization in the 1990s.

4. See Salgó and Török 1980.

5. See Petz 1993.

6. The Law on Economic Associations, the legal cornerstone of Hungarian privatization, was adopted in 1988. The transformation of some state firms (Medicor, Videoton, Ganz Danubius) into partly private, holding-based corporate structures started at the end of that year.

7. The legal package for privatization was almost complete by 1991 (Sárközy 1994); import liberalization was complete by the end of that year; and competition legislation has existed in its present form since 1990.

8. See, for example, Vissi 1994.

9. Our source for the statistical overview of the increase of the number of enterprises is a non-published working paper of the Ministry of Industry and Trade.

10. This issue cannot be discussed here in detail. For the theoretical fundamentals of the "boundary" problem, Coase (1937) and Williamson (1985) offer indispensable reading material. The special form of this problem in the transition has not been deeply analyzed by researchers yet.

11. See Brada, Singh, and Török 1994:14-17.

12. The explanations for the lack of data offered in this section are strongly supported by Ferenc Vissi, Chairman of the Hungarian Competition Office. In regards to the impact of privatization on Hungarian market structures, Vissi says: "Due to the lack of data, it is impossible to determine whether the new structure of competition means a positive or a negative change" (Vissi 1994:352). If the analyses of this leading and well-informed expert on competition issues suffer from inadequate data, problems in this regard must be truly dramatic.

13. See Borszéki, Gergely, and Páczi 1994.

14. A case in point was, until early 1994, the relationship between Renault and Volvo. The cross-ownership between Mazda and Ford is another good example from the car industry.

15. See Török 1992.

16. This and the next section draw widely upon Török (1994).

17. This agency is responsible for the freedom of competition, and for enforcing competition legislation. The Competition Office (more accurately, the Office of Economic Competition) is not part of the government. Its chairman is appointed by the Prime Minister for six years (the first appointment was in 1991), and has to report each year to the Parliament. With regard to dumping or other unfair trade practices, the Competition Office is represented in the Inter-ministerial Tariff Committee, which rules on complaints of dumping and can initiate such lawsuits (the credit for clarifying the Competition Office's role in dumping-related lawsuits belongs to Russell Pittman). In such cases, the Office can give consulting support to the Ministry of International Economic Relations. The latter might need the Competition Office if it cannot use its limited set of tools to protect Hungarian firms from "hit-and-run" entry on the domestic market.

18. See Sárközy 1993:122.

19. See Sárközy 1993:123.

20. See Sárközy 1993:124.

21. See Sárközy 1993:123, *Beszámoló...* 1993, Part II.

22. See Pogácsás and Stadler 1993:86.

23. See Sárközy 1993:123.

24. In Hungary, this is most commonly referred to as "antitrust policy."

25. See *Beszámoló...* 1993:13.

26. See Pittman 1992.

27. See *Beszámoló...* 1993:14.

28. Although any sort of "inheritance" from the Office of Prices and Materials is denied by Competition Office officials, the Competition Office's role in the post-1990 governmental structure is roughly comparable to that of the Office for Prices and Materials in the governmental structure prior to 1990.

29. Decisions prepared by the Competition Office are executed by the Competition Council. Council decisions can be appealed in court, and become valid only when the appeals process is completed. The Competition Council is thus a legal body, while the Competition Office is a regulatory body.

30. *Beszámoló...* 1993:i (Annex).

31. *Beszámoló...* 1994:i (Annex).

32. See Vissi 1993. A few months later, the same author published a slightly more updated analysis of the same problem in Hungarian (Vissi 1994). This newer version adds only the Matáv (Hungarian Telecom) privatization case to the cases reviewed in the 1993 paper. This has no real practical importance for our analysis, since this otherwise very important transaction did not as of yet have any considerable influence on the market structure yet. Therefore we still refer ourselves to his former paper.

33. While this term seems analogous to the notion of "contestable markets," this is not Vissi's intention. He has in mind "endangered market structures," implying that the "danger" is not one of entry for incumbents, but rather one of growing monopolization for potential entrants.

34. See Vissi 1993:8.

35. Kühn, Seabright, and Smith 1992:4.

36. Schwartz and Reynolds 1983.

37. Williamson 1985:56.

38. See Vissi 1993:10-14.

39. These barriers include: (1) trade barriers, (2) barriers that are normally neutral from the viewpoint of competition policy (e.g., economies of scale, capital requirements, or the access to certain natural resources), (3) no barriers to entry, and (4) excess capacity. This classification is similar to the triple system used in the literature: barrier (1) corresponds to "artificial" barriers; (2) to "natural" barriers; and (3) corresponds to one part of "strategic" barriers. (Other strategic barriers include the possibility of predatory behavior, the monopolization of physical assets, or efforts at monopolizing goodwill [Kühn, Seabright, and Smith 1992:4-5]).

40. Specifically, Hungarian customs duties on paper imports are higher than on imported pulp. This can be called "adversely effective customs protection."

41. According to the official statistics, the volume of Hungarian industrial output decreased by about 40 percent between 1987 and 1992. It grew, however, by 4 percent in 1993 (KSH 1993, 1994).

42. The argument developed here was first published in Somogyi and Török 1993.

43. Vissi 1992:118.

44. For example, the Meinl supermarket chain now offers Hungarian consumers only expensive French cheeses instead of Hungarian cheeses that are more price competitive. Rather than showing that Hungarian cheese producers can not compete with French firms, this example shows that foreign investors can use their control of sales channels to foreclose domestic producers' upstream abilities to compete.

45. Simply breaking monopolies up into several smaller units is normally not a good policy solution. This was the case with, for example, the MÉH recycling firm operating nationwide. Either the breakup is regional, creating smaller regional monopolies, or "oligopolistic tacit collusion" (Trebilcock 1992:108) results among the new smaller firms, with managers coming from the same managerial team. It is, on the other hand, not clear whether such arrangements necessarily result in uncompetitive market structures (the credit for this remark belongs to Professor Marvin Jackson).

46. Pogácsás and Stadler 1993:81.

47. Vissi 1994a:2-3.

48. Davidson, Knowles, Forsythe, and Jespersen 1987:1043.

49. 384 U.S. 563, 570-571, 1966; quotation supplied by Russell Pittman.

50. *Beszámoló...* 1994:19.

51. Vissi 1994a:3-4.

52. Neill and Brown 1992.

53. We were not allowed to indicate our industry sources with more precision.

54. See Brada, Singh, and Török 1994:85, 92.

55. The five regional firms are: TIGAZ, based in Hajdúszoboszló and serving seven counties in Northeastern Hungary; EGAZ, based in Győr and serving three counties in Northwestern Hungary; KÖGAZ, based in Nagykanizsa and serving three counties in Western Hungary; DDGAZ, based in Pécs and serving three counties of Southwestern Hungary; and DEGAZ, based in Szeged and serving three counties in South-Southeastern Hungary.

56. It should be pointed out that the maximum consumer price for natural gas is fixed by the government. This price currently covers only a small part of capital costs and depreciation.

57. *Beszámoló...* 1994:1-4.

58. See Sárközy 1993:123.

59. This case was registered with the Competition Council as case number Vj.-15/1993. Our source for this case study is *Versenyfelügyeleti Értesítő.* 1993 5:123-24.

References

Beszámoló az Országgyűlés részére a Gazdasági Versenyhivatal 1993. évi tevékenységéről és a versenytörvényalkalmazása során szerzett tapasztalatokról (Report to the Parliament on Competition Office Activities in 1993, and the Application of the Competition Act). 1994. Gazdasági Versenyhivatal. Budapest, March.

Beszámoló az Országgyűlés részére a Gazdasági Versenyhivatal 1992. évi tevékenységéről és a versenytörvényalkalmazása során szerzett tapasztalatokról (Report to the Parliament on Competition Office Activities in 1992, and the Application of the Competition Act). 1993. Gazdasági Versenyhivatal. Budapest, February.

Borszéki, Z., R. Gergely, and E. Páczi. 1994. *Piacvédelem! Piacvédelem?* (Protect the Domestic Market! Protect the Domestic Market?). Mimeo, Budapest, KOPINT-DATORG.

Brada, J., I. Singh, and Á. Török. 1994. *Firms Afloat and Firms Adrift. Hungarian Industry and the Economic Transition*. Armonk, New York: M.E. Sharpe.

Coase, R. 1937. "The Nature of the Firm." *Economica* 4: 386-405.

Davidson, D.V., B.E. Knowles, L.M. Forsythe, and R.R. Jespersen. 1987. *Comprehensive Business Law. Principles and Cases*. Boston: Kent Publishing Co.

KOPINT: Konjunktúrajelentés (Report on Business Conditions). 1994/1. Budapest: KOPINT-DATORG, April.

KSH (Monthly Bulletin of the Central Statistical Office). 1993/1. Budapest, March.

KSH (Monthly Bulletin of the Central Statistical Office). 1994/1. Budapest, April.

Kühn, K., P. Seabright, and A. Smith. 1992. *Competition Policy Research: Where Do We Stand?* CEPR Occasional Paper No. 8 (July 30). London: Centre for Economic Policy Research.

Losoncz, M., G. Papanek, and Á. Török. 1991. *Structural Adjustment, Changes of Export Markets, Support for Technical Development*. Economic Trends and Research Summaries, No. 4. Budapest: GKI Economic Research Institute.

NBH (National Bank of Hungary Monthly Report). 1993. Nos. 11-12, Budapest.

O'Neill, R.P., and A. Brown. 1992. "Privatization and Regulation of the Oil, Natural Gas and Electric Industries in Hungary." *Energy Law Journal* 13: 25-43.

Petz, R. 1993. "Szerkezetváltás a magyar gazdaságban 1988-1991 között" (Structural Change in the Hungarian Economy Between 1988 and 1991). *Ipargazdasági Szemle Struktúrák-Szervezetek-Stratégiák* 2: 46-60.

Pittman, R. 1992. "Some Critical Provisions in the Antimonopoly Laws of Central and Eastern Europe." *The International Lawyer* 2: 485-503.

Pogácsás, P., and J. Stadler. 1993. "Promoting Competition in Hungary," in C.T. Saunders, ed., *The Role of Competition in Economic Transition*. Pp. 78-89. New York: St. Martin's Press.

Salgó, I., and Á. Török. 1980. "Importverseny a gépipari fogyasztási cikkek belföldi piacán árutesztek tükrében" (Import Competition on the Domestic Market for Engineering Products for Consumption as Reflected in Goods' Tests). *Külgazdaság*. December.

Sárközy, T. 1994. *A privatizáció joga Magyarországon 1988-1993* (*Privatization Legislation in Hungary During 1988-1993*). Budapest: Közgazdasági és Jogi Könyvkiadó.

Schwartz, M., and R. Reynolds. 1983. "Contestable Markets: An Uprising in the Theory of Industrial Structure: Comment". *American Economic Review*. June.

Somogyi, L., and Á. Török. 1993. "Property Rights, Competition Policy and Privatisation in the Transition from Socialism to Market Economy," in L. Somogyi, ed., *The Political Economy of the Transition Process in Eastern Europe.* Pp. 208-26. Aldershot: Edward Elgar Publishing.

Statisztikai Tájékoztató: Ipar, 1993 március. (Statistical Information: Industry, March 1993). 1993. Budapest: Central Statistical Office.

Török, Á. 1994. *Industrial Restructuring and "Marketisation" in Hungary: An Assessment of Trends and Policies.* Manuscript, Leuven: LICOS Institute, Catholic University of Leuven.

_____. 1992. "Egy 'Értékcsökkentő' vállalat a magyar elektronikai iparban. (A 'Value-subtracting' Enterprise in the Hungarian Electronics Industry). *Közgazdasági Szemle,* December.

Trebilcock, M.J. 1992. "The Role of Competition Policy in Non-Market Economies in Transition: The Case of Hungary," in S.A. Rayner, ed., *Privatisation in Central and Eastern Europe.* Pp. 105-11. London: Butterworths.

Vissi, F. 1994. "A külföldi működőtőke-beruházások és a verseny" (FDI and Competition). *Közgazdasági Szemle* 4: 349-59.

_____. 1994a. "Kihívások és kérdőjelek a versenypolitika környékén" (Challenges and Question Marks Linked to Competition Policy). Forthcoming in *Ipargazdasági Szemle, Struktúrák-Szervezetek-Stratégiák.*

_____. 1993. *FDI and Competition.* Mimeo, written for the Blue Ribbon Commission. Budapest-Munich, September.

_____. 1992. "Privatisation and Monopolies in Hungary," in S.A. Rayner, ed., *Privatisation in Central and Eastern Europe.* Pp. 112-22. London: Butterworths.

Williamson, O.E. 1985. *The Economic Institutions of Capitalism: Firms, Markets, Relational Contracting.* New York: The Free Press.

3

Antimonopoly Policy and Monopoly Regulation in Russia

Vladimir Capelik and Ben Slay

Monopolies and De-monopolization: An Overview

When it was part of the USSR Russia had a highly monopolized economy. Management of the national economy was based on such monopolistic organizations as industrial ministries, their departments (*glavki*), and producer associations (*ob"yedinyeniya*). "One product, one producer" patterns dominated in numerous industries. According to data published by the Soviet State Commission on Statistics in 1989, out of 344 industrial product groups examined, the largest single firm was responsible for at least 50 percent of total output in 209 groups, and for more than 90 percent of total output in 109 groups.[1] According to disaggregated data supplied by the Soviet State Committee for Material and Technical Supplies, 87 percent of the items produced by the Soviet machine building sector in 1988 were manufactured by single firms. Machine building, ferrous and non-ferrous metallurgy, chemicals, and petrochemicals were among the most monopolized sectors. Lower product concentration levels, and thus better possibilities for competition, existed in the building materials, light industrial, civil engineering, and agricultural sectors.[2] Still, at the end of the Soviet period (1991), about half of industrial output was produced by some 1,000 large firms, which employed on average at least 8,500 workers.[3] During the course of the *perestroika* reforms (1987-1991), many of these organizations underwent gradual transformations into institutions of an apparently more market-compatible nature, such as trade associations, amalgamations, concerns, and holdings. In some cases, however, they remained responsible for the management of entire industries.[4] Russian reformers thus inherited a large number of monopolistic organizations from the command administrative system. Many were fundamentally inconsistent with the logic of competitive markets.

On the other hand, data of this sort exaggerate the extent of monopolization. Shortage pressures and the related drive for self-sufficiency created many "non-profile" extra-branch producers, whose in-house output was not captured by branch-oriented structural concentration data. Likewise, the official statistics rarely considered the implications of defense producers of analogous products. Nonetheless, until 1993, it was widely believed among both Russian and Western economists that Russia was afflicted with exceptionally high (if not the world's highest) levels of industrial concentration and monopolization.[5] And while more recent research indicates that levels of structural concentration in Russia may actually be comparatively low,[6] many other impediments to market competition are present in Russia.

The first important steps in de-monopolization occurred within the framework of the former USSR during 1990-1991, and were of a largely spontaneous nature. Many industrial enterprises expanded the production of goods that were highly valued in barter trade. A 1991 survey of machine-building enterprises found that managers were trying to reorient production towards products that could serve as "equivalents" in barter trade (i.e., shortage items like consumer goods and building materials).[7] The failure of the August 1991 coup provided further impetus, as all-union enterprises, ministries, and associations were pulled apart by the now independent republics. Single-industry entities were sometimes subdivided by sub-regional authorities. In Russia, the new instruments acquired by the local authorities in 1992 (for instance, in fiscal policy) made it easier for local governments to encourage multi-plant enterprises to "relocate" themselves in their locales, and to create difficulties for the local offices of firms based elsewhere. A large-scale restructuring among defense enterprises towards consumer goods production took place in 1992, due to sharp reductions in military orders. And many Russian industrial enterprises have since 1992 diversified their production in response to reduced supplies from other parts of the former Soviet Union, which has increased the number of potential competitors for many products. To be sure, many of these developments reflected a growing trend towards regionalization, which compressed markets and tended to reduce competition. However, if and when the ruble (and financial activities in general) are stabilized in Russia, the ensuing unification of the national market should reverse the trend toward compression, and increasing numbers of market actors should strengthen competitive forces. Indeed, the combination of relative macroeconomic stabilization after 1993, the beginnings of a working relationship between the center and the regions following the approval of the Russian constitution in December 1993, and traders' growing abilities to "avoid" administrative barriers to extra-regional trade, may by 1995 have reversed this trend towards market compression.

Although the reform program introduced by then Deputy Prime Minister Yegor Gaidar in January 1992 did not emphasize de-monopolization *per se*, some reform steps, such as price liberalization and the introduction of tighter budget constraints for small and medium-sized enterprises, were key prerequisites for the appearance of various forms of spontaneous de-monopolization. Some small and medium-sized enterprises responded by developing new products and/or withdrawing from larger producer associations. Price liberalization reduced shortage pressures, while the liberalization of commercial activity removed entry barriers. Many administrative monopolies were liquidated during numerous government reorganizations. Import liberalization increased competition in some markets, and if the pace of reform and Western aid accelerates in the future, import competition could lead to rapid changes in several monopolized industries.

The Kalinin Factory in Yekaterinburg offers an interesting example of enterprise restructuring resulting from the introduction of competitive forces. This enterprise, which had produced launchers and fuel systems for SS missiles, in 1992 underwent an internal decentralization that granted autonomy to its divisions producing tractors and timber-felling equipment (which was based on converted missile-launching technology), as well as its food-processing and industrial-refrigeration plants (which used converted rocket-fuel cooling technology). A second example is offered by the Leninetz Plant in Saint Petersburg, which makes avionics for Mig airplanes. Leninetz, which began conversion to the production of civilian goods in 1988, was broken up into 117 business units in 1992, each of which gained control over output and wage decisions. The headquarters staff of 250 guides the firm (with its 43,000 employees) by controlling cash flow. The Kirovskii Tank Plant in 1992 split itself into 27 pieces, and cut its central staff by 99 percent.[8]

Resistance to de-monopolization has been significant, and has been led by the management of large state enterprises and some ministers. The large industrial lobby was behind proposals issued in early 1992 by then Minister of Industry Alexander Titkin to establish 500-700 large "technologically-integrated production complexes," in order to facilitate the central management of state industries. In January 1992 former Deputy Prime Minister Vladimir Shumeiko proposed a version of price formation "by cartel agreements." In the beginning of 1993 another former deputy prime minister, Georgii Chizha, told a Japanese reporter that the government would maintain control over prices through "an agreement with industrial circles." Opposition by local government officials to the reductions in authority and control implied by liberalization and market competition has also been significant. Even reformist governments in Russia have been tempted to actively and directly influence the pricing behavior of large state enterprises.

The strong movement towards creating "financial industrial groups" (FIGs) is one of the more recent manifestations of this tendency.[9] A number of Russian government officials and industrialists have advocated the creation of financial industrial groups similar to those in South Korea. First Deputy Prime Minister Oleg Soskovets told the Russian press in June, 1995 that 15 FIGs were then in existence, and the creation of another 20 was anticipated by the end of the year.[10] The first financial industrial groups were established by local authorities, grouping industrial and construction enterprises, research institutes, investment funds, and banks. FIGs often combine firms producing similar goods, and when they are established from above, excessive regulation and reliance on government subsidies can result. Indeed, FIGs are often created by enterprises looking to improve their bargaining position vis-à-vis the center over subsidies and tax credits.

The Kuznetskaya Kompaniya FIG in Kuzbass is one such example. On March 15, 1994, the administration of the Kemerovo oblast' announced the creation of Kuznetskaya Kompaniya, which consisted of the local railroad, the Rosugol' corporation (previously the Ministry of the Coal Industry), two commercial banks, the local committee on state enterprise management, and about 40 large industrial enterprises (in the metallurgical, chemical, machine-building, and coal sectors). Each shareholder in the FIG's 4.5 billion ruble statutory fund held at least 100 million rubles, in the form of cash or a package of shares.[11]

Although FIGs can pose an obvious threat to competition, it is difficult to condemn them unequivocally. Structural concentration in some Russian industries is low by world standards, making the realization of scale and scope economies more difficult. More generally, the integration of activities characterized by important synergies is hardly inconsistent with the development of market forces. According to their proponents, FIGs can also serve as a decentralized bankruptcy mechanism, in which the assets and activities of chronically-unprofitable members can be gradually phased out or transferred to other firms within a given group. In some instances, FIGs could increase Russia's competitiveness. In any case, while such groups clearly represent a threat to competition, as of mid-1994, regional antimonopoly bodies had not intervened to stop the creation of a single FIG.

Holding companies can be another anticompetitive organizational manifestation. The Russian government during the 1992-1994 privatization campaign received numerous applications for the establishment of holding companies, many of which were denied by the State Property Committee (SPC). By contrast, the State Committee on Antimonopoly Policy (SCAP) was not very active in this area, and many experts believe that it did not perform this vetting function adequately, as the establishment of most holdings was approved without any particular difficulty. This vetting often seemed to be largely formal in nature, and obstacles to competition erected by the creation of horizontally-integrated umbrella organizations were frequently not considered. Moreover, because SCAP did not supply its regional departments with clear guidelines about policies concerning holding companies, holdings could be established locally if they had troubles with central authorities.

However, while the dissolution of pre-existing associations and enterprises was a rarity, the SPC did prevent numerous Soviet-era producers' associations from reestablishing themselves as holdings during the course of privatization. Many subsidiaries of industrial enterprises during privatization became autonomous of their parent firms as well. SCAP and its 80 regional offices did play an important de-monopolizing role in some privatization cases. SCAP's Moscow office figured prominently in the reorganization of the construction industry's Glavmosstroi and Promstroimaterialy associations in 1993, for example. All economic agents that had previously been subordinated to these associations became independent business entities during the course of the associations' privatizations, and the two associations' administrations were converted into municipal enterprises performing intermediary and consulting functions. SCAP and the SPC also cooperated in approving privatization plans for enterprises included in the "Register of Monopolistic Enterprises" (discussed below). On the other hand, the emphasis upon voucher privatization during 1993-1994 effectively precluded the dissolution or divestiture of many state enterprises, since ownership of these firms was transferred to voucher-holders in an essentially "as is" fashion.

In any case, the formidable economic problems of 1992-1994 were not directly related to the behavior of monopoly enterprises. Instead, these problems resulted from the failure to impose hard budget constraints on enterprises (especially large ones), irrespective of levels of monopolization. The difficulties encountered in macroeconomic stabilization meant that both monopolistic and non-monopolistic enterprises were able to reduce output and increase prices significantly. These price increases were in large measure determined by enterprises' inflationary expectations, and by accommodating fiscal and monetary policies. Indeed, in these circumstances only a few monopolistic producers were able to conspicuously reduce output and raise prices. However, the bigger state-owned enterprises (which, in a number of cases, are also the monopoly producers of certain products) were able to make their lives easier by getting cheap credits from the treasury, even while showing the same rate of price increases as small state-run firms.

The result was that monopolization in Russian manufacturing was still a serious problem at the end of 1994. "One product, one producer" patterns persisted in areas such as the manufacture of diesel locomotives, electric locomotives, and cement trucks. Wholesale trade was still monopolized in some spheres, and the regionalization of some markets where enough producers were present on national markets to provide potential competition also increased the extent of product-level monopoly. What role did competition policy play in this outcome?

Competition Policy: The Legal Framework

The first drafts of a competition law for the Soviet Union were prepared in 1988-1989 by economists and lawyers in the Soviet Academy of Sciences,[12] who were influenced primarily by the Polish competition law and American antitrust legislation. Experts from the OECD countries subsequently helped to improve the draft. The draft was then rewritten for Russia in 1990, with relatively minor changes. Following long discussions in the parliament, the Russian Federation law "On Competition and Limitation of Monopolistic Activity in Commodity Markets" was adopted in March 22, 1991. (This law was amended in some small but important ways in May, 1995.)[13]

Although some have argued that the Russian antimonopoly law is modeled on European legislation, it can more appropriately be described as a mixture of European and American competition policies. "Dominant position"—a concept taken from Western and Eastern European competition policy, rather than from the US—does play a key role in the Russian law, however. It is defined in Article 4 as the exclusive position of an economic subject[14] (or a group of economic subjects) on the market for a given product with no close substitutes. Such a position is one that allows an economic subject to exert decisive influence over the competition, create significant barriers to entry, or otherwise limit the scope for unfettered economic activity. Economic subjects whose shares of the relevant market exceed 65 percent are automatically viewed as having dominant positions; while economic subjects whose shares of the relevant market are between 35 and 65 percent may be considered dominant, if their market shares are stable, and barriers to entry are determined to be high. Economic subjects whose shares of the relevant market are less than 35 percent are not in any case regarded as dominant.

Article 5 concerns abuse of dominant position. It prohibits:

- the withdrawal of goods from the market in order to create shortages or raise prices;
- the imposition of onerous conditions on a contracting party that are unrelated to the subject of the contract;
- the setting of "monopolistically high or low prices";
- the creation of barriers to entry to (or exit from) the market; and
- violation of price-formation procedures established by state normative acts.

Evaluation of all such conduct is to be conducted under a rule of reason. That is, "in exceptional circumstances," firms may avoid culpability by proving that the positive effects of their actions, "including that in the socio-economic sphere...exceed the negative consequences for the commodity market under consideration."

While these strictures would seem to provide ample legal ammunition for the prosecution of predatory firms, they may also be general enough to be subject to abuse by SCAP. When should the "monopolistically low prices" set by dominant firms be viewed as predatory, as opposed to a manifestation of more efficient firms' competitive superiority?

Article 6, which focuses on horizontal and vertical agreements of a potentially anti-competitive nature, prohibits agreements among economic subjects that restrict competition through:

- fixing and maintaining prices and discounts;
- bid-rigging conspiracies at auctions;
- territorial segmentation of the market;
- forming amalgamations (i.e., trade associations) that may limit competition;
- joint imposition of barriers for new entrants to the market; and
- refusals to contract with certain buyers (boycotts).

Because it does not prohibit collusion in a *per se* fashion, this article has also been the subject of criticism. This is because this article: (1) only applies to firms that singly or jointly possess 35 percent of the relevant market; and (2) affords potential violators an efficiency defense, if they can prove that the agreement in question ("in exceptional circumstances," of course) provides net offsetting social benefits ("including the socio-economic sphere"). However, while the Russian law's treatment of such agreements does differ substantially from US practice, it is closer to the logic of competition policy in both Western and Eastern Europe.

Article 7 prohibits actions by administrative bodies (known as APAs)[15] that restrict competition, for example through narrowing the autonomy of, or creating discriminatory conditions for, economic subjects. It also prevents APAs from establishing limitations on trade between regions of Russia. Article 8 covers agreements (analogous to the agreements between economic subjects treated in Article 6) among APAs (or between APAs and economic subjects) that restrict competition. Article 7 was included in the law in order to circumscribe administrative organs' abilities to limit market access or restrict extra-regional exports. As such, this article could have decisive importance in ensuring free entry for new competitors, and its significance is likely to increase in the future.

Article 10 lists the prohibited forms of unfair competition. These include: (1) providing false or distorted information that results in losses for a competitor; (2) misleading consumers about product quality; (3) offering inaccurate comparisons of economic subjects' goods in advertising; (4) engaging in the arbitrary use of external trademarks and firms' names; and (5) the unauthorized use of intellectual property.

Articles 17 and 18 concern mergers and acquisitions. SCAP may veto the creation of an economic subject that would immediately acquire dominant market position. Economic subjects above some maximum size (usually expressed as assets relative to some multiple of the monthly minimum wage) must notify SCAP of merger intentions; SCAP must decide within 30 days whether to permit the merger.

Article 19 describes the factors that must be taken into account when the dissolution or divestiture of an economic subject is under consideration. These include the:

- organizational and territorial characteristics of the enterprise and its divisions;
- presence or absence of close technological links between the firm's divisions (e.g., the share of intra-firm turnover should comprise less than 30 percent of its gross output for a dissolution to be approved); and
- degree of intra-firm specialization within its individual divisions.

In dozens of rulings during 1992-1994, SCAP supported requests for independence via divestiture. For instance, a dispute between the Mosmetrostroi subway builder and one of its construction divisions in 1993 ended in a victory for the latter, with the active involvement of the SPC. In other cases, the initiation of a formal investigation by SCAP resulted in the parent enterprises permitting their sub-divisions to become independent, without SCAP having to issue a formal ruling.

Articles 22 through 26 set forth penalties for violations of the law. SCAP can order an economic subject or APA to terminate offending behavior, restore the initial *ex ante* situation, or dissolve or modify a contract. The compensation for losses resulting from restrictions on competition is determined by the courts. SCAP is charged with imposing fines on economic subjects (and their managers) and APA officials, while the courts execute payment for fines. Under 1992 amendments to the Criminal Code, APA officials and enterprise managers who are twice subjected to administrative sanctions for a given offense within a one-year period can be sentenced to two years of correctional labor.

Article 28 concerns appeals procedures. Like the US Federal Trade Commission, SCAP possesses both executive and judicial authority, so that initial competition-policy decisions take the form of rulings issued by SCAP or its territorial agencies. These rulings can be (and are) easily appealed to an arbitration court, however, and once an appeal has been filed, the ruling is held in abeyance until the court issues it verdict. The backlog of cases in many arbitration courts means that considerable delays (of a year or more) are not uncommon. And given the novelty of competition policy in Russia's nascent "independent" judiciary, SCAP officials argue that arbitration court decisions are frequently made in ignorance of the basic requirements of competition policy (not to mention basic economics). The upshot is that the appeals process, as it functioned during 1992-1994, significantly weakened the influence of SCAP decisions upon enterprise behavior.

The largest group of inquiries initiated by SCAP have concerned allegations of abuse of dominant position (Article 5). The imposition on contracting parties of onerous conditions unrelated to the primary subject of the contract, such as unjustified demands for the transfer of funds, raw and other materials, apartments, and labor, was also a frequently claimed violation. As the market economy gains in strength, the number of such abuses is likely to decline substantially, however.

Prosecution of price-fixing agreements (under Article 6) might be expected to increase as reform makes headway. The difficulties encountered in uncovering such collusion are obvious, however, as overt accords of this kind are rare. Most are deftly concealed, and much painstaking work is required to uncover them. Moreover, in Russian jurisprudence, the arbitration courts (to which SCAP rulings are frequently, and successfully, appealed) have generally ruled that, in order to obtain a conviction against collusion based on Article 6, SCAP must: (1) produce written documents unambiguously proving the existence of an agreement among firms jointly or singly comprising 35 percent of the relevant product market; and (2) explicitly demonstrate the specific anti-competitive consequences of the agreement in question. Needless to say, such rulings have made successful prosecution of collusive arrangements extremely difficult. It should also be pointed out that cartel agreements in Russia are frequently understood differently than in market economies. Along with horizontal agreements intended to restrict competition, cartel agreements in Russia often include vertical pricing restraints between suppliers and customers intended to slow the growth of prices for final outputs. While such vertical agreements can promote production efficiency and keener competition among producers, they can also disguise genuine cartels in which manufacturers of similar products agree to suspend competition in order to raise prices.

Barriers to entry are a key antimonopoly policy concern. Such obstacles remain very formidable. They are frequently associated with the decisions of governmental and administrative (rather than commercial) bodies, and may have become more numerous in many industries since 1992. The government's ordinance "On the Powers of Executive Authorities of Regions, Autonomous Areas, and Cities of Federal Significance to License Individual Activities" (No. 492 of June 27, 1993), for instance, tightened local administrative restrictions on access to commodity markets in 27 of the most profitable production and investment activities. Presidential Decree No. 918 (of June 11, 1993) "On the Restoration of the State Monopoly on the Production, Storage, Wholesaling, and Retailing of Alcoholic Products" had similar effects. And while import competition can help combat monopoly abuses, auto, electronic, instrument-making, and textile companies in the summer of 1993 demanded exorbitant tariffs (from 50 to 150 percent, depending on the product) on imports competing with their output. The AvtoVAZ car maker in November-December 1993 secured the adoption of high duties on vehicle imports by legal entities and prohibitive duties on imports of both new and used cars by individuals.[16] A new tariff regime introduced in March 1994 increased average nominal tariff rates from 8 to 14 percent.[17]

In theory, such activities could be treated as violations of Article 7, which pertains to "actions by legislative and executive authorities that restrict competition." However, investigation (not to mention prosecution) of these practices (the most common of which were bans on the establishment of new firms or changes in enterprises' production profiles, prohibitions on extra-regional exports, and the provision of unjustified benefits to individual firms that distorted competition) have been extremely infrequent. Given the strong opposition to de-monopolization apparent in the behavior of many central, regional, and local governmental and administrative bodies, inactivity in this area points perhaps to the greatest weakness in competition policy to date.

The "State Program for Demonopolizing the Economy and Developing Market Competition in the Russian Federation" was adopted by the government on March 9, 1994. The program's main goals are altering the monopolized structures that were formed under the administrative-command system, and creating an environment conducive to the development of competition. The program set forth guidelines and long-term priorities for antimonopoly policy, with special emphasis on trade, construction, telecommunications, transportation (except for the railways), and machine-building. The Interdepartmental Commission on Competition Policy, headed by then Deputy Prime Minister Oleg Soskovets, was established and charged with coordinating regional and industrial de-monopolization programs.

The need to update the legal framework for competition policy has been widely acknowledged, especially in light of the developments that have occurred since the 1991 law. Most of the amendments that were passed into law in May 1995 were prepared in 1993, but the volatile political situation in the second half of the year prevented their consideration by parliament. Article 4 was amended by the Russian Supreme Soviet in June, 1993, however. The amendment recast market definition procedures by emphasizing "the buyer's economic capacity to acquire a particular good within the relevant geographic area, and the absence of such possibilities outside of this area." The intent was to specify more clearly the geographic boundaries of markets, since the courts had generally acted on the presumption that markets could only exist within large administrative-territorial regional entities. Many specialists also believe that the arbitration courts have often defined "the buyer's economic capacity" too broadly, enabling local monopolies to avoid the competition law's strictures.

The State Committee on Antimonopoly Policy (SCAP)

The State Committee of the Russian Federation for Antimonopoly Policy and Support of Economic Structures (SCAP) was established in August 1990. Its creation signalled the start of competition policy in

Russia, as well as the training of appropriate personnel (mostly economists and lawyers). The establishment of SCAP's 82 territorial offices (roughly one in each of Russia's *oblasti* and autonomous republics) in early 1992 represented another important landmark in the institutional development of Russian competition policy. SCAP's territorial offices are formally subordinated to the central office in Moscow, and initially the territorial offices received their marching orders from Moscow. Since 1992, however, a good deal of power has devolved from the central to the territorial offices, as competition policy has *de facto* been increasingly made by officials in the region.[18]

According to Article 3 of the 1991 competition law (as amended in May 1995) the chairman of SCAP's central office in Moscow is appointed (or removed) by the president upon the nomination of the Prime Minister.[19] The SCAP board (which is approved by the government) consists of the SCAP chairman and his deputies, heads of departments, and leading scholars and specialists. Four expert councils, consisting of scholars, SCAP staff, and specialists from other ministries and departments, develop competition promotion measures, and analyze market structures and conditions. Although (according to the resolution of August 24, 1992) employment in SCAP's central office is supposed to be 350, by mid-1994, employment stood at 200; likewise, employment in the 82 regional offices, which should number 2,500, stood at only 1,700 at the end of 1993,[20] and was not expected to increase quickly. SCAP's failure to grow to its designated size results from a lack of financial resources and skilled specialists in Russia.

Moreover, SCAP since its inception has been involved with functions not directly related to competition policy (as understood in the West); initially, only 20 of the 100 employees at SCAP's central office were directly involved with competition policy issues *per se*.[21] Formally, these other functions have included regulating free economic zones, promoting entrepreneurship, overseeing commodity exchanges, and monitoring protection of intellectual property rights. Informally, the territorial offices have often seemed caught up with matters more properly understood as industrial-policy concerns, such as keeping unprofitable firms in operation, slowing price increases for foodstuffs and other "socially sensitive" products, and preventing rapid increases in local unemployment rates. On the other hand, some aspects of competition policy are legally outside of SCAP's purview—the maintenance of competition in the banking sector is under the jurisdiction of the Ministry of Finance, for example.

The above-mentioned resolution of August 24, 1992, outlines SCAP's basic tasks, functions, and authority. These include promoting the development of competition; limiting monopolistic activities;

preventing unfair competition; and protecting consumer rights. More specifically, SCAP activities can be divided into the following areas:

- SCAP supervises the enforcement of competition legislation, and investigates violations. SCAP analyzes competition policy making in other countries (including in the other members of the Commonwealth of Independent States),[22] summarizes domestic enforcement and practices, develops legal acts concerning antimonopoly policy. SCAP also submits to the president findings on draft laws and other normative acts, analytical materials, and proposals concerning monopolistic activities, the development of product markets, competition, and the protection of consumer rights. SCAP and its territorial offices are supposed to have unimpeded access to information on the activities of economic subjects and APAs.
- SCAP conducts preliminary monitoring of mergers of economic subjects holding dominant market positions. It also performs these functions during the commercialization, privatization, and dissolution of state enterprises. In cooperation with the State Property Committee (SPC), SCAP provides a unified methodological framework for the creation of competitive markets, and coordinates industrial and regional de-monopolization programs. SCAP provides opinions on plans for privatizing state enterprises occupying dominant positions on product markets.
- SCAP may issue cease-and-desist orders, order offenders to restore the situation in force prior to the illegal activities, and dissolve or amend agreements among economic subjects and APAs. SCAP makes decisions regarding the imposition of fines on economic subjects, their managers, and APA officials. It brings suit in court, participates in the investigation of violations, and sends evidentiary materials to prosecutorial organs. SCAP also presents the appropriate ministries with proposals for introducing mandatory licensing and prohibiting or terminating export-import operations for economic subjects found to be in violation of antimonopoly legislation. SCAP may order the dissolutions or divestiture of economic subjects in dominant market positions that engage in monopolistic activity.
- SCAP organizes the implementation of measures aimed at protecting consumer rights and preventing unfair competition. It also organizes the work of the Commission for Commodity Exchanges in keeping with the 1992 Russian Federation legislation "On Commodity Exchanges and Exchange Trade."

- SCAP organizes competition policy research. In doing so, it may establish analytical institutions and specialized off-budget funds. Funding is drawn from the state budget, and from the Fund for the Support of Entrepreneurship and the Development of Competition. SCAP participates in the training of specialists, and informs the population through the mass media of developments in antimonopoly policy.
- SCAP maintains the State Register of Monopoly Associations and Enterprises on Product Markets (the Register). It makes decisions concerning the inclusion of economic subjects in, and their removal from, the Register. Decisions are based on information provided by the State Statistical Committee (Goskomstat), and the results of previous investigations of possible violations of antimonopoly legislation.
- SCAP is authorized to approve the establishment of new holding companies, concerns, and other umbrella organizations. Many experts have criticized SCAP's performance in this area, as the establishment of most such associations were approved in a largely perfunctory manner; impediments to competition associated with the creation of horizontally integrated umbrella organizations were frequently not considered.

While this laundry list may seem to be rather unexceptional, its emphasis upon "competition advocacy" is especially noteworthy. Because of its legal and institutional role in the complex of Russian economic policy making, SCAP is uniquely positioned to advocate pro-competitive policy solutions—and oppose anti-competitive measures. Whether it has exercised its competition advocacy function as effectively as it might is a matter of some debate.[23]

The "Register," "Monopoly" Regulation, and Price Controls

Four important decrees and resolutions on "monopoly" regulation were introduced during the winter of 1991-1992.[24] These documents were the legal manifestation of what has been described as a "cavalry charge against monopoly" that followed the price liberalization of January 1992;[25] they were meant to facilitate the application of tough measures against enterprises found to abuse their market power. These measures included:

- the mandatory restoration of contracts cancelled economic subjects in dominant market positions;
- obligatory deliveries of a portion of enterprise output to the state reserve fund at controlled prices;
- the elimination of subsidies and preferential credits for monopolistic enterprises;
- the cancellation of contracts with heads of state enterprises by the ministries; and
- the forced restructuring of monopolies.

Despite the fierce regulatory stance implied by these decrees, competition policy has not generally been consistent with the principles behind them. This initially resulted in 1992 from the Gaidar government's liberal, pro-business orientation, and then from declines in executive authority in the center and the regions, the lack of skilled specialists, and poor coordination between SCAP and the price authorities. Instead, these developments resulted in the creeping reintroduction of price regulation during 1992-1993, under the guise of "competition policy." This was largely due to political initiatives of anti-market forces, rather than the need to restrict the predatory conduct of natural monopolies. The political heterogeneity of the Russian governments after mid-1992 contributed the success of these initiatives, as cabinet members close to the industrial lobby were able to use the regulation of "monopoly prices" as a justification for retaining central administrative influence over state enterprise pricing and output decisions.

The "Register of Monopoly Enterprises"[26] was introduced by SCAP in February 1992 as part of this cavalry charge, and thereafter underwent periodic (frequently monthly) updates. Some 2,000 enterprises and associations suspected of occupying dominant positions on federal or regional product markets and engaging in anticompetitive activities were initially listed in the Register—many without sufficient justification. As one observer noted:

> During 1992, local [SCAP] administrations, striving to lower the level of social tensions in their regions, made active use of the levers of anti-monopoly regulation for this purpose. That is why a large number of enterprises in the food and light industries, which were traditionally orientated to their local markets, immediately appeared in the regional divisions of the register of monopolies. Typically, these producers at times did not occupy a dominant position on their markets. Quite often this policy was accompanied by a variety of prohibitions on selling consumer goods and food products outside of the *oblast*.[27]

Relevant markets were arbitrarily defined, since SCAP's central office did not issue the documentation for proper market definitions until 1993.[28] Shares exceeding 35 percent in these poorly-defined markets were at that point the only (formal) grounds for inclusion in the Register. The firms and APAs listed in the Register included state-controlled associations involved in wholesale trade, as well as industrial enterprises and amalgamations. By January 1993, according to Goskomstat figures, the number of enterprises and APAs in the Register had increased to more than 6,000.

Inclusion in the Register during 1992-1993 influenced both pricing and privatization decisions. In addition to being subject to various forms of price regulation by the central government, firms included in the Register were generally bypassed for privatization by the SPC, in favor of enterprises whose privatization did not require SCAP approval. For these and other reasons, enterprises generally tried to secure their removal from the Register, and many were successful. Others were not. For example, Mosintur (a Moscow tourist agency specializing in international tourism) estimated its share in the market of hotel services at less than 35 percent, and in December 1992 it requested its removal from the Register. Nevertheless, on the basis of SCAP data showing that Mosintur controlled (directly and indirectly) about 90 percent of the business done by Moscow hotels, the company's request was rejected.[29]

Price regulation (or reregulation) based on the Register began in earnest on May 8, 1992, when the State Price Committee adopted Resolution number 2, requiring that "monopolistic firms" obtain permission for price increases. Appropriate instructions were drawn up for the Price Committee's regional offices, which were charged with the task of scrutinizing increases in prices that had been liberalized in January. The price and cost estimates documented immediately before the resolution went into effect were adopted as the basis for price regulation.

In August, 1992 the government issued a resolution (signed by then Prime Minister Gaidar) "On State Regulation of Prices and Tariffs for the Products and Services of Monopoly Enterprises in 1992-1993." This resolution set maximum profit rates for "monopolies" (i.e., firms that met the 35 percent market-share test); and it delineated five forms of price regulation for enterprises listed on the Register: (1) setting actual prices; (2) setting maximum prices; (3) linking maximum price increases to inflation-related coefficients; (4) linking prices to profitability levels; and (5) setting maximum limits on price increases. Instruments (1) through (3) were applied to products included in the Register, while (4) and (5) were applied to other products manufactured by "monopolistic" enterprises. Violations of these regulations could result in double-damage sanctions, payable to the state budget. Exceptions to restrictions on profitability levels (4) were, however, granted by the Ministry of the Economy, in order to stimulate technological progress and to help arrest the decline in production.

In practice, these regulations were usually ineffective and/or counterproductive.[30] Enterprises have many ways of inflating production costs to avoid showing high profits, and price controls can be avoided by engaging in barter trade. Administered or maximum prices can cause enterprises to reduce production or stop producing altogether. In practice, it proved virtually impossible to determine how cost-based prices should be set when joint costs that can not be easily allocated across individual products constitute an appreciable share of a multi-product enterprise's total costs. Since appropriate cost estimates were frequently absent, price officials established arbitrary rates of price increase relative to the levels registered in preceding periods. Further, because of the mass of paperwork associated with enterprise price and cost data, administrative approval of price increases could not be realistically required for all enterprises included in the Register. The requirement was therefore initially limited to a special list of products. Even so, obtaining approval for price increases was a constant headache for enterprises. While most firms initially sought to obtain approval for price increases once a quarter, many companies began insisting on obtaining approval for price increases on a monthly basis, in order to keep pace with rising input costs. Queues developed, so that enterprises had to wait for up to two months for decisions from the relevant offices of the Price Committee. Petitions for price increases often became outdated in the interim, and new requests had to be submitted. Despite these problems, the Price Committee during 1992 was preparing measures that would have subjected virtually all prices to reregulation. At the end of December 1992, the new Prime Minister Viktor Chernomyrdin signed the infamous price regulation decree that would have done just this.

This decree was repealed on January 18, 1993, however, after liberal ministers managed to explain to the new Prime Minister that such procedures had proven to be ineffective even in the case of "monopolistic" enterprises. This repeal represented something of a watershed in Russian competition policy, in that the inability of the largely-unreformed pricing authorities to set well-grounded prices via administrative methods was increasingly accepted.[31] Moreover, it was increasingly understood that policies justified by the need to combat monopoly in many cases did exactly the opposite. Policy makers saw that price regulation in 1992 had not been limited to natural monopolies, and that genuinely natural monopolies were regulated through old-fashioned administrative methods. Arguments that the gas and oil industries should be divested of their distribution networks, so that the latter could be regulated as natural monopolies while the former could be subjected to competitive forces, therefore began to receive an increasingly favorable reception. So did proposals to create specialized regulatory agencies to oversee pricing and output in those industries that could genuinely be regarded as natural monopolies.

Much of the ineffectiveness of monopoly regulation was linked to the nature of the Register of Monopoly Enterprises itself, and the number of firms and APAs included in the Register declined sharply after reaching its peak (of 6,000) in early 1993. As one observer put it:

> Facing the prospect of a mass of arbitration hearings, and with a high probability of losing them, the anti-monopoly administrations themselves began to remove enterprises which had not abused their dominant position from the register. With such enterprises agreements were usually concluded whereby they would supply a certain proportion of their output to the local trade network (Rostov) or would provide regular information about the volume of production and the state of the market (St. Petersburg).[32]

By the end of 1993, the central Register listed only 582 enterprises and amalgamations as "monopolists of national significance," while some 1,600 companies were listed on regional Registers. These two groups constituted 2.7 percent of all enterprises in Russia, producing about 7 percent of total industrial output.[33]

On the other hand, the Register did help SCAP to define itself on Russia's economic landscape, and spurred work on problems of market definition. One observer has argued that, as the number of dominant firms on the Register has declined, the firms that have remained on the Register have generally been those firms that genuinely abuse their market power. This situation "notably reduced the extent of regulation and increased its effectiveness."[34] The fact that the regulation of "monopoly prices" during 1992-1993 was attempted via methods thought to be consistent with Western practices (such as price caps, limits on prices, rates of price increases, profitability, or seller's mark-ups) may also have had some significance. Still, many of the rulings that were actually issued, such as the mandatory restoration of traditional economic ties and patterns of product distribution, compulsory deliveries of enterprise output to state reserves at controlled prices, the dismissal of managers, and the forced reorganization of enterprises, clearly belonged to the command system, and on balance probably damaged the development of market competition.

Along with reduction in the numbers of firms on the Register, the emphasis in price regulation during 1993 shifted to a more flexible indicator—limits on profitability relative to prime costs.[35] These limits ranged between 10 and 50 percent, depending on the sector. This more flexible price regulation mechanism also had a number of drawbacks that were predictable from Western regulatory experience, and were subsequently confirmed in Russian practice. Enterprises kept profit rates under the ceilings by maximizing expenses, for example. In the Russian case, this problem was compounded by the fact that the indicator used by regulators was the ratio of profits to prime costs, rather than the ratio of profits to assets, which generally remain an unknown quantity. Also, enterprises manufacturing products sold at both regulated and unregulated prices have incentive to shift costs associated with the production of unregulated products to the production of regulated ones. Firms can reduce or halt regulated activities, or reduce their quality. Finally, actual profitability can be deliberately understated, in order to keep nominal profit rates within regulatory limits. Russian enterprises, for example, ask customers to delay payments for sales when the sellers are about to exceed the profitability limit.

Entry into markets where incumbents' prices are subject to regulation is often restricted in Western countries. In Russia, however, the doors to these markets have generally been wide open.[36] But while incumbent firms have faced disadvantages regulated in the form of controlled prices, they have also enjoyed the advantages of large size (if not of regulation itself), such as political influence, access to centrally-subsidized inputs and credit, and entrenched market positions. Subsidized input sales have in fact frequently been used to support enterprises whose output prices are regulated. State agencies also grant numerous other concessions to "their" enterprises, such as discounts on (or exemptions from) the profit tax, water charges, fees for the use of service lines, rent, and land payments. By contrast, while entrants may make their own pricing and production decisions, they are more likely to face firmer demand and financial constraints, and are frequently prevented (by regulation) from competing with protected incumbents on the entire expanse of the market. As a result, small ventures outside of the state sector frequently find themselves at a competitive disadvantage, even if their prices are not regulated. Such arrangements have tended to keep large enterprises with depreciated equipment and obsolete technologies afloat, which works to prevent adjustment in sectors that could otherwise have turned more quickly from monopoly to competition.

In any case, the August 1992 profit-regulation ordinance expired in late 1993, and was not renewed in 1994. The continuation of this form of regulation of "monopolistic" enterprises' prices and profitability by the central government seems therefore to have ended. On the other hand, the monopoly Registers maintained by SCAP's central and local offices seem likely to continue for the indefinite future. These Registers have provided one of the legal pretexts that allowed many local and regional governments to maintain formal (not to mention informal) controls on prices, profits, and production profiles into 1994 and beyond.[37] According to one estimate, 20 percent of Russia's prices in 1994 were still regulated at the national level, and another 30 percent were regulated by the local authorities.[38] While many factors brought this situation about, competition policy is certainly one of them. Moreover, should political developments in Russia take an unfavorable tack, a return to all manner of regulatory schemes, covering more than just natural monopolies, would be quite possible. The conservatives abilities' to exploit the regulation of "natural monopolies" as a disguise for regression towards increased state and administrative influence in enterprise decision making should not be overlooked.

Natural Monopoly Regulation

The problem of regulating natural monopolies still exists, the overregulation of previous years notwithstanding. Until now, most regional natural monopolies have been regulated by the local authorities via traditional administrative means. The prices charged by many natural monopolies have often been well below costs, necessitating subsidies from local budgets. While progress in privatization and price liberalization should ultimately provide certain answers to these difficulties, local and regional regulatory schemes should be developed well in advance of their completion. On the other hand, some natural monopolies have used their dominant position in ways that are genuinely harmful for consumers. The prices of many goods and services supplied by natural monopolies have increased significantly in relative terms since the general price liberalization of January 1992. For example, in 1993, when the general industrial price index increased 8.2 fold, electricity prices increased 13.8 fold, heating prices 14.8 fold, and railroad freight tariffs 18.6 fold. These price increases frequently outpaced growth in costs as well. In the first quarter of 1994, for example, telecommunication prices increased 2.7 fold, while energy prices increased 1.5 fold, wage costs increased 2.4 fold, transportation costs increased 2.5 fold, and other input costs rose 1.8 fold.[39] Likewise, regional data indicate that wages in natural monopoly enterprises are significantly higher than average industrial wages. In the electricity industry, for example, wages in natural monopoly enterprises exceeded average industrial wages 5.1 fold in Stavropol' krai, 4.4 fold in Penza oblast', and four-fold in the Dagestan Republic. In railroads, the ratios were 4.1 fold for Tambov oblast', 3.8 fold for Bryansk oblast', and 2.6 fold for Tula oblast'. In telecommunications, the ratios were 1.5—2 fold in the Ryazan, Vladimir, and Ivanovo oblasti.

These trends can be partly explained by the difficulties industries with homogeneous products face in hiding incomes from the fiscal authorities. It is very difficult to sell electricity or telephone services on the black market. Other state enterprises can sell part of their output for cash, do not pay taxes, and pay wages in cash while keeping these operations "off the books." Also, these increases in relative prices for natural monopoly industries may have themselves been a correction driven by the losses these firms incurred prior to price liberalization.

The draft law "On Natural Monopolies" was prepared by the Russian Privatization Center and SCAP during 1993-1994, and was presented to the Duma (parliament) by the government in late July 1994. As of mid-1995, the law had received parliamentary approval, been vetoed by President Yeltsin (apparently at the behest of his advisors) and passed again by the Duma. If approved by the presidential administration, the law would replace the August 1992 ordinance and promote efficiency in natural monopoly enterprises, while simultaneously protecting consumers from the abuses of monopoly prices made possible by price liberalization. Other (non-natural) "monopoly" enterprises would not be regulated under this law, and would instead fall under the general framework of competition policy. Thus, regulatory methods for natural monopolies would not be applied to firms or industries that should more appropriately be classified as competitive or contestable.

The draft law defines a natural monopoly as a market situation in which demand is satisfied more efficiently in the absence of competition, and products cannot be easily substituted because of relatively low price elasticity of demand. The draft law regards the following sectors as natural monopolies: (1) pipeline transportation for gas and oil; (2) the production and transmission of electricity; (3) the railroads (both passenger and freight); (4) transportation to and within remote regions; (5) services of transport terminals, sea- and airports; (6) some telecommunication services; (7) water and sewage; and (8) management of air transportation.

This scheme would narrow the class of firms that can be defined as natural monopolies and therefore be subject to regulation. If enacted, it would substantially reduce the list of regulated sectors. Indeed, the list of natural monopolies could be further reduced as industries that in time lose their natural monopoly characteristics, due to technological change or the emergence of new substitutes, would be removed from the list. The draft law also envisions the creation of federal agencies to regulate natural monopolies, although the actual establishment of these bodies would require additional legislation or executive decrees. Such organs, which could be regarded as prototypes, already exist in some sectors, such bodies resembling the US Federal Energy Commission, charged with regulating regional electricity rates. These regulatory agencies should be independent, and should apply specific regulatory instruments on the basis of the above-mentioned draft legislation.[40] In applying these instruments, the agencies must take into account the opinion of ministries, enterprises and their trade associations, SCAP and its regional offices, and consumer protection organizations. According to the draft legislation, each agency is to be headed by a seven member board of directors. The chairman of the board is to be appointed by the government for a three year term. Should a regulated industry lose its "natural monopoly" status, due to the development of new technologies or substitute products, its regulatory body would be liquidated.

The instruments to be applied by agencies regulating natural monopolies include:

- determination of groups of users to whom the natural monopolies must provide certain services;
- price regulation (via price caps or rate-of-return regulation);
- requirements concerning the quality of products (and services);
- regulation of entry;
- regulation of investment activities; and
- review of mergers, acquisitions, and sales of shares.

Although these regulatory agencies would have exclusive jurisdiction over the regulation of "their" natural monopolies, they could choose to employ little or no regulation in the appropriate circumstances. Regulatory programs would be determined by the agencies after considering proposals from industrial management bodies, enterprises, and consumer protection organizations. Agencies would be authorized to require regulated entities to supply information necessary for the regulatory process, and would also prescribe regulatory accounting rules.

In the event of a violation, the regulated monopoly enterprises would have to:

- cease and desist actions judged to be inconsistent with the law;
- restore the situation existing prior to the violation;

- cancel management decisions;
- sign a new or change an existing agreement with a consumer;
- pay fines;
- provide compensation to injured parties for damages resulting from the offending behavior; and/or
- transfer to the state budget the profit received as a result of the offending behavior.

Regulatory decisions could be annulled in court if regulators were to exceed their authority, or fail to perform their functions.

Conclusions

This chapter suggests the following conclusions concerning competition policy in Russia.

While the Russian portion of the former Soviet economy was highly monopolized, the extent of industrial concentration was not as high as widely believed. Moreover, some spontaneous de-monopolization has taken place since 1991.

The State Committee on Antimonopoly Policy (SCAP) was created in 1990, and Russia's first antimonopoly law was adopted in 1991. This helped reduce the scale of the monopoly problem, and has promoted de-monopolization. However, SCAP's central and territorial offices have encountered a number of problems in enforcing this legislation, due mostly to SCAP's and the courts' lack of skilled personnel (economists and lawyers), to difficulties in financing the training of specialists, and to SCAP's inability to forestall anticompetitive behavior by other state and administrative institutions. Progress in removing barriers to entry has also been insufficient, especially in terms of reducing cumbersome licensing procedures and promoting import competition. Only a few direct antimonopoly measures have been implemented, and not all of them have been unblemished successes. In fact, SCAP's structural de-monopolization efforts have generally been less successful than those undertaken by the State Property Committee (SPC), which prevented the establishment of some industry-wide holding companies during the course of privatization. Although the 1991 Law on Competition and subsequent presidential and government decrees empowered SCAP to prevent the emergence of such holding companies, it rarely did so. So while competition policy has not been particularly ambitious in practice, liberalization and privatization have promoted competition among enterprises.[41] Still, SCAP has often played an important role as an advocate for the development of market forces, and as an opponent of anti-competitive policy measures proposed by other administrative bodies.

SCAP's central and territorial offices should seek to strengthen their links to, and work more closely with, the SPC appropriate SPC offices on the de-monopolization of industries during the course of their privatization. In terms of competition policy *per se*, SCAP should focus on such problems as developing notification and registration systems for mergers and acquisitions, dismantling barriers to entry, ensuring proper enforcement of competition legislation, and improving co-ordination between and among the central and regional offices. Consumer protection efforts might also be reduced, in light of the activities of many consumer protection organizations such as the International Confederation. Despite the fact that it is one of the most important institutions for promoting competition, SCAP has not worked effectively with the mass media. Indeed, information on competition policy is not provided to either the general public or outside experts in an open, transparent manner. SCAP should therefore work more closely with mass media and consumer protection organizations in the enforcement of the antimonopoly law.

Much energy was devoted to developing the Register of Monopoly Enterprises. The original inclusion of some 2,000 enterprises occurred in a largely arbitrary manner, which then necessitated extensive inclusions into and removals from the Register. This shifted attention away from promoting competition towards regulating (and frequently protecting) firms that were frequently far from being natural monopolies. Also, SCAP did not aggressively oppose the anti-competitive activities of regional, and local governments, in terms of their monopolization of real estate markets, barriers to entry, and restrictions on inter-regional trade. Although the 1991 Law on Competition provides SCAP with a legal basis for opposing such activities, SCAP's territorial offices are often tied to local and regional government bodies (who, for example, provide the SCAP offices with office space and facilities) even though SCAP employees are paid by the federal government. Not surprisingly, such arrangements limit the zeal with which SCAP offices combat local governments' anticompetitive behavior. Similar problems could appear if the specialized agencies that are to be established to regulate the natural monopolies currently controlled by the local and regional authorities must also rely on these authorities' goodwill.

Although much attention has centered on the regulation of prices and profit rates recorded by monopolistic firms, such regulation frequently resulted from conservative initiatives intent on slowing the pace of reform. The sphere of regulation was defined too broadly and the methods used in regulating these firms had numerous short-comings. Nevertheless, beginning to control natural monopolies by limiting their autonomy and selecting the most suitable regulatory measures is essential, and legislation pending presidential approval in mid-1995 would do just this.

In sum, competition policy in Russia has been a dynamic, evolutionary process, characterized in large measure by trial and error, experimentation, and learning by doing. The devolution of authority away from SCAP's central office in Moscow towards the territorial offices has been an important part of this process. The 82 territorial offices themselves experienced first hand the problems of the Monopoly Register, for example, and their search for solutions to these problems has effectively determined much of the competition policy that has been made since 1993. As market infrastructure and processes take hold with time, and as communication and cooperation among and between SCAP's central and territorial offices improve, Russian competition policy is likely to move (in tandem with the rest of the Russian economy) towards something a Western antitrust specialist might increasingly regard as "normality."

APPENDIX: CASE STUDY

"Tassel" versus the "Oktyabr' Railroad Company"[42]

Ben Slay and Vladimir Capelik

The railroads were one of the industries whose rapacious behavior led to the creation of competition policy the United States in the nineteenth century. Small businesses, farmers, and entire communities found themselves at the mercy of railroad companies, whose market power could not be controlled without redress to the Sherman Act and the courts. As the case of the "Oktyabr' Railroad Company" shows, similar forces appear to be at work a century later in the Russian economic transition.

Tassel Inc., a privately-held corporation located in Petrodvorets outside of Saint Petersburg, specialized in the export of wood products to Finland. In 1992, Tassel signed a shipping contract with the Oktyabr' Railroad Company, according to which "Oktyabr'" would transport Tassel's wood products to the Finnish border. Tassel then contracted with its Finnish clients for the export of 15 freight cars of wood, for delivery in August 1993.

According to Russian press reports, upon learning of Tassel's new export contract, Oktyabr' demanded the renegotiation of the shipping contract, arguing that unless Tassel paid fees for "additional services," the railroad would be unable to fit Tassel's wood shipments "into the plan." Payments for these additional services would have increased Tassel's shipping costs by a factor of 60, from 25,000 to 1.5 million rubles per ton.

Tassel turned to the local office of the State Committee on Antimonopoly Policy (SCAP) in Saint Petersburg which, upon the conclusion of its investigation, found that the Railroad had violated Article 5 of the law "On Competition and Limitation of Monopolistic Activity in Commodity Markets," Russia's basic competition policy legislation (of March 1991). Oktyabr' was classified as a "dominant firm" since it controlled at least 35 percent of the local shipping market. The railroad was found under this Article to have "imposed onerous conditions on a contracting party that were unrelated to the subject of the contract." Furthermore, evidence uncovered during the course of the investigation indicated that other small shippers had encountered similar problems with Oktyabr'. The SCAP office issued a cease-and-desist order which, according to press reports, the railroad company simply ignored.

Officials from the Saint Petersburg SCAP office appealed in April 1994 to SCAP's national office in Moscow for assistance in executing the judgment. The imposition of a one million ruble fine (approximately $400 at prevailing exchange rates) on the Oktyabr' Railroad Company was also requested. A special SCAP commission was formed in June to investigate the "Oktyabr' Affair." Hearings were held in August, which confirmed both the facts and the propriety of the Saint Petersburg office's handling of the case. (Although the railroad's attorneys were present at the hearing, they apparently did not dispute the facts.) According to SCAP officials, Oktyabr''s attorneys "did not take the proceedings seriously," and responded to the charges against the railroad by arguing that the railroad was not being paid by its clients, and that "railroad men have to make a living somehow."

The fine was then levied, and Oktyabr' was ordered to pay within 30 days. When the railroad ignored this verdict as well, SCAP took the matter to an arbitration court in Moscow. Meanwhile, Tassel demanded compensation from Oktyabr' for damages resulting from the railroad's behavior which had been judged to be in violation of the law. No response was forthcoming: Tassel's letters to the railroad company came back marked "return to sender."

Tassel seemed likely to be decimated by its inability to honor its Finnish export contracts, since rail was regarded as the only feasible means of transporting wood in bulk, and Oktyabr' apparently faced no serious competition from other railway lines in the region. Thus, what could be regarded as a battle between Tassel and Oktyabr' over the division of the profits (and foreign exchange) generated by the Finnish exports seemed likely to result in a net loss to the Russian economy (in the form of lost export revenues), not to mention the destruction of an apparently enterprising private firm at the hands of a state-owned quasi-monopoly, and the demonstration effect these developments could have on small shippers.

This case illuminates three important points about competition policy in Russia. First, regardless of how prospects for the spontaneous development of competitive markets are assessed in general, the case shows that competition policy has a critical role to play in promoting post-communist de-monopolization. To be sure, railroads in many developed capitalist economies long ago lost their monopoly status (natural or otherwise) due to the development of other modes of freight transportation, especially trucking. However, Russia is a long way from being a developed capitalist economy, and for reasons of history, geography, and climate, railroads are likely to continue to occupy a dominant position in Russia's transportation system for the foreseeable future. Some 70 percent of all freight shipped in Russia is transported via rail; this includes intra-city shipments, as well as inter-city and inter-regional freight.

Second, this case shows how the failure to develop effective mechanisms for natural monopoly regulation is likely, in the transitional economy context, to spill over into antitrust policy. To be sure, the difficulties the authorities face in controlling the behavior of firms like Oktyabr' can be seen as another example of the problems governments everywhere face in regulating natural monopolies. However, if increasing market contestability, either through the spontaneous development of new products and technologies, or via policy-induced reductions in barriers to entry and exit, is to be regarded as the general solution to such problems, then its application in Russia would require the elaboration and funding of a multibillion dollar transportation program. Such a program would seem to be highly unrealistic for the foreseeable future.

Third, this case shows how, as with many other aspects of the Russian economic transition, increasing the effectiveness of competition policy hinges on further progress in the development of the rule of law. SCAP's local and central offices both found that the Oktyabr' Railroad Company had violated the basic law on competition, but were unable to impose sufficiently-stringent penalties upon the railroad to evoke a change in its behavior. This is a political as well as legal issue, since the conduct of Oktyabr' (and many other state-owned monopolistic firms) belies a certain (not unreasonable) faith in its own political impregnability. Further progress in Russian competition policy may therefore require the creation of a different political context, in which reformers will not be chronically overmatched against large state enterprises that use market and public power to resist privatization, restructuring, and market competition.

Notes

1. Yevstigneyev 1993:90.

2. See Capelik 1992, Yakovlev 1991.

3. These data come from *The Economist*, December 5, 1992.

4. "By 1992, almost no branch ministries were left in Russia; most of them had transformed themselves into trade associations" (Joskow, Schmalensee, and Tsukanova 1994:327).

5. See Capelik and Yakovlev 1990, and Kroll 1991.

6. See Brown, Ickes, and Ryterman 1993, and Joskow, Schmalensee, and Tsukanova 1994:312-313.

7. Boyeva, Dolgopyatova, and Shironin 1992.

8. These figures comes from *The Economist*, November 28, 1992.

9. See Joskow, Schmalensee, and Tsukanova 1994:348-351, and Starodubrovskaya 1994:13.

10. Thomas Sigel, "Yeltsin Meets with Financial-Industrial Groups," *Daily Digest*, Open Media Research Institute, June 22, 1995.

11. This information comes from *Segodnya*, March 17, 1994.

12. See Capelik *et al.* 1990.

13. Other legal acts forming the basis for competition policy include the law "On Consumer Rights Protection," which was adopted in the spring of 1992; "Methodological Recommendations for Determining Market Boundaries and Size," an order issued by SCAP on October 26, 1993; "On the Procedure for Regulating the Acquisition of Shares, Participating Stock and Registered Common Stock of Joint Stock Companies and the Procedures for Recognizing Persons Controlling One Another's Assets," an order issued by SCAP on January 18, 1994; "Methodological Recommendations for Determining the Dominant Market Position of Economic Agents," an order issued by SCAP on March 6, 1994; and the "State Program for Demonopolizing the Economy and Developing Market Competition in the Russian Federation," which was adopted

by the government on March 9, 1994; as well as the privatization acts issued during 1992-1993. On the whole, these laws meet the requirements of a market economy, but they need to be continuously updated to reflect the changing economic situation.

14. Economic subjects are private, state, and other enterprises, including joint-stock companies, as well as associations of enterprises and institutions possessing the rights of juridical persons.

15. APAs ("administrative power agencies") are federal and local state agencies, as well as trade associations, concerns, and other groupings of enterprises whose functions are administrative (such as supervising the fulfillment of state orders, or allocating quotas of material supplies) rather than commercial.

16. See Joskow, Schmalensee, and Tsukanova 1994:304.

17. Rutland 1995:18.

18. This would seem to be a recent application of the old Russian proverb: "God is high, and the tsar is far away." For more on the evolution of SCAP's territorial offices and their role in Russian competition policy, see Yakovlev 1994.

19. The question of the government agency to which SCAP has been a matter of some political controversy. Following a period of struggle between President Yeltsin and the Supreme Soviet, a resolution linked to presidential decree number 915 (of August 24, 1992) made SCAP a central executive organ of the Russian Federation. Likewise, while the 82 territorial offices are formally subordinated to SCAP's central office and funded by the central budget, a significant degree of control over their activities is often wielded by the regional authorities, who provide the territorial offices with such critical logistical support as office space, telecommunications, and the like.

20. Joskow, Schmalensee, and Tsukanova 1993:335-336.

21. See Fornalczyk and Hoffman 1993.

22. Competition policy officials from the CIS countries met with increasing frequency during 1993-1994, and the standardization of antimonopoly legislation was initiated. The inter-republican economic integration inherited from the Soviet period implies that monopolization on many product markets can be more effectively tackled within the framework of the CIS, rather than in individual republics.

23. For critical views, see Capelik 1994, Leitzel 1994, and Yakovlev 1994.

24. These were: (1) the Resolution of the Ministry of the Economy and Finance of December 29, 1991 (number P-424) "On Price Regulation Procedures for Monopoly Enterprises"; (2) the Resolution of the Supreme Soviet Presidium of January 20, 1992 (number 2218-1) "On Regulation of Monopoly Enterprise Activities"; (3) the President's Decree of February 20, 1992 (number 165) "On Measures to Stabilize Russian Federation Industry in 1992"; and (4) the government resolution of February 27, 1992 (number 132) "On the Temporary Measures for the Special Regulation of Monopoly Enterprise Activities in 1992."

25. See Yakovlev 1994:36-38.

26. Although the "Register" is generally referred to in the singular, a plethora of such registers are in fact used by SCAP's central and regional offices.

27. Yakovlev 1994:37.

28. This was "Methodological Recommendations for Determining Market Boundaries and Size," an order issued by SCAP on October 26, 1993.

29. See *Business MN*, no. 6, 1993.

30. See Capelik 1994, and Yakovlev 1994:37-38, for more on this.

31. See Joskow, Schmalensee, and Tsukanova 1994:355-358.

32. Yakovlev 1994:39.

33. *SCAP Rossii Report* 1994.

34. Yakovlev 1994:39.

35. The large-scale regulation of enterprise profitability was based on Ordinance number 576, "On the Regulation of Prices and Profit Rates on Products and Services of Monopolistic Enterprises in 1992-1993," issued August 11, 1992.

36. See Chapter 7 for description of some of the difficulties this "open door" policy has caused for the Russian telecommunications sector.

37. See Joskow, Schmalensee, and Tsukanova 1994:341.

38. See Rutland 1995:13.

39. Goskomstat Rossii data.

40. See Chapter 6 for more on the pluses and minuses of independent regulatory institutions for natural monopolies in the post-communist context.

41. This point is made even more strongly by one observer, who argues (Yakovlev 1994:33): "Where real demonopolisation of markets has been observed it has by no means always been attributable to deliberate action by the anti-monopoly organs."

42. The information in this case study comes from "GKAP suditsya s Oktyabr'skoi zheleznoi dorogoi" (SCAP Takes the Oktyabr' Railroad Company to Court), *Business MN*, October 19, 1994, p. 23.

References

Annual Report 1993. 1993. Moscow: State Committee on Antimonopoly Policy. (Also published in *Ekonomicheskaya Gazeta* 1993:3).

Boyeva, I., T. Dolgopyatova, and V. Shironin. 1992. *Gosudarstvennye predpriyatiya v 1991-1992 g.* (State Enterprises in 1991-1992). Moscow: Economic Policy Institute.

Boycko, M., A. Shleifer, and R.W. Vishny. 1993. "Privatizing Russia." *Brookings Papers on Economic Activity* 2: 139-92.

Brown, A.N., B.W. Ickes, and R. Ryterman. 1994. "The Myth of Monopoly: A New View of Industrial Structure in Russia." Policy Research Working Paper No. 1331. Washington D.C.: World Bank.

Capelik, V. 1994. "Should Monopoly Be Regulated in Russia?" *Communist Economies and Economic Transition* 1: 19-32.

_____. 1992. "The Development of Antimonopoly Policy in Russia." *Radio Free Europe/Radio Liberty Research Report* 34: 66-70.

Capelik, V., and A. Yakovlev. 1990. "Monopoliya v sovetskoi ekonomike" (Monopoly in the Soviet Economy). *Problems of Economics* 33: 31-42.

Capelik, V., et al.. 1990. "Proyekt antimonopol'nogo zakona SSSR" (The Draft of the Antimonopoly Law of the USSR). *Material'no-technicheskoye snabzheniye* No. 4.

Estrin, S., and M. Cave, eds. 1993. *Competition and Competition Policy: A Comparative Analysis of Central and Eastern Europe.* London and New York: Pinter Publishers.

Fornalczyk, A., and R. Hoffman. 1993. "Demonopolization and Deconcentration of Russia's Economy," in M. Dąbrowski, ed., *The Gaidar Program: Lessons for Poland and Eastern Europe.* Pp. 83-86. Warsaw: CASE Publishers.

Fox, E.M., and J.A. Ordover. 1992. "Free Enterprise and Competition Policy for Central and Eastern Europe and the Soviet Union," in Stephen A. Rayner, ed., *Privatization in Central and Eastern Europe.* Boston: Butterworths.

Hanson, P. 1991. "The Dimensions of the Monopoly Problem." *Radio Liberty Report on the USSR* 17: 5-6.

International Monetary Fund/World Bank/Organization for Economic Cooperation and Development/European Bank for Reconstruction and Development. 1991. *A Study of the Soviet Economy.* vol. 2. Paris: OECD.

Joskow, P.L., R. Schmalensee, and N. Tsukanova. 1994. "Competition Policy in Russia during and after Privatization." *Brookings Papers: Microeconomics 1994.* Boston.

Kroll, H. 1991. "Monopoly and Transition to the Market." *Soviet Economy* 2: 143-174.

Leitzel, J. 1994. "A Note on Monopoly and Russian Economic Reform." *Communist Economies and Economic Transition* 1: 45-53.

Petrov, A. 1993. "Privatization and Antimonopoly Policy." *Radio Free Europe/Radio Liberty Research Report* 30: 19-22.

Pittman, R. 1992. "Some Critical Provisions in the Antimonopoly Laws of Central and Eastern Europe." *The International Lawyer* 2: 485-503.

Program for Deepening the Economic Reform. 1992. Moscow: Russian Government. June.

Russian Economic Reform: Crossing the Threshold of Structural Change: A World Bank Country Study. 1992. Washington D.C.: The World Bank.

Rutland, P. 1995. "A Twisted Path Towards a Market Economy." *Transition: Events and Issues in the Former Soviet Union, East-Central and SouthEastern Europe* 2: 12-18.

Rynok i antimonopol'noye zakonodatel'stvo Rossii. (The Market and Russia's Antimonopoly Legislation). 1992. State Committee on Antimonopoly Policy. Moscow: Justitsinform.

SCAP Rossii Report ("On the Activities of SCAP Rossii in 1993 and Objectives for 1994"). 1994. Moscow: State Committee on Antimonopoly Policy. February.

Slay, B. 1992. "Privatizatsiya i demonopolizatsiya" (Privatization and De-monopolization). *Voprosy ekonomiki* 3: 58-68.

Starodubrovskaya, I. 1994. "The Nature of Monopoly and Barriers to Entry in Russia." *Communist Economies and Economic Transition* 1: 3-18.

_____. 1990. *Ot monopolizma k konkurentsii* (From Monopoly to Competition). Moscow: Izdatel'stvo Politicheskoi Literatury.

Yakovlev, A. 1994. "Anti-Monopoly Policy in Russia: Basic Stages and Prospects." *Communist Economies and Economic Transition* 1: 33-44.

_____. 1991. "Monopoliya v sovetskoi ekonomike i obuslovivshiye ee faktory" (Monopoly in the Soviet Economy and its Determinants). *Vestnik statistiki* 1: 4-7.

Yevstigneyev, R. 1993. "Creating a Competitive Environment in Russia," in C.T. Saunders, ed., *The Role of Competition in Economic Transition*. Pp. 90-100. New York: St. Martin's Press.

4

Antitrust and the Evolution of a Market Economy in Mongolia[1]

William E. Kovacic and Robert S. Thorpe

Introduction

In 1990, after seventy years of communism, Mongolia began the transition from central planning to a market economy. One element of the transition process has consisted of preparing and enacting an antitrust statute. In taking this step, Mongolia has joined a large and growing number of formerly socialist countries for which antitrust legislation is an ingredient of economic reform.[2] Under the auspices of the University of Maryland's program on Institutional Reform and the Informal Section (IRIS) and the United States Agency for International Development (USAID), we made trips to Mongolia in November 1992 and February 1993 to assist Mongolian government in drafting an antimonopoly law.[3] In July 1993, the Mongolian Parliament adopted an antitrust measure, and attention then shifted to implementing the new competition policy mandate. In June 1994, one of the authors returned to Mongolia and reviewed the status of implementation efforts with officials of the Mongolian government.

There is an active debate among specialists about how regulatory reform should proceed in transition economies. One aspect of this debate is whether transition economies should adopt antimonopoly legislation and, if such legislation is appropriate, what form such measures should take.[4] We believe that the process and the substantive results of the drafting effort in Mongolia yield useful conclusions about competition policy and legal reform for transition economies generally, whether they be former communist economies or economies recovering from longstanding, failed attempts by the state to orchestrate economic development.

This chapter uses the Mongolian antitrust law drafting experience as a vehicle for considering optimal approaches for accomplishing regulatory reform in transition economies, and for providing external technical assistance to that end. We also address the role that an antitrust system can play in facilitating the movement from planning to free markets in Mongolia and other transition economies. We begin by briefly discussing the origin and current status of economic adjustment in Mongolia. The second section reviews the drafting process that resulted in the proposal to the Mongolian Parliament for a Mongolian antitrust statute. The third section describes Mongolia's antitrust statute, as enacted by the Mongolian Parliament in July 1993. The fourth part examines the prospects for successful implementation and considers how the development of an antitrust system can encourage the emergence of market institutions and processes.

Economic Adjustment in Mongolia: Background

Mongolia evokes images of fierce horsemen, pastoral settings, and Genghis Khan. An independent country located between the People's Republic of China and Russia, Mongolia is now in the throes of transition from central planning to a market economy. Its population of about 2.2 million people occupy a cold, dry land mass that is relatively large for the population. Its pastures support roughly 25 million livestock, the largest proportion being sheep and goats. Agriculture has accounted for approximately 20 percent of Mongolia's gross domestic product (GDP) and 30 percent of its work force.[5] Mongolia is remote and landlocked, and its transportation and communications networks are rudimentary.

Once "Outer Mongolia" in the Chinese state, Mongolia asserted its independence in 1911 with the demise of the ruling Chinese dynasty, and became independent in 1921 when the Soviet Red Army allied with Mongolians defeated a White Russian force then occupying the Mongolian capital. For the next seventy years Mongolia was a client state of the Soviet Union. Ruled by the Mongolian People's Revolutionary Party (MPRP), Mongolia suffered the rigors of Stalinism and the rigidities of a socialist economy. During these seventy years the country developed several cities, including its capital Ulaanbataar, and was transformed from an essentially nomadic and pastoral livestock economy of herders to an economy that also had some light agricultural processing and extractive industries.[6]

In 1990 with the general collapse of the socialist economic model, political and economic change began in Mongolia.[7] Demonstrations in

Ulaanbaatar led to the relaxation of monolithic Communist rule, the adoption of a new Constitution, the development of political parties, elections, and major changes in government policy. Mongolia still remained heavily dependent on the Soviet Union for direct aid and loans, essential imports, and export markets. The impetus for change therefore came in no small measure from the effects on Mongolia of the Soviet economic collapse. Before the upheaval of the late 1980s and early 1990s, Soviet aid accounted for 25 percent of Mongolia's GDP, and 90 percent of Mongolia's foreign trade took place with the Eastern Bloc.

Economic change in Mongolia meant that the socialist model was officially abandoned, private property and private enterprise were endorsed, and a privatization process for state-owned enterprises was begun.[8] A coalition reform government took power, with young economists in the forefront supporting radical reform. Mongolia thus joined the countries of Central and Eastern Europe in escaping from the Soviet system. As these countries did, Mongolia suffered major declines in its standard of living and faced the necessity of taking its economy apart and reassembling it.

Mongolia depended more heavily on the Soviet Union than most Soviet bloc countries.[9] With the socialist penchant for building large plants that could serve broad geographic areas, privatization and the demise of central planning yielded industry structures that were far from atomistically competitive, and led to increasing worries about the effects of monopoly.

In 1992 the coalition reform government was replaced after national parliamentary elections by the MPRP. Although no longer a communist party and having committed itself officially to reform, the MPRP ran on a platform criticizing the speed with which the previous government had pursued the transition. Among other tactics, the MPRP sought to associate the languid condition of Mongolia's post-communist economy with efforts to institute economic reforms.[10]

Drafting a New Antimonopoly Law

IRIS[11] began working in Mongolia in early 1991 under the leadership of Peter Murrell, a University of Maryland Professor of Economics and a specialist in comparative economic systems and the evolution of economies. Before the antimonopoly project began, IRIS conducted a series of workshops for Mongolian policy makers on the institutions of a market democracy, and undertook advisory activities related to issues considered in the workshops.[12] Georges Korsun, an IRIS economist, lived for more than a year in Ulaanbataar and worked with Mongolian policy makers on a variety of economic reform issues. Korsun was instrumental in shaping the thinking of Mongolian officials about the possible role for an antitrust system in the broader framework of economic reform. Korsun's work demonstrated the benefits to legal reform efforts of technical assistance programs that use a sustained, in-country presence to identify and define specific projects of interest to the host country.

As noted above, the literature on economic reform in transition economies features a growing debate about what role, if any, antitrust legislation should play in the establishment of market systems. Commentators raise essentially three objections to adopting antitrust legislation. The first is that the effort to devise and implement antitrust policy deflects attention away from higher priority reforms, such as the creation of mechanisms for defining, exchanging, and protecting property rights.[13] A second criticism is that, as a safeguard against private efforts to restrict output, antitrust is an inferior tool compared to other policy approaches, including the dismantling of legal barriers to trade such as controls on imports and foreign investment.[14] The third objection is that antitrust mechanisms are excessively prone to misapplication, through error or corruption, by government enforcement bodies and courts, or to strategic abuse by private actors.

These concerns warrant caution in creating antitrust systems in transition economies. There is general agreement that efforts to delineate and transfer property rights deserve a high (perhaps the highest) priority.[15] It is also apparent that removing import trade restrictions can provide a valuable spur to competition, especially where state-owned enterprises or newly privatized firms control domestic production.[16] The weakening of regional or local trade restrictions that inhibit intra-national commerce also can eliminate significant barriers to competition among domestic firms.[17] And there is always the danger that, unless its functions and operations are carefully delimited and monitored, a new antimonopoly apparatus could become simply another form of growth-suppressing state intervention.[18]

Though formidable, critiques of antitrust as an element of market modernization tend to overlook some important aspects of legal reform in many transition economies. Enacting no antitrust system may be politically infeasible or unwise. The alternative to an antimonopoly system may be far more intrusive controls on economic activity, including broad-based price controls. Thus, the policy issue often will be what type of antitrust system will do the most good (or least harm). Despite its positive attributes, trade reform may have little competitive impact on local markets or in countries (such as Mongolia) where geographic barriers and a frail transportation infrastructure preclude robust import competition, at least in the short and medium term.[19] Finally, antitrust may provide a useful tool for dismantling or resisting government policies that obstruct trade or otherwise curb rivalry.[20]

The IRIS advisors and Mongolian officials involved in the legal reform process envisioned that the antitrust system would serve three basic aims in Mongolia. The first would be the creation of a mechanism for challenging efforts by the state, acting either through government ministries or state-controlled business enterprises, to hinder the development of competitive markets. Among the greatest impediments to the functioning of markets in Mongolia are state policies that restrict entry, curb imports, and favor established state-owned firms. An antitrust system could serve as an important counterweight to competition-suppressing measures or to the adoption of new exclusionary statutes, rules, or policies.[21]

The second purpose would be to discourage private efforts to replicate the type of central coordination and single-firm control of markets that characterized economic organization under Communist rule. This role would assume particular significance in industries where the subjects of privatization will be single-firm monopolies or tight oligopolies accustomed to centrally-orchestrated, industry-wide production decisions.[22] For example, without some controls on horizontal collaboration among separate entities, firms simply might substitute private agreements for central ministerial control in selecting products, choosing output levels, and establishing prices. By providing the public assurance that private entities will not be permitted to distort the market process through output-restricting arrangements, the implementation of an antitrust system also could assist in deflecting public demands for maintaining or bolstering a comprehensive system of price controls.

The third goal of an antitrust system in Mongolia would be to facilitate a basic adjustment in the nature of public intervention in the economy, by moving away from an expansive conception of government as the central planner of economic activity and moving toward a narrower role of government as arbiter and rulemaker. As conceived in most countries, antitrust legislation embodies a preference for the primacy of market forces as the means of organizing economic activity. Antitrust enforcement contemplates that the government will continue to intervene in the affairs of business, but such intervention is viewed as exceptional (rather than routine) and must be justified by its capacity to correct market failures. Seen this way, an antitrust system can become an institutional force for redefining perceptions about the government's proper role in the economy.

The effectiveness of external assistance to the Mongolians charged with drafting an antimonopoly law benefitted substantially from long-term IRIS activities in Mongolia, and from a sustained period of assistance designed to pave the way for law drafting. Mongolia mirrors the IRIS experience in several other countries, notably Poland, where long-term and sustained assistance, research, and education have improved the chances that Poles will accomplish institutional reform as part of the country's progress toward free markets and democratic structures. There has been rightful criticism of technical assistance projects that consist chiefly of quick "parachute" visits by external consultants.[23] Such endeavors may yield paper reforms, but the absence of sustained in-country activity before and after the participation by consultants often means that nominal reforms quickly are remitted to a back shelf with no implementation and a strong residue of cynicism about the rule of law and governmental processes.

The Law Drafting Process: The First Trip

In November 1992, an IRIS team including the authors spent two weeks in Mongolia making specific preparations for drafting an antimonopoly law. The initial visit focused on three activities. The first was providing Mongolian academics and government officials with a basic orientation to the economic and legal ingredients of an antitrust system. Lectures were given to the Mongolian Law Drafting Group on microeconomic theory as it applies to competition policy, on substantive antitrust law and procedure, and on the organization of antitrust enforcement. These lectures were videotaped and were followed by question and answer periods.

The second objective of the visit was to gather data on the industrial organization of the Mongolian economy and the regulatory framework in which Mongolian business managers operate. As is the case in many transition economies, existing data on industry structures and performance are scarce, fragmentary, and often unreliable. To develop a better basis for analyzing business behavior and identifying possible subjects for competition policy scrutiny, we led Mongolian researchers in performing studies of competition in three major industry sectors—telecommunications, livestock slaughter/meat production, and wool spinning.[24] For these studies we asked Mongolian researchers and representatives of the industries to assemble data about sales, costs, and prices. The studies consisted mainly of interviews of industry managers, plant tours, and discussions with government officials with oversight duties for the industry sectors.

The case studies provided several useful perspectives on the Mongolian economy. One result was a sketching of the structural outlines of some of Mongolia's most important sectors. In many instances, the studies revealed significant possibilities for competition. Mongolia has three principal meat-processing plants which operate as independent, "privatized" entities, although the government holds a majority interest in each. We made preliminary efforts to construct concentration data based on inputs (numbers of animals slaughtered) and outputs (sales).[25] Efforts to assess the competitive significance of the three firms depended heavily on geographic definitions of the market, as well as the reliability of data on slaughtering and sales activity. Despite limitations in the data, and assuming relatively high levels of concentration (with Herfindahl-Hirschman Indices at or above 4,000) measured on a national or local scale, there appeared to be important cases of new entry and significant possibilities for potential entry or expansion by small meat processing operations.

The case studies also identified business conduct and government interference that an antimonopoly law might address. In both the wool spinning and meat processing industries, we saw evidence of efforts by incumbent producers to collude to depress the price of raw material inputs (raw wool and animals). Our written studies described the government's pervasive interference in the development of markets.[26] In all three sectors that we studied, government officials acting without clear authority or in violation of existing laws or decrees often intervened to influence managers' pricing, production, and marketing decisions. While this result may be unremarkable in view of Mongolia's history and circumstances, it still provides a reminder of how difficult reforms are to achieve and how much Western advisors sometimes take for granted.

The third focus of our visit could be loosely defined as a form of industrial organization technology transfer. We met with the Mongolian researchers to discuss the methodology we had used for the industry case studies and to review what we had learned. These meetings provided an opportunity to consider antitrust issues that might arise in specific industry settings, to analyze how antitrust principles might be applied to these industries, and to help guide the Mongolian researchers in undertaking studies of competitive conditions in other industries. We left behind treatises and papers on antitrust, and a schedule of activities for the Law Drafting Group to pursue in the next few months. This included reviewing existing Mongolian laws for relevance to an antimonopoly draft, conducting additional competitive studies, and preparing a draft of the antimonopoly law. The plan was set for us to return in February 1993 to advise on the final drafting process.

In the succeeding three months, IRIS had regular contact with our Mongolian colleagues from the Law Drafting Group. Three important IRIS documents were prepared and sent to Mongolia. One was a short discussion of alternative organizational structures for an enforcement agency—should it be an independent agency, or should it be located within an existing ministry? The second was a detailed review of antimonopoly laws adopted or being considered by other countries undergoing the transition from communism to market systems, with commentary comparing these measures to the American antitrust laws.[27] The third document critiqued two earlier unsuccessful draft Mongolian antimonopoly laws.

The Law Drafting Process: The Second Trip

Upon our arrival in February, we found that a smaller core unit had been formed within the Law Drafting Group. This unit was chaired by Amarsana, a former Minister of Justice, but its organization and daily activities were supervised by Bailykhuu, a senior advisor to the Mongolian Privatization Commission.[28] The drafting group also included two economists and a lawyer. The core unit had prepared an eminently workable draft that became the basis for two weeks of intensive collaboration among ourselves and our Mongolian colleagues. The core unit had absorbed all the background materials we had prepared, and more.[29] The IRIS memoranda discussing organizational structures and comparing antimonopoly laws in transition economies had been translated into Mongolian (no small achievement)[30] and had been distributed with drafts of the law to government officials, members of Parliament, and private sector representatives. The draft law that emerged from our collaboration had a definite European flavor, showing a concern with dominant firms and, as compared with American antitrust law, a relatively lesser concern about agreements between horizontal competitors.

Four specific features of the draft legislation stand out. Among the paramount concerns of the Law Drafting Group was the definition of "dominance," which affected the operation of the draft law's controls on single-firm conduct and its restrictions on horizontal collaboration by rival entities. Large state-controlled or recently-"privatized" concerns dominate the Mongolian economy. Mongolia has not experienced the dramatic development of a private sector that has occurred, for example, in Poland. In these circumstances, our Mongolian colleagues did not want to hinder the private sector in any way, and saw little reason to regulate agreements among horizontal competitors as long as collectively they did not hold a dominant position. The draft legislation defined dominance as accounting for more than 50 percent of commercial activity in a relevant market.[31] The application of a market share screen to horizontal arrangements is one area in which the draft Mongolian law departs from traditional practice in the United States and mirrors antimonopoly statutes adopted by a number of formerly socialist countries.[32] The result reflects a concern all of us shared: that the law be attuned to Mongolian circumstances.

A second noteworthy feature of the draft legislation involved merger enforcement. Again, reflecting concern about interfering with market activities as opposed to preventing harmful government actions, the Mongolians felt that restrictions on mergers should be narrowly cast. The draft legislation condemned horizontal transactions only if they yielded a dominant market position and banned vertical arrangements only if a vertical merger yielded a single entity with a dominant position in two or more vertically-related stages of a market. Moreover, the draft statute enabled the merging parties to raise efficiency defenses to sustain transactions that otherwise would be deemed unlawful through the application of the structural dominance criteria.[33]

A third important area involved the choice of enforcement mechanism. The draft statute vested enforcement and adjudication responsibility in an independent Competition Commission, whose decisions were made appealable to the Supreme Court of Mongolia. The Law Drafting Group believed the enforcement authority should not reside within an existing government bureau, lest the new antimonopoly authority be hindered in performing the competition advocacy function described below. Because Mongolia's courts of original jurisdiction lack expertise in adjudicating commercial disputes, placing decision making authority (subject to judicial review) in an independent agency dedicated to formulating and applying competition policy seemed more likely to create a body of antitrust expertise and to generate a coherent, sensible body of competition doctrines.[34] Violations of the statute were to be remedied by decrees forbidding specific conduct, by the payment of actual damages to victims of illegal behavior, and by fines to be imposed upon economic entities, government agencies, or individual managers of such organizations.

The fourth significant feature of the draft legislation was the role of the independent Competition Commission in opposing actions by other government agencies that reduce competition. The Law Drafting Group strongly supported an expansive competition advocacy function for the new agency, in the belief that the most serious threat to the emergence of competitive markets would not come from privately-imposed restraints, but from competition-suppressing government intervention.[35] Specific focal points of advocacy activity would include government-imposed trade barriers and regulatory restrictions that inhibit entry, as well as efforts by state-owned or state-controlled enterprises to prey upon private rivals. In designing the advocacy role, the working group envisioned that the antimonopoly body would function as a "constitutional court" that could object to state intervention that suppressed competition, and could issue decrees that support the operation of a market economy.[36]

Early in our two weeks it became clear that the issue of regulating monopolies had risen on the Mongolian political agenda, and there was great interest in the work of the Law Drafting Group and the "American experts." We attended a roundtable discussion sponsored by the committee of the Mongolian Parliament which would consider the draft legislation. During the meeting, we responded to a raft of shrewd, intelligent questions about the draft law and its likely impact on the Mongolian economy. Similar sessions were held with representatives of the office of the President, the office of the Prime Minister, a council of managers of privatized businesses, and others.

We finished the drafting process with the realization that Mongolians had drafted the law with our help, which they had been free to accept or reject. It was their draft, not ours.[37] The Mongolians saw it as their draft and their proposed law. We had engaged in an intellectually stimulating process, but it had not happened by accident nor without sustained preparation by both the external advisors and the internal drafting group.

Content of the Mongolian Antitrust Statute

We also had no illusions about the difficulties the draft might face in its way through the legislative process.[38] Although we very much would have liked to have had an IRIS team present during those deliberations, for various reasons this proved impossible. As described below, our inability to consult regularly and first hand with the Law Drafting Group and other government officials may have been costly.

Following extended discussion, the Mongolian Parliament adopted the Law of Mongolia on Prohibiting Unfair Competition in July 1993.[39] The new statute has four principal operative elements: substantive antitrust prohibitions governing the conduct of business entities; restrictions on the ability of government bodies to adopt competition-suppressing regulations and policies; consumer protection mandates; and provisions concerning the enforcement mechanism. Each of these elements is summarized below.

Substantive Antitrust Provisions

The statute's substantive antitrust prohibitions largely resemble the Law Drafting Group's proposal. The statute's chief focus is the conduct of firms that unilaterally or collectively hold a dominant market position. Article 3.1 (Dominance, Monopoly, and Monopolistic Activities) defines dominance as a market share of over 50 percent in a relevant market.[40] The law does not specify a methodology for defining markets or measuring market power, leaving these issues for administrative elaboration. All of the statute's antitrust provisions create a safety zone for unilateral or collective conduct where the market share of the economic entities in question falls below 50 percent. The statute's prohibitions apply equally to private and state-controlled firms.

Article 4 spells out restrictions on unilateral conduct. Among other provisions, dominant firms may not:

- restrict production or sales for the purpose of creating an artificial shortage and raising prices;
- impose contractual terms that discriminate among similarly situated suppliers or customers;
- engage in sales below cost for the purpose of impeding entry or excluding existing rivals;
- refuse to deal with other economic entities without a business justification and for the purpose of driving such entities from the market;
- impose tying arrangements or resale price maintenance agreements; or
- demand that suppliers provide inputs at price levels that might lead such suppliers to reduce production and sales of such goods or services.

Article 5 bars certain joint actions by firms that collectively occupy a dominant market position. It also bans the following types of conduct where such arrangements are designed to hinder competition:

- Agreements to fix prices, rig bids and tenders, or to otherwise restrict output;
- Agreements to allocate markets according to geographic territories, customers, products, or suppliers;
- Agreements to impede competitors from joining organizations facilitating efficient business operations; and
- Agreements to refuse unreasonably to deal with other economic entities in order to drive such entities from the market.

Article 7 prohibits certain mergers. This provision bars dominant economic entities from buying the capital stock or shares of its rivals. Article 7 does not appear to apply to transactions by which two non-dominant firms merge to create a single dominant firm, nor does it contain any limitations on vertical mergers. Article 7 also allows the merging parties to overcome a finding of illegality by showing that the merger's benefits in increasing production "in sectors of the national economy of prime concern to the population," or in increasing the competitiveness of Mongolian firms in achieving sales in export markets, exceed any harm to competition.

Controls on Government Efforts to Suppress Competition

The Mongolian Unfair Competition statute retains the draft legislation's suspicion of government intervention that stifles the competitive process. The prominent concern about government-imposed controls is evident in Article 1, in which the law's basic aim is described as regulating relations concerned with prohibiting and restricting state control over competition among economic entities in the market, as well as monopoly and other activities impeding fair competition.

Article 9 takes two approaches to curbing government intervention that reduces rivalry. First, it forbids national or local government bodies from acting unilaterally to adopt a variety of competition-suppressing measures, unless such measures are explicitly authorized by an act of the Mongolian Parliament. Government agencies are forbidden to bar or restrict market entry by new or existing firms, to set production levels, or to treat any economic entity in a preferential or discriminatory manner. The second approach is to prohibit government entities from acting in concert with other government agencies or with affected firms to restrict competition, unless such action is explicitly authorized by an act of the Mongolian Parliament. Forbidden actions include decisions to set price levels, divide markets, restrict market entry by an economic entity, or to compel exit by an economic entity.

Consumer Protection Features

Although most of its substantive features involve antitrust commands, the Mongolian Unfair Competition Law also contains consumer protection safeguards.[41] Unlike the antitrust strictures, the consumer protection measures apply to dominant and non-dominant economic entities alike. Among other features, Article 8 condemns:

- the dissemination of false or misleading advertising that causes losses to competitors or diminishes their reputations;
- engaging in the unconsented copying of trademarks, brand names, packaging, or labels of other firms;
- misappropriating the intellectual property (e.g., production and customer information) of other firms; or
- concealing product quality defects or dangerous product characteristics.

Enforcement Mechanism

The most worrisome aspect of the new law is the mechanism established for its enforcement. On its face, the Unfair Competition Law ambiguously distributes enforcement-related power across four institutions: Parliament, the heads of central government ministries, the Department of National Development (DND), and the Mongolian courts. Article 10 of the statute gives Parliament (the Great Hural) responsibility for enforcing prohibitions against anticompetitive behavior by instrumentalities of the national government. Under Article 11.1, agencies of the central government must also consult with Parliament when they adopt decisions concerning price regulation of industries considered to be natural monopolies or concerning restrictions on import or export activities.

For all other matters arising under the Unfair Competition Law, Article 11 delegates enforcement authority jointly to the heads of Mongolian national government ministries and to the DND Chairman.[42] Article 11 directs these bodies to:

- present proposals to the national government concerning the supervision and enforcement of the Unfair Competition statute, and about procedures for its enforcement;
- submit proposals to the Prime Minister about overruling decisions by local government authorities that violate the Unfair Competition statute;
- require businesses and government bodies to supply information concerning whether individual firms are monopolies, natural monopolies, or dominant firms;
- demand that monopolies or dominant firms engaged in illegal conduct be dissolved; and
- publish their decisions concerning efforts to redress prohibited conduct.

As discussed more fully below, the Mongolian Government has assigned the DND responsibility for drafting rules to implement the Unfair Competition Law. It presently appears that Mongolia's antimonopoly bureau will reside within the DND.

The Unfair Competition Law appears to vest all authority to adjudicate violations with the Mongolian courts. Article 12 gives the courts power to decide the market status of individual economic entities (i.e., monopoly, natural monopoly, dominant firm, or non-dominant firm), to demand that economic entities cease violating the law, and, more generally, "to settle disputes arising from violating" the statute's prohibitions. Article 12 suggests that the national ministries and the DND have no independent adjudicatory authority and must prosecute all complaints involving violations by economic entities in the Mongolian courts. Thus, unlike the Law Drafting Group proposal, which contemplated a combination of independent agency adjudication and appellate review, the Unfair Competition statute places all adjudicatory authority in the Mongolian courts.

Article 14 presents the main remedial tools of the enforcement process. Article 14.1 entitles injured parties to actual damages for injuries suffered as a result of law violations. However, this provision does not specify whether damages may be assessed against economic entities, government bodies, or both; nor does it indicate which instrumentality (i.e., a government ministry, the DND, or the court) is responsible for calculating and awarding damages. Article 14.2 permits the court to impose fines upon business owners and firm managers for law violations, for failure to comply with court decrees, or for refusing to supply required information. Unlike the Law Drafting Group proposal, the statute imposes no fines on government entities which engage in law violations. Indeed, the statute does not indicate how government agency violators are to be punished.

Prospects for Implementation

Implementation issues arose repeatedly throughout our work with the Mongolian Antitrust Law Drafting Group. It is impossible to overemphasize the importance of sustained effort and preparation in assisting other countries to achieve legal reform. Implementation is the Achilles heel of legal reform in transition economies, and experience in many countries has shown quick fixes and shortcuts to be utterly unavailing. Close attention to implementation is a central element of a successful reform process.[43]

Experience with the passage of Mongolia's Unfair Competition Law shows why legal reform efforts are prone to founder without sustained concern with implementation as legislation is being drafted, debated, and approved. As enacted, the Unfair Competition Law ignores a number of important enforcement issues and leaves other ingredients of the enforcement apparatus ill-defined. Perhaps the most significant deficiency is the new statute's failure to specify the structure and location of the enforcement bureau and to provide resources for its operation.

The DND currently is responsible for drafting rules to implement the Unfair Competition Law. Although the DND has yet to issue final rules, preliminary drafts suggest that the government antimonopoly bureau will consist of a small office residing within DND. At least in its early stages, the antimonopoly office will consist of a small number of engineers who previously have been responsible for overseeing the operations of Mongolia's state-owned energy and telecommunications firms.[44] The DND rules drafting group anticipates that the national antimonopoly office eventually would be supplemented by personnel assigned by Mongolia's regional government authorities. As of early 1995, however, the Mongolian Parliament had not yet authorized the creation of new positions to enforce the Unfair Competition Law. Thus, it seemed likely that personnel to staff the national bureau and its local adjunct offices would have to come from existing government agencies.

As adopted, the Unfair Competition Law contains a number of potentially useful substantive commands, particularly dealing with the role of the state in the economy. However, as of early 1995, it was not clear that the provisional implementation plan would be able to put them into effect. There is a danger, therefore, that the antimonopoly experiment may join the roster of nominally impressive reform measures whose practical impact is slight. Moreover, because adopting laws without serious efforts to apply them can corrode public confidence in the rule of law, the failure to pursue implementation seriously could be counterproductive.

Such gaps in the new legislation might have been avoided, or their implications realized more fully, if an IRIS team had been present in-country while Parliament debated the statute, and if outside experts had been present at the beginning of implementation efforts. External advisors cannot dictate the terms of legislation to lawmakers, but they may exert a valuable influence in ensuring that crucial issues are recognized and confronted. They can best play this role by combining attentiveness to distinctive national conditions with close familiarity with how other countries have adopted and implemented similar statutes. Also, while their ideas and suggestions may ultimately be rejected, the advisors can serve as a valuable sounding board for identifying the implications of different policy choices.[45] A practical lesson from the Mongolian experience is the importance of having expert external advisors on-hand in the critical stages of the law enactment process.[46]

The lack of a clear implementation scheme in Mongolia raises the question of whether the new antitrust statute can serve as a platform for developing a useful national competition policy. Implementation efforts must currently take into account at least two fundamental institutional constraints. First, the Mongolian government is likely to be able to commit few resources to enforcement. Not only does the country face enormous pressure to cope with other national needs and financial obligations, but only a relative handful of Mongolians have familiarity with the legal concepts or industrial organization economics that underpin the operation of an antitrust system.[47] A second and related point is that many institutions essential to effective enforcement will need to be built virtually from the ground up. A new enforcement bureau will have to be created (either within an existing ministry or as a stand-alone body), a professional staff must be assembled and trained, and judges of the courts that will hear antitrust disputes must be given at least a rudimentary education in legal and economic principles that are certain to be alien.[48]

In light of these constraints, we suggest an Unfair Competition Law implementation program built upon a hierarchy of four priorities. The first priority would be to build an austere enforcement apparatus around a small cadre of Mongolian experts, such as the core members of the Antitrust Law Drafting Group. It is important to assign at least one lawyer and one economist to the bureau's staff.[49] The Mongolian officials would benefit from assistance provided by external competition policy advisors resident in-country, and from competition policy workshops conducted by external advisors either in Mongolia or in other countries. Such workshops could also be offered to judges who will adjudicate disputes under the statute.

The second priority would be for the newly-created competition bureau to devote its efforts in its first year of operation to performing an education and publicity function within and outside the government about the new competition policy system. Through media interviews, pamphlets, and seminars, the competition policy bureau could inform business leaders, government officials, and Mongolian citizens about the new statute.[50] In dealing with internal and outside constituencies, the new office would declare that its main goal for the first year of the statute will be education rather than the prosecution of cases. Such an approach could raise public awareness of the statute, provide visible evidence of the government's commitment to implementation, create the sense among affected actors that the legal regime is fair because it will be applied only after notice of its requirements has been given, promote the virtues of market-oriented public policy, and give the new office time to devise an enforcement strategy.

The third priority would be to begin to perform the competition advocacy function contemplated by provisions of the statute that seek to discourage government intervention that impedes market rivalry. Among other specific targets, a competition advocacy program could attack regulatory controls and policies that restrict entry and favor incumbent firms. More generally, the antitrust bureau could use the competition advocacy program to create an institutional force to foster the adoption within the government of market-oriented reforms.

The fourth priority would be to begin initiating cases to challenge violations of the statute's commands. A possible target of such enforcement might be efforts by large, formerly state-owned enterprises to use cartels to restore the regime of planned production and marketing that prevailed in the era of central controls. Here too, the new antimonopoly bureau could benefit substantially from the assistance of external advisors in choosing possible cases and prosecuting violators.

Conclusion: Lessons for Regulatory Reform in Transition Economies

Our experience suggests seven general conclusions about the process of legal reform in transition economies. First, effective legal reform requires sustained effort over a substantial period of time. There will be failures and false starts. Successful participation by external advisors is unlikely to flow from visits by consultants who "parachute" into the country, make a few quick lectures, and head for home. Particularly for programs involving legislative reform, consultants are likely to have the greatest impact where they participate extensively in preliminary fact-gathering as a prelude to law drafting, assist in drafting, remain available to monitor and advise in the legislative process, and help with implementation.

The second lesson relates closely to the first. Legal reform is most likely to take root within an overall context of ongoing relationships with a country and as part of a larger process of teaching and interaction. It is an enormous advantage if the legal reform team can rely on colleagues who are resident in the country. A long-term in-country presence does not ensure the success of reform efforts. For example, a sustained in-country presence cannot ensure that sudden political shifts in the host country do not undermine or derail even the most carefully devised and well-conceived reforms. But the in-country presence is crucial to diagnosing economic and legal problems correctly, proposing sensible cures, assisting in implementation, and in anticipating political changes that may dictate adjustments in strategy. We would call the sustained in-country presence a necessary, but not sufficient, condition for successful legal reform.

Third, reform experts coming to a country cannot spend all their time "whispering in ministers' ears." The reform process needs to involve encompassing interests. There is much a reforming country can learn from an open and transparent legal reform process, where the consumers and users of the law are involved in the reform process.

Fourth, reform ultimately has to be generated by citizens of the reforming country. Foreign experts can serve as catalysts, teachers, and expert advisors, but reform efforts will fail if groups and leaders in the country do not take major roles in achieving reform.

Fifth, laws and regulatory processes must be adapted to the host country's environment. It is insufficient for reformers to adopt an American law, or even the "best" law on the subject.[51] Indeed, it sometimes may be necessary for outside advisors to accept provisions that are "bad" in their eyes, because such provisions might be the only ones that have a chance of being passed and implemented and might improve the existing situation. A crucial ingredient of the catalytic and teaching process is to help the drafters choose from among alternatives adapted to the country's distinctive circumstances.

Sixth, implementation must be a priority from the beginning. There are plenty of fine-sounding laws in the world, and even constitutions, that sit on shelves and never are implemented. The drafting process for the Mongolian Unfair Competition Law could serve as a model for other law drafting exercises. Nonetheless, important questions remain as to whether the new statute's attractive substantive features will be applied effectively.

Finally, antimonopoly legislation can play a valuable role in facilitating the adjustment from controls to markets. We acknowledge that the usefulness of an antimonopoly law to transition economies remains controversial. There is reason to fear any regulatory bureaucracy in a transition economy. However, one of the most important lessons to be learned is the proper role of the state in a market economy. The process of adopting and implementing an antimonopoly law can be a centerpiece in the transition from government as central planner and manager of the economy, to government as arbiter and rulemaker for private competitors.

APPENDIX: CASE STUDY

The Meat Processing Sector in Mongolia

*Karen Turner Dunn, William E. Kovacic,
and Robert S. Thorpe*[52]

To provide a foundation for drafting Mongolia's antimonopoly law, the IRIS-Mongolia Project and the Privatization Commission of the Government of Mongolia performed an assessment of existing industry structure and government regulatory behavior. In November 1992, the authors (as a study team of IRIS researchers) studied three of Mongolia's primary industries: meat processing, telecommunications, and wool spinning. The studies were based principally upon interviews with industry managers, plant tours, and discussions with government officials who had oversight responsibilities for the industries. Mongolian researchers and industry representatives also gathered data on sales, costs, and prices to identify business conduct and government intervention that an antimonopoly statute might address, and to analyze the potential for competition in the three industries.

The Role of Meat in the Mongolian Economy

Mongolia is a country of about 2.2 million people and 25 million livestock—sheep, goats, cattle, horses, and camels. Sheep and goats account for about 19 million of the 25 million livestock. According to one estimate, agriculture in 1989 constituted 20 percent of Mongolia's Net Material Product, and livestock accounted for about 70 percent of agriculture's contribution.[53] Meat is a dietary staple with important cultural significance in Mongolia. This fact serves as a note of caution about drawing conclusions as to the proper functioning of the Mongolian meat production system.

Mongolia has vast pasture lands. It is a relatively dry, cold country, with a short growing season. It has inadequate roads and transportation facilities, and a frail communications infrastructure. These conditions affect the meat industry—for example, instead of being shipped, animals are herded or "trailed" to slaughter at the largest meat plants. (In the United States, by contrast, animals are usually shipped to slaughter by truck, and a slaughter plant will often purchase most of its animals within a 150-mile radius of the plant. Adequate transportation and communication facilities tie together markets that are otherwise separated geographically and permit wide dispersion of information about prevailing market prices in various regions.) Mongolia's largest meat plants only slaughter in the period July to December, when animals can be trailed and when they must be slaughtered, because there is insufficient fodder during the winter. There is also a phenomenon in Mongolia called "traditional slaughter," which is done manually or on a household basis rather than at a meat processing facility.

Parts of the Mongolian economy were in various stages of transition from socialism to capitalism at the time this study was written. For example, where the state once owned all livestock, nearly all herds are now privately owned. But while the largest meat plants were in various phases of privatization, the central government holds, and apparently intends to retain, a majority ownership share in each. Meat is subject to rationing in major urban areas. The General Director of the Darkhan meat plant explained that city central procurement agencies place orders with the meat plant for meat to be supplied at a fixed price. A meat plant has to satisfy these orders first, before it can sell meat at negotiated, market prices. There were indications that the prices at which plants sold meat had doubled between 1989 and 1991.

The Meat Processing Industry

Meat Production

The IRIS Study Team focused on the production of fresh meat, which is sold or frozen for later use. The production of fresh meat is a relatively low value-added process: animals are typically purchased and slaughtered, and their meat is sold. Animals are often bought by the live-weight pound, and meat is sold by the pound. The entire production process, from purchase of animal to sale of meat, often takes only a few days. The largest component of meat processing costs by far are the costs of acquiring animals for slaughter. Meat processing can also include the production of processed meats, such as sausage.

There are three large Mongolian meat processing plants, located in the cities of Ulaanbaatar, Darkhan, and Choibalsan. These plants slaughter sheep, cattle and goats, as well as some hogs, horses and camels. There are also smaller plants at Saynshsaud in Dornogovi Aimag (region) southeast of Ulaanbaatar and at Ulastay in Dzavhan Aimag west of Ulaanbaatar. Aimag centers are apparently important meat processors as well: according to one estimate,[54] approximately 60 percent of the total Mongolian live-weight supply of meat in 1989 was slaughtered in the aimags or by home slaughter, all for local consumption. Another 14 percent was exported as live animals or meat products; the remaining 26 percent was supplied to the cities. However, of this 26 percent almost one-third was slaughtered locally and delivered to the cities. So even though there is a single meat plant in each of the three cities, meat is supplied to the cities from other sources as well. Moreover, entry into meat processing appears to be relatively easy.

The Purchase of Livestock

Under the old central planning system, the state owned all livestock. Government officials issued allocation and delivery orders to the aimag centers, which then arranged for animals to be delivered as specified to the various meat plants. Elaborate scheduling charts were worked out in May for the coming slaughter season at the big urban meat plants.

With the privatization of the herds and the nominal elimination of the central allocation system, central allocation and delivery orders no longer control the procurement of livestock for meat plants. While it is by no means clear what has replaced the old system, there appear to be many opportunities for competition in procurement.

In May 1992, an effort was apparently made by two or three of the urban meat plants acting in concert to acquire the animals needed for slaughter during the 1992 season at a single price, to which it was hoped all livestock owners would agree. According to the General Director of the Ulaanbaatar meat plant, this price was 20 tugriks per live kilogram of sheep delivered for slaughter. By contrast, the Study Team learned that the current price for live sheep on the Ulaanbaatar Commodity Exchange was 40 tugriks per live kilogram.

The General Director of the Ulaanbaatar meat plant said that of the 18 aimags in Mongolia, his plant was assigned and drew animals from ten of them, from aimags ranging in proximity from 45 to 1,200 kilometers. The Darkhan meat plant drew from four aimags. However, in some instances where an aimag was located approximately midway between two urban meat plants, animals from that aimag might go to either plant.

One other phenomenon was described: the use of custom slaughter when meat plants could not acquire animals. In Darkhan and in other areas around the Darkhan meat plant, city governments were able to acquire animals for slaughter by paying more for the animals in cash or barter than the meat plants were willing to pay. The cities would then have the animals slaughtered on a custom basis for a fee by the urban meat plants, taking the meat for sale under rationing in the cities and arranging with the meat plants to sell or otherwise utilize the by-products. Cities and other local government units apparently had control over items of value to livestock owners and thus were in a better position than the meat plants to bargain for animals for slaughter. The General Director of the Darkhan meat plant expected that soon his plant might purchase animals only for meat to be exported, and that most of its slaughter would be on a custom basis for owners of animals.

According to the Vice Minister of Agriculture, the difficulties the urban meat plants were experiencing in buying animals stemmed from the privatization of herds. The old system of allocation and central delivery orders was no longer viable. An attempt was made to place state orders for delivery, and it failed. Then special price levels were attempted to maintain the supply of animals. The Vice Minister expected that efforts would be made to keep sheep slaughter prices at 20 tugriks per live kilogram, but that herders (livestock owners) were then wanting 25 tugriks per live kilogram. He added that city governments have some advantages in getting animals for slaughter because they can pay in cash, which meat plants often find difficult to get from banks, and they can barter with consumer goods that would otherwise be unavailable to the herders. Cities also have better contacts with livestock owners and more people to send out to buy animals than do meat plants.

Competitive Analysis

The Mongolian meat industry during this time was not operating in a competitive fashion. Meat plants had to sell a substantial amount of their production at prices fixed by the government. The meat plants agreed among themselves and with the government about the prices they would bid for slaughter livestock. The meat plants were parties to formal or informal territorial divisions concerning where meat would be sold and where efforts would be made to buy animals. The government had a majority ownership interest in the three largest meat plants. The competitive spur of profits and expanding market share is largely absent.

At the same time, there were great opportunities for expanding competition in the Mongolian meat industry. Meat plants could compete for slaughter animals. On the selling side, meat was already being shipped into the large cities where the largest meat plants are located.

Although data limitations make the construction of Herfindahl-Hirschman Indices (HHIs) for the Mongolian meat processing industry

Table 4.1 Sample Herfindahl-Hirschman Indices (HHIs) for the Mongolian Meat Processing Industry, 1989 and 1991

	1989		*1991*	
City	*Market Share*	*HHI*	*Market Share*	*HHI*
Ulaanbaatar	62%	3,844	69%	4,761
Darkhan	21%	441	17%	289
Choibalsan	17%	289	14%	196
TOTAL	100%	4,574	100%	5,246

SOURCE: DANAGRO 1991.

difficult, plausible ranges can be estimated. If the three large meat plants are assumed to be the only sellers of meat and purchasers of animals in the appropriately-defined geographic area, the HHIs would be as shown in Table 4.1 above.

These HHIs in the 4,000 to 5,000 range indicate that this is a concentrated market, as would be expected with only three competitors. However, if these three entities competed vigorously against each other, the result could be competitively satisfactory. Vigilance against collusion would be important in such a concentrated market. It is also noteworthy that, while the Ulaanbaatar meat plant here shows a market share in the range of 62-69 percent, its General Director said that this plant did not provide more than 50 percent of the meat consumed in Ulaanbaatar.

Additional data obtained by the Study Team from interviews with representatives of the Ministry of Agriculture, and from the owner of a private meat plant in Boganu (a "satellite" town about 130 kilometers from Ulaanbaatar), can help provide a more accurate picture of market concentration. Both respondents said that some 7 million animals are slaughtered in Mongolia each year. While we know that these three plants accounted for about 1.5 million of the 7 million animals slaughtered, we don't know the individual market shares of the other slaughterers. However, we do know the other slaughterers are all smaller than the smallest of the three plants, Choibalsan, which had about a 5-percent share of the total slaughter in 1989 and a 4-percent share in 1991. More accurate HHIs may therefore be calculated by assuming that all the remaining slaughter is done by plants holding a 5-percent market share in 1989 and a 4-percent market share in 1991.

Table 4.2   Modified Herfindahl-Hirschman Indices (HHIs) for the Mongolian
Meat Processing Industry, 1989 and 1991

| | 1989 | | 1991 | |
City	Market Share	HHI	Market Share	HHI
Ulaanbaatar	18%	313	16%	243
Darkhan	6%	35	5%	21
Choibalsan	5%	27	4%	17
SUB-TOTAL	29%	375	24%	281
Others	70%[a]	350[a]	76%[b]	304[b]
TOTAL	100%	725	100%	585

[a]Assuming that there are 14 other firms, each with 5-percent market shares.
[b]Assuming that there are 19 other firms, each with 4-percent market shares.

SOURCE: DANAGRO 1991, plus interview data.

(These assumptions will tend to overstate the HHIs, but are sufficient for our purposes.)[55] The results, shown above in Table 4.2, indicate an unconcentrated market.

Care must be used in interpreting both sets of HHIs. The first set, based on sales data, assumes that the three plants are in the same geographic market, both for selling meat and purchasing animals. It is not clear that in a market economy these three plants would compete with each other over the same geographic area. The second set, based on data for animals slaughtered, assumes that *all* Mongolian meat plants are in the same geographic market, which consists of all of Mongolia. This assumption is surely too strong, given Mongolia's underdeveloped transportation and communications systems. Hence, these HHIs understate concentration and can be interpreted as lower bounds.

One might also examine the potential for competition in the sale of meat in Ulaanbaatar by using assumptions similar to those employed above. According to the general director of the Ulaanbaatar meat plant, his plant supplied approximately 50 percent of the meat consumed in Ulaanbaatar. This plant's market share can therefore be assumed to be 50 percent. The source of the other 50 percent is not known for sure, but if it were produced by ten other plants each accounting for a 5-percent market share, the HHI for the sale of meat in Ulaanbaatar would then be 2,750 ($50^2 + 10 \times 5^2$). This would be a moderately concentrated market, and one likely to be performing satisfactorily.

There are a number of areas where more information about the Mongolian meat industry would be useful in evaluating the tentative conclusion that there is substantial room for competitive forces that are not now being realized. These areas include:

- the meat rationing system and government allocation orders;
- the trailing system and the extent to which livestock owners can choose among slaughter options;
- transportation costs;
- retail meat establishments, and the manner in which such shops acquire meat;
- the role of exports of live animals and of meat;
- the effects of seasonality on the potential for competition;
- significant competitive differences in the markets for sheep, goats, cattle, horses, hogs, and camels and their meat;
- the livestock procurement process and the role of custom kill arrangements; and
- local slaughter capacity in the aimags.

Suggestions for Competition Policy

This study provides evidence of the kinds of practices Mongolian competition policy should address. As is the case in other areas of the Mongolian economy, government regulations undermined the potential for competitive behavior in this industry. Rationing, restrictions on exports, and allocation orders obstructed the development of markets. Further, there was common majority ownership (by the Government of Mongolia) of the three largest plants. Competition policy could ensure that even where there is common government ownership, the plants must behave as independent competitors.

Competition policy should also address anticompetitive conduct perpetrated by the meat plants themselves, should such conduct be documented. Agreements between competitors to fix prices, to allocate markets, and to divide selling areas usually are condemned in a market economy, and there are signs that such practices threaten competition in the Mongolian meat industry. Competition policy could prohibit these practices, regulate mergers, and provide for divestiture when appropriate. Again, however, anticompetitive conduct by firms in the industry can be sensibly addressed only after firms are truly allowed to set prices independently, and are given time to adjust to this process. Care must be taken to prevent antimonopoly efforts themselves from reinforcing traditions of government intervention.

Notes

1. Authors' Note: This publication was made possible through support provided by the U.S. Agency for International Development under Cooperative Agreement No. DHR-0015-A-00-0031-00 to the Center on Institutional Reform and the Informal Sector and administered by the Office of Economic and Institutional Reform, Center for Economic Growth, Bureau for Global Programs, Field Support and Research.

2. See Boner 1995, and Gray and Davis 1993.

3. These trips are described in Kovacic and Thorpe 1993.

4. See Godek 1992, Rodriguez 1994, Rodriguez and Coate 1994, Rodriguez and Williams 1994, and Rubin 1994:45-46, for critiques of programs encouraging transitional economies to develop antitrust systems; see Boner and Langenfeld 1992, Boner 1995, Conrath and Freeman 1994, Jatar 1995, Langenfeld and Blitzer 1991, Waller and Muente 1989, and Willig 1991, favoring use of antitrust policy as one element of reform.

5. Dunn, Kovacic, and Thorpe 1994:25.

6. See Library of Congress 1991, World Bank 1991, and Milne *et al.* 1991.

7. See Shapiro 1992.

8. See Denizer and Gelb 1992, Korsun and Murrell 1993 and 1994, Murrell 1991, Murrell *et al.* 1992a, and Whytock 1992.

9. Mongolia borders Siberia, and in many respects is similar to newly independent Central Asian states located to the west.

10. See, for example, McGregor 1993.

11. IRIS is a USAID-funded affiliate of the Economics Department at the University of Maryland, College Park. Its Principal Investigator is Distinguished Professor of Economics Mancur Olson. IRIS conducts a substantial research program and a number of field programs supporting institutional reform in countries undergoing a transition from central planning to a market system. For IRIS, "institutions" are the rules of the game governing economic and political actors in a society, including laws, regulatory procedures, and patterns of behavior. In addition to Mongolia, IRIS has institutional reform programs in Armenia, Chad, India, Madagascar, Nepal, Poland, Russia, and Ukraine.

12. A number of the members of the Mongolian Antitrust Law Drafting Group previously had attended IRIS Workshops on market institutions, as had Mongolian Prime Minister Jasrai and Tsedendagva, a member of Parliament and Chair of the Parliamentary committee responsible for antimonopoly legislation. Our work on a Mongolian antimonopoly law took root in an IRIS workshop whose main topic was the role of prices in a market economy.

13. See Godek 1992, and Rubin 1994.

14. Slay (1994:30) argues that:

> Privatization, increased import competition (mostly in manufacturing, less so in other areas), the liberalization of prices and business activity, and the virtual eradication of shortage pressures, have done more to promote competitive forces than structural competition policies.

Although similar institutional and legal frameworks for competition policies have been created in Poland and Hungary, the significance of these policies in the overall transition has been relatively minor.

15. See Olson 1995, Pitofsky and Goldschmid 1991:4-5, Rubin 1994, and Starodubrovskaya 1994:14. Projects to promote the establishment of legal institutions for recognizing and exchanging property rights have figured prominently in IRIS legal reform programs, including those in Mongolia.

16. Competition policy authorities in formerly socialist countries recognize this point and see trade liberalization as a crucial element of market-oriented reform. See Bělehrádek 1993:49-50, where the Chairman of the Czech Competition Office cites trade reform as a central means to promote market competition. See also Pogácsás and Stadler 1993:79, where officials of the Hungarian Competition Office state that "[f]or a small country like Hungary competition from imports must play a decisive role in breaking down monopolistic and dominant positions."

17. See Brown *et al.* 1994:38-39 for a description of how eliminating regional and local restrictions on entry and the movement of goods could improve Russia's system of distribution and increase competition.

18. This possibility has not been lost on commentators inside countries experimenting with new antimonopoly systems. Yevstigneyev (1993:98), in discussing Russia's antimonopoly law, observes that "there is a danger that an antimonopolistic policy...could itself encourage the revival of command methods."). Similar points are made in Capelik's discussion of the problems of Russia's "Monopoly Register" (1994:22-24, 27-31; see also Chapter 3); and by Starodubrovskaya (1994:15-16) who criticizes the Russian regulation of firms with market shares of 35 percent or more.

19. See Hoekman *et al.* 1994:2-3, and Kovacic 1992:260 on collusion in the services sector in Zimbabwe.

20. See Kovacic 1995.

21. For example, Flassik (1993:74-75) notes how the Czechoslovak Federal Competition Office used its competition advocacy authority to achieve a reduction in tariffs for automobiles, in order to bring competitive pressure to bear upon the country's sole domestic car producer.

22. See Dunn, Kovacic, and Thorpe 1994:2, 13-14. In our first visit to Mongolia in November 1992, we interviewed officials in the country's meat packing industry. During one meeting, a manager described how herders had begun to obtain better prices for their herds by exploiting bidding by the country's three principal meat packing plants for the best animals. The manager predicted that this outbreak of bidding would cease because he had obtained assurances from his counterparts in the other plants that they would offer herders a uniform price in the coming year.

23. See Klitgaard 1990:185.

24. See Dunn, Kovacic, and Thorpe 1994.

25. The results of the meat processing industry study, including tables on concentration data, are found in the case study accompanying this chapter.

26. Price controls and administered pricing by government agencies were central features of socialist economies. One of the most difficult problems for transition economies is abolishing price controls and trusting market outcomes. Price controls continue in one form or another in Mongolia in many sectors. (For example, some Mongolian meat and flour products were subject to government rationing in February 1993). In addition meat is a dietary staple with important cultural significance in Mongolia, and the three largest meat production plants, although "privatized", were each majority owned by the Mongolian government. (See Murrell *et al.* 1992a, 1992b). Of course, price regulation to control monopoly power or to achieve other public purposes is hardly unknown in the United States, as can be seen in the 1992 cable television price control statute, or in proposals to regulate pharmaceutical drug and other medical prices as part of health care reform.

27. The chief resource for this review was Pittman 1992.

28. In addition to privatizing state-owned enterprises, the Mongolian State Commission for Privatization has been a leading force for market reforms, and it had umbrella responsibility for drafting an antimonopoly law. Gerelchuluun, its Secretary, also attended an IRIS Workshop.

29. Two incidents demonstrate the depth of the core unit's preparation. At one point, Badarch, an economist in the core unit, referred to a recent article by an official of the U.S. Federal Trade Commission's Bureau of Competition. This article had been translated into Russian and had been published in a Russian journal, which Badarch had read. The article prompted him to ask whether our advice was simply "main-line" or whether it reflected the "new trends" in antitrust analysis. At another point, Badarch asked us to compare and contrast the Japanese and Korean antitrust models as an aid for considering alternatives for Mongolia.

30. We spoke no Mongolian, and most of our Mongolian colleagues spoke no English (although many spoke Russian). We relied on a superb translator/interpreter, Yanjemaa, who is well-known and respected in Mongolia. All oral presentations (and most conversations between Mongolians and Americans) were in simultaneous translation. Yanjemaa has translated for IRIS workshops and knows the jargon of law and economics. As Mongolian is not a particularly commercial language, Yanjemaa often "invented" Mongolian phrases to convey Western ideas affecting commerce. Two other Mongolians, Batsettseg and Minjin, also provided valuable translation assistance.

31. The use of a 50 percent dominance threshold is closer to European Union practice than to U.S. antitrust doctrine, which ordinarily requires a showing that the firm or firms in question hold a market share of 65 percent or more before a condition of dominance will be deemed to exist. (See Gellhorn and Kovacic 1994). The preference for the 50 percent test reflects the tendency of many transition economies—especially those in Central or Eastern Europe, or those (such as Mongolia) whose legal systems have been shaped by Eastern European (i.e., Soviet) models—to draw upon European experience.

32. The antitrust statutes of a number of transition economies mandate the use of market share thresholds in the evaluation of horizontal conduct. For example, Hungary's antitrust law prescribes a rule of reason analysis for horizontal agreements where the participants' collective market share does not exceed 30 percent and efficiency rationales support the collaboration (Pogácsás and Stadler 1993:86-87). The Russian antitrust law also requires antimonopoly agencies to show that participants in an anticompetitive agreement collectively hold at least 35 percent of the market. Some commentators (see Joskow *et al.* 1994: 361-62) have proposed that this dominance threshold be abandoned if it proves in practice to seriously impede prosecution of naked cartel arrangements.

33. Many other transition economy antimonopoly laws have created efficiency defenses for otherwise illegal mergers. See Brzezinski 1994, and Pittman 1992.

34. Transition economies vary greatly in their receptivity, at least in the short to medium term, to mechanisms that permit private entities to enforce public laws. Partly due to its civil law structure, Mongolia has no tradition of private enforcement of public laws. Creating private rights of action would entail a relatively drastic departure from existing practice and, consequently, might prove especially difficult to implement. By contrast, Zimbabwe has a well-developed tradition of private enforcement of public laws and would be a suitable candidate for a scheme of private enforcement of public antimonopoly commands. See Kovacic 1992:264.

35. See Rodriguez and Williams (1994:227-31) for a discussion and critique of the potential benefits for transition economies of competition advocacy programs that attack public restrictions on market rivalry. See also Conrath and Freeman (1994:243-45), who conclude that competition advocacy can be a valuable component of antimonopoly policy in transition economies. Freeman (1994:9-10) argues that competition advocacy is useful in implementing privatization programs and criticizes government efforts to limit trade liberalization. See also Hoekman *et al.* (1994:16-18) who argues that competition authorities in Central and Eastern Europe should actively oppose import restrictions. Joskow *et al.* (1994:359-60) strike a similar note in the Russian case, arguing that regional antimonopoly authorities in Russia "could play a more useful role here if they became advocates for policies that promote competition" in regulated sectors such as energy, telecommunications, and transportation. See also Kovacic 1992 for a discussion of the value of competition advocacy in the context of Zimbabwe's consideration of new antimonopoly law.

36. The Law Drafting Group attributed a "constitutional" character to the antimonopoly body's advocacy work because it believed that market principles were fundamental to legal reform, and that government-imposed departures from such principles warrant close scrutiny.

37. Compare Klitgaard (1990:79), who observes that, in working on economic reform projects in transition economies, "decisions are improved by collegial efforts to lay out issues, clarify choices, and separate the value judgments and the factual questions."

38. Even though some members of the Law Drafting Group had strong ties to the Privatization Commission (the government body charged with drafting the antimonopoly law), the Law Drafting Group was clearly not an instrument of the highest levels of the Mongolian government. Moreover, in our experience, mechanisms by which policy choices are shepherded through the law enactment process are not well developed in Mongolia.

39. The discussion in this part of the paper is based upon a draft, unofficial translation of the Mongolian statute.

40. Article 3.2 defines "monopoly" as single-firm control over all production or sales in a market. The statute does not provide a definition for the concept of "relevant market."

41. The Law Drafting Group's proposed antimonopoly law also had included consumer protection provisions.

42. The statute creates no private right of action, but permits (in Article 13) individual firms, citizens, or organizations representing consumer or producer interests to register complaints with the Hural (concerning legal violations by national government agencies) and with the government ministries and the DND (concerning legal violations by local government bodies and by business enterprises).

43. See Boner 1995, and Kovacic 1995.

44. The implementation rules drafting team consists of four engineers, who are to receive periodic assistance from the Ministry of Justice.

45. For example, during the parliamentary deliberations on the Unfair Competition Law in Mongolia, an IRIS team might have helped ensure that Parliament's attention remained focused on implementation concerns.

46. There is also the issue of when a country should be left "on its own" in pursuing policy reform. In this context, we note that the United States has provided technical assistance on antimonopoly law implementation to transition economies in Eastern Europe and the NIS, including Bulgaria, Estonia, the Czech Republic, Kazakhstan, Latvia, Lithuania, Poland, Romania, Russia, Slovakia, and Ukraine—which are already better equipped (in terms of an institutional infrastructure and resources) than Mongolia to deal with such issues (see McDermott 1991).

47. Mongolia is not unique among transition economies in facing difficult challenges in developing the expertise and institutions to execute an antimonopoly program: see Capelik 1994a, Joskow *et al.* 1994:336, Khemani 1994, and Langenfeld and Yao 1993:205-09.

48. Our interviews with judges and practitioners in Mongolia's legal community have indicated that Mongolia's courts historically have served chiefly as forums for deciding criminal cases, and therefore have little experience in adjudicating commercial disputes. However, discussions with Mongolian judges who participated in the IRIS Workshop on the Development and Implementation of Business Law in Ulaanbataar in June 1994 revealed that a number of Mongolian judges have acquired an impressive level of sophistication in analyzing the legal and economic issues arising in commercial law disputes.

49. On the importance of assembling a suitable mix of legal and economic expertise, see Langenfeld and Yao 1993.

50. See Langenfeld and Yao (1993:214) for a discussion of the value of speeches and other forms of educational outreach activities by competition policy authorities.

51. See Rubin 1994, and Waller 1994.

52. Robert Thorpe was the principal researcher and author of this study which is derived largely from Dunn, Kovacic, and Thorpe 1994.

53. DANAGRO 1991.

54. DANAGRO 1991. These data are roughly consistent with information derived from the Study Team's interviews with Surenjargal, Mongolia's Vice-Minister of Agriculture; Deleg, the General Director of the Ulaanbaatar meat plant; Lhundev, the General Director of the Darkhan plant; and Dovdon, former Deputy Director of the Ulaanbaatar meat plant, and then owner of a private meat plant. Dovdon's success in establishing a private processing facility suggested the feasibility of new entry in this sector.

55. These numbers are modified to account for data on horses slaughtered at the Ulaanbaatar and Darkhan meat plants. For the Ulaanbaatar plant, the horse figures were 3,238 in 1989 and 2,400 in 1991; for the Darkhan plant, the figures were 2,400 and 95, respectively.

References

Bělehrádek, S. 1993. "Competition Policy and Privatisation in Czechoslovakia," in C.T. Saunders, ed., *The Role of Competition in Economic Transition*. Pp. 49-54. New York: St. Martin's Press.

Boner, R.A. 1995. "Competition Policy and Issues in Transitional Economies," forthcoming in Frischtak, C., ed., *Regulatory Policies and Reform in Industrializing Countries*. Washington D.C.: World Bank.

Boner, R.A., and J. Langenfeld. 1992. "Liberal Trade and Antitrust in Developing Nations." *Regulation* (Spring): 5-6.

Brown, A.N., B.W. Ickes, and R. Ryterman. 1994. "The Myth of Monopoly: A New View of Industrial Structure in Russia." Policy Research Working Paper No. 1331. Washington D.C.: World Bank.

Brzezinski, C. 1994. "Competition and Antitrust Law in Central Europe: Poland, the Czech Republic, Slovakia, and Hungary." *Michigan Journal of International Law* 4: 1129-78.

Capelik, V.E. 1994a. "Development of Antimonopoly Policy and Monopoly Regulation in Russia." Mimeo. Moscow: Institute for Economy in Transition.

_____. 1994b. "Should Monopoly be Regulated in Russia?" *Communist Economies and Economic Transition* 1: 19-32.

Conrath, C.W., and B.T. Freeman. 1994. "The Effectiveness of Proposed Antitrust Programs for Developing Countries—A Comment." *North Carolina Journal of International Law and Commercial Regulation* 2:233-45.

Cooter, R.D. 1993. "Market Modernization of Law: Economic Development Through Decentralized Law." Mimeo. Berkeley: University of California.

DANAGRO ADVISER A/S. 1991. "Consulting Study of the Mongolian Meat Industry."

Denizer, C., and A. Gelb. 1992. *Mongolia: Privatization and System Transformation in an Isolated Economy.* Washington D.C.: World Bank.

Dunn, K.T., W.E. Kovacic, and R.S. Thorpe. 1994. "Analysis of Competition in Mongolia: Three Case Studies." College Park, Maryland: Center for Institutional Reform and the Informal Sector, Country Report No. 14 (April).

Flassik, I. 1993. "Priorities of the Czechoslovak Anti-Trust Office," in C.T. Saunders, ed., *The Role of Competition in Economic Transition.* Pp. 73-77. New York: St. Martin's Press.

Freeman, B.T. 1994. "The Political Economy of Competition Policy for Eastern Europe." Mimeo. Washington D.C.: U.S. Federal Trade Commission, Bureau of Economics.

Gellhorn, E., and W.E. Kovacic. 1994. *Antitrust Law and Economics in a Nutshell,* 4th ed. St. Paul: West Publishing Co.

Godek, P.E. 1992. "One U.S. Export Eastern Europe Doesn't Need." *Regulation.* (Winter): 20-21.

Gray, C.S., and A.A. Davis. 1993. "Competition Policy in Developing Countries Pursuing Structural Adjustment." *Antitrust Bulletin* (Summer):425-67.

Hoekman, B.M., and P.C. Mavroidis. 1994. *Linking Competition and Trade Policies in Central and Eastern Europe.* Policy Research Working Paper No. 1346. Washington, D.C.: World Bank.

Jatar, A.J. 1995. "Competition Policy in Latin-America: The Promotion of Social Change." Mimeo. Washington D.C.: The Inter-American Dialogue.

Joskow, P.L., R. Schmalensee, and N. Tsukanova. 1994. "Competition Policy in Russia during and after Privatization." *Brookings Papers: Microeconomics 1994.* Boston.

Khemani, R. (Shyam). 1994. "The Administration of Competition Law and Policy in Transition Economies: The Case of Russia." Mimeo. Washington D.C.: The World Bank.

Klitgaard, R. 1990. *Tropical Gangsters.* New York: Basic Books.

Korsun, G., and P. Murrell. 1995. "The Effects of History, Ownership and Pre-Privatization Restructuring on Post-Privatization Governance." College Park: IRIS Working Paper No. 147.

_____. 1993. "Ownership and Governance on the Morning After: The Initial Results of Privatization in Mongolia." Mimeo. College Park: IRIS.

Kovacic, W.E. 1995. "Designing and Implementing Competition and Consumer Protection Reforms in Transitional Economies: Perspectives from Mongolia, Nepal, Ukraine, and Zimbabwe." *Depaul Law Review* 4 (forthcoming).

_____. 1992. "Competition Policy, Economic Development, and the Transition to Free Markets in the Third World: The Case of Zimbabwe." *Antitrust Law Journal* 1: 253-65.

Kovacic, W.E., and R.S. Thorpe. 1993. "Antitrust Law for a Transition Economy." *Legal Times* (August 2): 41.

Kroll, H. 1991. "Monopoly and Transition to the Market." *Soviet Economy* 2: 143-74.

Langenfeld, J. and M. Blitzer. 1991. "Is Competition Policy the Last Thing Central and Eastern Europe Need?" *American University Journal of International Law and Policy* 3:347-98.

Langenfeld, J. and D.A. Yao. 1994. "Competition Policy and Privatization: An Organizational Perspective," in H.J. Blommestein and B. Steunenberg, eds., *Governments and Markets*. Pp. 195-218. Dordrecht, Netherlands: Kluwer Academic Publishers.

Library of Congress, Federal Research Division. 1991. *Mongolia: A Country Study.* Washington, D.C.:U.S. Government Printing Office.

McDermott, K.E. 1991. "U.S. Agencies Provide Competition Counseling to Eastern Europe." *Antitrust* (Fall/Winter): 6-7.

McGregor, J. 1993. "In the Post-Soviet Era, A Nation of Nomads Wanders Into Oblivion." *The Wall Street Journal* (March 16): A1.

Milne, E., J. Leimone, F. Rozwadowski, and P. Sukachevin. 1991. *The Mongolian People's Republic: Toward a Market Economy*. International Monetary Fund Occasional Paper 79. Washington D.C.: International Monetary Fund.

Murrell, P. 1991. *Reform Issues in Mongolia*. College Park: IRIS, Country Report No. 1.

Murrell, P., G. Korsun, and K. Dunn. 1992a. *Price Policy in Mongolia: A Chronology of Developments*. College Park: IRIS, Country Report No. 6.

_____. 1992b. "The Culture of Policymaking in the Transition From Socialism: Price Policy in Mongolia." College Park: IRIS, Working Paper No. 32.

Olson, M. 1995. "The Devolution of Power and the Societies in Transition: Therapies for Corruption, Fragmentation, and Economic Retardation." Mimeo. College Park: University of Maryland.

Pitofsky, R., and H.J. Goldschmid. 1991. "Azerbaijanian-American Symposium: The Road to Economic Renewal." *International Merger Law* (September): 2-6.

Pittman, R. 1992. "Some Critical Provisions in the Antimonopoly Laws of Central and Eastern Europe." *International Lawyer* 2:485-503.

Pogácsás, P., and J. Stadler. 1993. "Promoting Competition in Hungary," in C.T. Saunders, ed., *The Role of Competition in Economic Transition*. Pp. 78-89. New York: St. Martin's Press.

Rodriguez, A.E. 1994. "Antitrust Policy in Recently Liberalized Economies." Mimeo. Washington D.C.: U.S. Federal Trade Commission, Bureau of Economics.

Rodriguez, A.E., and M.B. Coate. 1994. "Limits to Antitrust Policy for Reforming Economies," Mimeo. Washington D.C.: U.S. Federal Trade Commission, Bureau of Economics.

Rodriguez, A.E., and M.D. Williams. 1994. "The Effectiveness of Proposed Antitrust Programs for Developing Countries." *North Carolina Journal of International Law and Commercial Regulation* 2:209-32.

Rubin, P.H. 1994. "Growing a Legal System in the Post-Communist Economies." *Cornell International Law Journal* 1: 1-47.

Shapiro, F.C. 1992. "Starting From Scratch." *The New Yorker*: January 20.

Slay, B. 1994. "Industrial Demonopolization and Competition Policy in Poland and Hungary." Middlebury, Vermont: Middlebury College Working Paper No. 94-9.

Starodubrovskaya, I. 1994. "The Nature of Monopoly and Barriers to Entry in Russia". *Communist Economies and Economic Transition* 1: 3-18.

Waller, S.W. 1994. "Neo-Realism and the International Harmonization of Law: Lessons from Antitrust." *University of Kansas Law Review* 3: 557-604.

Waller, S.W., and R. Muente. 1989. "Competition Law for Developing Countries: A Proposal for an Antitrust Regime in Peru." *Case Western Reserve Journal of International Law* 2: 159-84.

Willig, R.D. 1992. "Anti-Monopoly Policies and Institutions," in C. Clague and G. Rausser, eds., *The Emergence of Market Economies in Eastern Europe.* Pp. 187-96. Cambridge, Massachusetts: Blackwell Publishers.

World Bank, Country Operations Division. 1991. *Mongolia Country Economic Memorandum: Towards a Market Economy.* Washington D.C.: The World Bank.

Whytock, C.A. 1992. *Mongolia in Transition: The New Legal Framework for Land Rights and Land Protection.* College Park: IRIS, Country Report No. 7.

Yevstigneyev, R. 1993. "Creating a Competitive Environment in Russia," in C.T. Saunders, ed., *The Role of Competition in Economic Transition.* Pp. 90-100. New York: St. Martin's Press.

5

Industrial De-monopolization and Competition Policy in Poland

Ben Slay

This chapter examines the development of competitive markets in Polish industry during the late 1980s and early 1990s, the critical years of Poland's transition from Soviet-type socialism to capitalism. Four specific topics are considered: (1) the nature of the "monopoly socialism" in Poland before and during the transition; (2) officially-measured changes in structural concentration in Polish industry, particularly during 1987-1992; (3) the evolution of competition policy in Poland; and (4) conclusions.[1] These include the following:

- The Polish transition has witnessed an important degree of spontaneous de-monopolization. Expanded import competition, price liberalization, state enterprise deregulation, and rapid growth of the private sector have reduced entry barriers and significantly increased the numbers of actual and potential competitors in most sectors.
- Structural deconcentration activities by the Antimonopoly Office have been relatively unimportant, and competition policies *per se* have often taken a back seat to privatization, trade, and industrial policies. The focus of competition policy has been on preventing anti-competitive behavior, especially by dominant firms, and on promoting market competition in general, rather than on effecting changes in industrial structures.
- The relevance of these conclusions is somewhat ambiguous for Russia and (to a lesser degree) other post-communist economies. On the one hand, reforms introduced in Poland during the 1980s had begun to condition state enterprises to function in a partially marketized environment. Once the full-

fledged transition to capitalism began, these earlier reform steps promoted spontaneous deconcentration and de-monopolization tendencies, to a degree not present in many other transitional economies.[2] On the other hand, because the Polish economy is much smaller and more open than the Russian economy, Poland can not, even in the long run, rely on large domestic markets and numerous potential (if not actual) competitors to provide market discipline for producers in concentrated industries. In contrast to Russia, competition policy in Poland must therefore be closely linked to the maintenance of a relatively open trade regime. For Russia, however, external liberalization may not be a precondition for successful de-monopolization, although the liberalization of domestic prices and economic activity, as well as privatization, almost certainly are.

- The governments of Prime Ministers Waldemar Pawlak (from October 1993 to March 1995) and Józef Oleksy (since March 1995), which were formed by parties descended from the pre-1989 (communist) political system, adopted a decisively more interventionist, anti-competitive economic philosophy than the Solidarity cabinets that had held power during 1990-1993. Both governments favored protection from competitive forces for industrial and agricultural lobbies to a much greater degree than their predecessors. Still, wholesale reversals in either de-monopolization in general or competition policy in particular after 1993 have not been forthcoming.

"Monopoly Socialism" in Poland

The establishment of Soviet-type socialism in Poland was accompanied by reductions in numbers of firms and increases in industrial concentration. A mixed economy, characterized by a multitude of state-owned, cooperative, and private industrial firms, had emerged during the 1945-1948 reconstruction period. With the onset of Stalinism after 1948, however, private enterprise was driven to the margins of economic life. The private-sector share of total industrial employment fell from 24 percent in 1946 to 5 percent in 1960,[3] for example; while the number of private industrial firms declined from 16,000 in 1948 to 4,200 in 1955.[4] Simultaneously, industrial plants and firms in the "socialized sector" (consisting of state and cooperative enterprises) were increasingly merged into larger entities. The share of small state-owned industrial firms (with less than 100 employees) in the

Table 5.1   Changes in Numbers of Polish State and Cooperative Industrial
Enterprises, 1970-1992

Year	Number of State Firms	Average Employment	Number of Cooperative Firms	Average Employment
1970	3058	3485	2489	413
1975	3036	3954	2043	552
1976	2879	3973	1557	564
1977	2849	4015	1500	570
1978	2861	4013	1502	569
1979	2878	4016	1599	556
1980	2887	4001	1711	546
1981	2999	3987	2143	552
1982	3040	3769	2217	531
1983	3077	3724	2260	535
1984	3121	3700	2304	543
1985	3116	3674	2309	541
1986	3116	3684	2348	539
1987	3140	3666	2392	534
1988	3177	3597	2400	527
1989	3224	3468	2336	503
1990	4317	753	n.a.	n.a.
1991	4737	580	2475	138
1992	4599	525	2341	117

Sources: *Roczniki Statystyczne: Przemysł* 1985:20-21, 1990:2-3, 1991:1, 1992:1, 1993:1.

total number of state-owned industrial firms declined from 37 percent in 1960 to 11 percent in 1975, while the share of large state-owned industrial firms (with more than 1,000 employees) rose from 9.5 percent to 24 percent during this time.[5] At the end of this period, organizational decisions were being made under the influence of the so-called "WOG" (*wielkie organizacje gospodarcze*) reform, in which state enterprises were amalgamated into vertically- and horizontally-integrated "large economic organizations." In many respects, this "reform" represented the zenith of concentration tendencies in Polish industry.[6] As Table 5.1 shows, the numbers of state and cooperative enterprises were smallest, while aggregate concentration levels in these sectors (as measured by average employment per firm) were highest, during 1977-1979.

The establishment of the institutions of central planning was at least as important as changes in industrial structures *per se*. Such institutions as the intermediate-layer *zjednocznenia* and the branch industrial ministries to which they were subordinated, or the material supply bureau and its agents, were themselves monopolistic organizations with control over production and investment decisions in wide sections of the Polish economy. More importantly, these institutions were intrinsically linked to the system of centralized planning and administration that was incompatible with the commercial autonomy and entrepreneurship needed for competitive markets to function. In fact, the shortage economy and its associated seller's-market phenomena endowed even small firms with *de facto* monopoly power, since their customers were (nominally) prevented by central allocation mechanisms from finding multiple sources of supply.

While the market-socialist economic reforms introduced during the early and mid-1980s were the first steps away from the traditional system, they also heralded new developments in the evolution of "monopoly socialism" in Poland. Legislation adopted during 1981-1982 reduced the number and size of the branch ministries, partially decontrolled some prices, and began the deregulation of state and cooperative enterprises. The intermediate-layer zjednocznenia were replaced by trade associations (*zrzeszenia*),[7] in which membership was voluntary for some firms (especially outside of heavy industry). However, because these reforms did not make a clean break with socialist paternalism or with the branch-oriented logic of industrial structures, they gave rise to two new aspects of monopolization. First, as market forces began to take hold and as the intermediate-layer organizations became more dependent on their constituent enterprises, attention turned to the development and maintenance of cooperative pricing and output arrangements.[8] Second, the industrial ministries responded to their reduced influence enterprise behavior by creating new monopolistic organizations directly under their control. Some of these entities, such as the *Wspólnota Węgla Kamiennego* and the *Wspólnota Energetyki i Węgla Brunatnego* created in 1987, amalgamated all the enterprises in three industrial branches into two nation-wide concerns.[9] These developments made Polish reform economists more aware of the institutional impediments to competitive markets, and of the need for more serious efforts at de-monopolization.[10]

The pace of economic change began to accelerate in the late 1980s. In addition to the abolition of the branch industrial ministries and the *zrzeszenia* (during 1987-1989), legislation passed in December 1988 permitted all firms, regardless of ownership, to engage in any legal business activity, and to form equity partnerships with firms from other sectors. Important steps in import liberalization, and in increasing the convertibility of the zloty, were also begun in 1989. Combined with the 1988 liberalization of restrictions on joint ventures (which in turn were further liberalized in 1991) and the still valid 1934 Commercial Code, these changes effectively removed numerous barriers to entry, and provided a strong boost to spontaneous privatization processes as well.[11] These developments led to the rapid expansion of limited- and unlimited-liability corporations which, after 1989, remade much of Poland's industrial landscape.[12] Extensive price liberalization, which began with food products in August 1989 and was then extended to most of the rest of the economy (except for labor markets) in 1990, provided another key element of the de-monopolization processes. Last but not least, the Antimonopoly Office (*Urząd Antymonopolowy*) was established in 1988, first as a division of the Finance Ministry, later (in 1990) as an independent government agency.

Changes in Industrial Concentration

The official data on industrial concentration published in the Polish statistical yearbooks leave much to be desired, as Tables 5.2 and 5.3 indicate.[13] Although the yearbooks contain Gini coefficients and what might be described as modified concentration ratios measuring concentration (by gross sales and employment), these data do not reflect the activity of firms with less than 50 employees. Prior to 1989-1990, these statistics apparently did not reflect the activities of private industrial firms at all. While these problems may not have introduced a particularly serious bias into the concentration data in 1984, they almost certainly did so by 1992. This is because private industrial firms (which have traditionally operated on relatively small production scales) were officially accounting for some 25 percent of industrial production by 1992, and many new small state-owned and cooperative firms had appeared as well. And since the data for 1989-1992 do not reflect industrial activities conducted by enterprises employing less than 50 people, information about a disproportionately large share of private (and other) small-scale industrial activities continued to be excluded from the official statistics on concentration.

Moreover, concentration ratios and Gini coefficients are highly imperfect measures of market concentration and monopolization in any economy. Concentration ratios provide little information about the extent of concentration below the i-th firm cut-off, while Gini coefficients are essentially measures of inequality, not concentration. Most important, neither measure incorporates information about

Table 5.2 Gini Coefficients for Polish Industry,[a] 1984-1987,[b] 1989-1992[c]

Industrial Branch	1984	1985	1986	1987	1989[d]	1990	1991	1992
Coal	.246	.236	.209	.487	.082	.069	.063	.231
Fuels	.923	.911	.916	.147	.601	.642	.579	.235
Electric power	.837	.830	.829	.450	.347	.286	.297	.398
Ferrous metallurgy	.506	.482	.461	.285	.243	.252	.282	.521
Non-ferrous metallurgy	.391	.310	.272	.111	.261	.307	.301	.531
Metals	.918	.920	.922	.709	.339	.399	.315	.723
Engineering	.736	.732	.727	.622	.423	.438	.451	.667
Precision tools	.938	.937	.935	.671	.488	.453	.387	.600
Transportation equipment	.933	.929	.925	.729	.647	.606	.608	.803
Electrical appliances	.894	.888	.883	.639	.363	.445	.424	.704
Chemicals	.828	.824	.821	.640	.572	.606	.618	.731
Building materials	.752	.756	.751	.545	.368	.380	.278	.641
Glass	.901	.902	.907	.568	.465	.523	.519	.656
Ceramics	.639	.649	.656	.496	.393	.371	.452	.611
Wood	.801	.806	.816	.618	.133	.185	.226	.669
Paper	.779	.788	.782	.561	.473	.538	.581	.768
Textiles	.846	.840	.834	.574	.201	.221	.260	.604
Clothing	.816	.813	.815	.546	.012	.057	.019	.592
Leather	.941	.940	.937	.686	.238	.246	.129	.613
Food processing	.874	.869	.730	.675	.293	.256	.215	.668
Animal feed	.608	.611	.703	.283	.198	.202	.354	.574
Printing	.773	.777	.784	.502	.113	.139	.801	.550
Other branches	.763	.766	.773	.412	.198	.267	.304	.576
AGGREGATE	.899	.896	.885	.719	.405	.439	.415	.784

[a]These coefficients are derived from gross industrial sales data in current prices, reported by firms with at least 50 employees.

[b]The coefficients for 1984-1987 were complied from state-enterprise and cooperative data; private-sector industrial activities were not included.

[c]The coefficients for 1989-1992 reflect private-sector, as well as state-enterprise and cooperative data.

[d]The inclusion of private-sector data is apparently responsible for the abrupt declines in the coefficients for 1989. If private industrial activities are not included in these data, the coefficients for 1989 are quite similar to those for 1988. The aggregate Gini coefficient for 1989 without the private-sector data is officially listed as .765 (*Roczniki Statystyczne: Przemysł* 1990:27), for example, although this figure was exceeded by the coefficient for only one industrial branch (transportation equipment).

Sources: *Roczniki Statystyczne: Przemysł* 1985:19, 1986:22, 1987:22, 1988:35, 1990:27, 1991:21, 1992:13, 1993:13.

Table 5.3   Polish Industrial Concentration Ratios,[a] 1987, 1991, 1992

				Number of firms whose gross sales jointly exceed:					
				50% of total branch sales			*80% of total branch sales*		
	Number of firms								
Industrial Branch	*1987*	*1991*	*1992*	*1987*	*1991*	*1992*	*1987*	*1991*	*1992*
Non-ferrous metallurgy	9	19	25	1	4	0	2	4	6
Energy	11	84	91	1	12	12	3	33	33
Fuels	20	25	25	1	1	1	6	7	3
Coal	18	85	84	2	21	21	5	45	44
Ferrous metallurgy	37	44	48	3	3	2	11	12	11
Animal feed	14	33	44	4	5	16	7	12	16
Ceramics	30	38	40	5	4	4	14	14	14
Paper	54	89	93	6	4	3	16	18	16
Transportation equipment	232	310	302	8	10	5	32	42	36
Precision tools	116	155	138	9	15	15	30	49	45
Glass	79	91	87	11	10	8	27	26	25
Leather	198	298	285	12	28	31	44	86	90
Engineering	429	656	684	19	50	50	110	176	194
Printing	118	134	118	20	17	15	51	50	45
Electronics	252	325	329	21	23	21	65	81	82
Metals	412	496	512	24	31	29	88	105	116
Chemicals	356	445	455	27	23	24	83	81	90
Food processing	732	1130	1228	27	86	82	159	347	355
Building materials	240	463	487	33	45	38	95	166	157
Other branches	167	153	145	36	18	16	85	57	52
Wood	384	535	527	44	41	38	110	126	129
Clothing	343	677	643	52	67	63	182	240	224
Textiles	370	417	393	55	50	50	130	131	131
AGGREGATES	4712	6702	6783	141	232	207	853	1129	1097

[a]Derived from data on gross industrial sales in current prices, as reported by firms employing more than 50 workers.

Sources: *Roczniki Statystyczne: Przemysł* 1988:36, 1992:14, 1993:14.

demand and supply elasticities, which are extremely relevant to considerations of market definition and contestability.

Market definition is made especially problematic by the Polish methodology employed in measuring concentration levels. Because market concentration is essentially reduced to taking shares of gross sales within an industrial branch concentrated in the sales of the branch's largest firms, concentration levels are measured within industrial branches, rather than in appropriately-defined markets. Actual levels of market concentration are therefore overestimated when a given market is supplied by firms from different branches. It may either be overestimated or underestimated when firms in a given branch supply more than one market.[14] This methodology also implicitly equates industrial branches with national markets rather than local or regional markets, which may underestimate actual concentration present at the local and regional levels.[15] Finally, because export and import data are not included, the Polish statistics tend to overstate concentration in net importing branches, and may either understate or overstate concentration in net exporting branches (for the reasons explained in the previous note).

Although the Polish experience with economic reform can be traced back to the late 1950s, industrial deconcentration efforts played virtually no role in these reforms until the 1980s. The numbers of state and cooperative industrial firms increased during the 1980s, and their average employment levels decreased (see Table 5.1), in part because of reforms increasing the number of organizations authorized to create new state enterprises (e.g., existing state firms, local government bodies, banks, etc.). The weakening of central political and economic structures in the second half of the decade, the resurgence of market reform ideologies, and growing financial pressures on firms to find more efficient organizational forms began to result in divestitures by large state enterprises of some plants and activities of tertiary importance. Meanwhile, the private sector entered a phase of development that prepared it for the post-communist transformation in the 1990s.[16] Although data on industrial concentration during the 1980s are difficult to interpret unambiguously, Gini coefficients for gross industrial sales fell from .899 in 1984 to .719 in 1987, indicating declines in aggregate industrial concentration during that time (see Table 5.2).[17] Deconcentration measures were implemented in the central administration as well: many of the branch industrial ministries were abolished in 1987, as were the *zrzeszenia* intermediate-layer organizations in 1989; and the precursor to the Antimonopoly Office was established in 1987.

The picture of industrial deconcentration during the 1980s was not clear cut, however. The large declines in the Gini coefficients during the second half of the decade (see Table 5.2) are somewhat suspect, for two reasons: (1) it is difficult to account for the aggregate industrial Gini coefficients (i.e., the bottom row in Table 5.2) on the basis of the coefficients for individual branches given in the other rows;[18] and (2) statistics showing structural deconcentration trends are difficult to reconcile with the reformers' inabilities to tackle problems of large, monopolistic enterprises and, prior to 1987, monopolistic elements of the central administration.[19]

Did the developments in 1989-1990, associated with the collapse of the communist political system and the introduction (on January 1, 1990) of the "big bang" program for a rapid economic transition, mark a watershed in industrial deconcentration? On the one hand, the statistical yearbook data clearly show structural deconcentration between 1987 and 1991. According to the concentration ratio data shown in Table 5.3, structural concentration (as measured by the number of firms in a given branch whose joint sales exceed 50 percent of the branch total) increased in only 9 of 23 branches during this time; when measured as the number of firms in a given branch whose joint sales exceed 80 percent of the branch total, concentration levels increased in only 5 of 23 branches. Moreover, despite the official start of state enterprise privatization in mid-1990, the number of state industrial enterprises actually increased from 3,224 to 4,737—a 47 percent increase—during 1989-1991.[20] Overall, the total number of state enterprises (not just in industry) increased by some 28 percent between January 1990 and June 1992, despite the fact that privatization removed more than 1,000 firms from the rolls of state enterprises during this time.[21] While numerous factors were responsible for the growing numbers of state firms, it is clear that these numbers reflected in part sharpening pressures on enterprise management to find more efficient organizational forms, which resulted in the spontaneous divestiture and dissolution of many large state enterprises into larger numbers of smaller state firms.

On the other hand, the official Gini coefficient data depict what can only be described as a staggering increase in concentration levels between 1989 and 1992, mostly due to a seemingly inexplicable jump in the coefficients for 1992 (see Table 5.2). According to these data, the aggregate industrial Gini increased from .415 in 1991 to .784 in 1992, as 22 of 23 industrial branches reported increases in their coefficients for that year. If taken at face value, these increases would imply that structural concentration in Polish industry had in 1992 suddenly returned to levels of the mid-1980s!

These increases should not be taken at face value, however, for at least two reasons. First, they are not consistent with the official concentration-ratio data presented in Table 5.3. When measured as the number of firms in a given branch whose joint sales exceeded 50 percent of the branch total, concentration ratios increased in only 13 of 23 branches between 1991 and 1992; when measured as the number of firms in a given branch whose joint sales exceeded 80 percent of the branch total, concentration ratios increased in only 12 of 23 branches. Thus, the scale of the increase in the concentration-ratio data poorly matches that of the Gini coefficients. While the Gini for the clothing industry, for example, increased from .019 in 1991 to .592 in 1992 (exceeding even the .546 coefficient recorded in 1987), the number of firms responsible for 50 and 80 per cent of branch sales registered only small declines (of 6.0 and 6.7 percent, respectively) from 1991 to 1992. Although the total number of clothing firms declined slightly (by 5.0 percent) from 1991 to 1992, the 1992 figure was still nearly double the number of clothing firms listed in 1987.

While concentration in the clothing industry appears to have moderately increased in 1992, the whopping increase for the 1992 Gini coefficient could easily have resulted from entry by small producers which, while not affecting the situation of the largest incumbents (and therefore concentration ratios), would have increased the share of the industry's sales originating in the "small" end of the distribution, thus increasing the dispersion between the industry's "haves" and "have nots," thereby increasing the value of the Gini for 1992. Most importantly, because imports and exports accounted for a significant share of the clothing purchased and produced in Poland in 1992, the difference between the clothing "industry" and the "market" is likely here to be especially important. What this example really illustrates, therefore, are the drawbacks of using Gini coefficients as measures of industrial, and especially market, concentration.[22]

Second, this chapter has until now regarded declines in Polish industrial concentration as generally desirable in and of themselves. This proposition is most defensible for the 1987-1991 period, when industrial structures were clearly undergoing market-driven deconcentrating tendencies, correcting for the effects of excessive centralization and the gigantomania of the socialist period. By 1992, however–the third year since the collapse of Soviet-type socialism in Poland–other trends, linked to Polish firms' need to increase competitiveness on world markets by capturing economies of scale and scope, had probably become increasingly important. Thus, to the extent that declines in industrial concentration may have been arrested after 1989-1991, this may have been neither undesirable nor inefficient.

Industrial De-monopolization After 1989

The previous section introduces some confusion into the assessment of industrial deconcentration in Poland after 1989. However, when factors other than structural concentration in the state sector are considered, the political and economic developments in 1989-1990 clearly do constitute a watershed in industrial de-monopolization. The rapid growth in the numbers of private industrial firms, which had reached 351,401 by the end of 1992,[23] made a significant contribution to structural deconcentration. While state firms continued to officially account for the majority of Polish industrial production, the private share of industrial production had reached 38 percent at the end of 1994,[24] and the unofficial private share was certainly much higher. (By way of comparison, only 8.1 percent of the industrial labor force was officially employed in the private sector at the end of 1984; in 1980, this share was 5.1 percent.[25]) Also, Poland achieved important increases in current-account convertibility during 1990 which, when combined with significant import liberalization and the abolition of administrative supply allocation, meant significant increases in import competition. Poland's agreement on associate membership status in the European Union (initialed in November 1991, and which went into effect in January 1994), membership in the Central European Free Trade Association (as of March 1992), as well as in the General Agreement on Tariffs and Trade and Poland's accession to the World Trade Organization (in late 1994), seemed likely to lock in place a relatively open trading regime.

To be sure, there were some problematic developments. The trade liberalization upon which this import competition was based was partially rolled back after mid-1991.[26] Average (nominal) tariff rates were tripled in August 1991 (to 18 percent), and generally continued to increase during 1992-1993, while quotas and concessions were introduced for food, fuel, alcohol, and ferrous metal imports. Although import-competing lobbies certainly had a lot to do with this erosion in Poland's open trade regime, pressures applied (often successfully) by Western corporations for increased protection of the domestic market, as the price for investing in politically influential (and often monopolistic) Polish industrial (invariably state-owned) firms, also played an important role. This was most apparent in the automobile industry, where General Motors and Fiat were able to extract significant increases in protection on domestic automobile markets as the price for investing in (and thereby rescuing from bankruptcy) Polish auto firms such as FSO and FSM. Also, while import competition increased significantly on consumer goods markets during 1989-1991, it remained much weaker on producer goods and raw materials markets throughout 1989-1994. It is also noteworthy that, according to one observer, 70 percent of the product lines produced by state industry remained in the hands of 25 per cent of the firms in 1991.

Still, on the whole, the price liberalization, deregulation, and privatization policies pursued after 1989 essentially eradicated shortage pressures, and dramatically lowered entry barriers for domestic firms from all sectors. (Indeed, much of this happened in 1990, the first year of the Polish "big bang.") Needless to say, these developments reduced the scale of product-level monopoly as well. The net effect was that most non-structural barriers to entry–the state's foreign trade monopoly, paternalistic enterprise regulation, currency inconvertibility, shortage pressures–virtually dropped by the wayside after 1989. Moreover, the relatively passive posture adopted by the Antimonopoly Office (discussed below) strongly indicates that many of these changes occurred in a largely spontaneous manner, as endogenous derivatives of the transformation. The implication is that the anticipated difficulties in attaining rapid progress in de-monopolization were overestimated, at least in the Polish case.[27] It also raises questions about the nature and relevance of the competition policies pursued during this time.

The Evolution of Competition Policy in Poland

The Polish Antimonopoly Office (*Urząd Antymonopoly*) is the oldest of the post-communist competition agencies. Its precursor, which began to function in January 1988 as a division of the Finance Ministry, under whose auspices rulings were made and enforced, was originally created by legislation passed in January 1987.[28] This legislation was updated by a second law approved by the Polish parliament in February, 1990.[29] This law, which constitutes the basic legal framework for Polish competition policy, was written with an eye towards European Union (EU) competition law, especially Articles 85 and 86 of the 1957 Treaty of Rome, as well as the 1989 Concentration Control Regulation.[30] It also gives the Antimonopoly Office fairly broad powers, including a mandate to concern itself with "the formation of organizational structures." The basic law of February 1990 was amended slightly on June 28, 1991, and again in 1993; other amendments were awaiting parliamentary approval in early 1995.[31]

Like the US Federal Trade Commission, the Antimonopoly Office possesses both executive and judicial powers, so that its rulings have the force of law. The Office's decisions may be appealed to the Antimonopoly Court, a department of the Warsaw region court established especially to hear competition-policy appeals. In exceptional cases, decisions may be appealed to the Supreme Court. Approximately 15 percent of the Office's cases were appealed to the Antimonopoly Court during 1990-1993; the Court partially or completely reversed the Office's findings in about 6 percent of the cases. Only three cases were appealed to the Supreme Court during this time.[32] However, in contrast to the Russian case, the Polish Antimonopoly Office's decisions are binding unless and until they are overturned by a court ruling.[33] In addition to imposing fines on offending firms and their managers, the Office may order a firm to lower its price or cease and desist a certain activity.

The February 1990 law made the Antimonopoly Office a government body independent of the Finance Ministry (and other central agencies) whose President and Vice President are appointed by the Prime Minister. The Antimonopoly Office's first President, Anna Fornalczyk (who headed the Office from 1990 until mid-1994), is an economics professor from Łódź University and one of Poland's leading specialists on competition policy. Although Fornalczyk brought other knowledgeable specialists to the Antimonopoly Office, much of the Office's initial staff was composed of former employees of the central and local offices of the Pricing Commission. Seven regional divisions of the Antimonopoly Office were established during 1990-1991 to handle cases within their geographic jurisdictions. In contrast to the Russian Antimonopoly Committee, the Antimonopoly Office's central office in Warsaw clearly plays the dominant policy-making role.

The Antimonopoly Office came into existence during a period of heightened organizational and economic instability in Poland. The Office's first years of operation took place in economic conditions frequently described in terms such as "hyperinflation" and "catastrophic declines" in production and incomes.[34] 1989-1991 was also a period pregnant with the anticipation, and then the realization, of the large-scale privatization of state-owned industrial enterprises. Finally, the Office's first years also marked what could be described as the zenith in popular and official antipathy towards large state enterprises, which were often regarded as combining the worst features of capitalist monopolies (disdain for smaller suppliers, customers, and competitors) and socialist monopolies (chronic unprofitability, and insensitivity to prices, costs, and other market pressures).

Competition policy in Poland can be considered in six distinct areas: (1) structural policy; (2) dominant-firm regulation; (3) monopolization; (4) policy against collusion; (5) competition advocacy; and (6) competition policy's overall effectiveness.

Structural Policy: The Deconcentration–Privatization Trade-off

Under the 1990 law, the Antimonopoly Office is empowered to order the divestiture, dissolution, or liquidation of state, private, and cooperative firms that both: (1) occupy dominant market positions; and (2) "permanently restrict actual or potential competition." The Office may transform state enterprises into (state-owned) corporations, thus giving it the authority to dissolve or restructure monopolistic firms during the privatization process.[35] Activist merger policies are also sanctioned: all mergers involving firms possessing (either singly or jointly) dominant market positions must be reported to the Antimonopoly Office. Mergers are automatically approved if the Office does not object within two months, however.

Although it possesses a relatively broad mandate in monitoring mergers and privatization for possible threats to competition,[36] the Antimonopoly Office has not adopted what might be called an activist deconcentration agenda. Instead, privatization and other policy concerns have taken precedence over competition policy issues *per se*.[37] The Antimonopoly Office essentially admitted this in its 1992 Annual Report:

> The Antimonopoly Office attempted to introduce provisions that would guarantee emergence of a competitive structure within the industry...or deter excessive concentration as a result of privatization. Often in these efforts, the requirements of competition policy had to give way to the necessity of introducing capital to the industry or to the needs of social policy (recession, unemployment).[38]

Moreover, competition policy has tended to focus on issues of conduct–especially dominant-firm regulation, monopolization, and anti-cartel policies–rather than structural questions. So although Polish competition law would seem to authorize activist deconcentration policies, they have not been forthcoming. Instead, as former President Fornalczyk wrote:

> The caution of the Office was a result of the belief that division procedures are very slow by their nature and there is a major threat of making a mistake, since it is hard to define a proper balance between a more competitive structure and possible loss of advantages of economies of scale and scope.[39]

This caution is apparent in the official data on the Antimonopoly Office's activities (see Table 5.4). Of the 1906 "structural decisions" in which the Antimonopoly Office participated during 1990-1992, formal

Table 5.4   Activities of the Polish Antimonopoly Office, 1990-1992

	Behavioral decisions		Structural decisions			
Year	Total	Finding of monopolistic practices	Total	Approval of transformation	Prohibition of transformation	Division
1990ᵃ	70	32	119	17	8	0
1991	116	17	974	63	4	12
1992	113	42	740	9	9	4
TOTALS	299	91	1906	89	21	16

ᵃBeginning April 13, 1990.

Source: Urząd Antymonopolowy 1993, Appendix 2.

rulings were only issued by the Office in some 126 of those (less than 7 percent). Of those 126 rulings, 89 were classified as "approvals of structural transformation," while rulings mandating the "prohibition of structural transformation" and "division" (i.e., dissolutions and divestitures) of an enterprise were limited to 21 and 16, respectively. Other evidence of this caution can be cited: one observer noted in early 1991 that virtually no divisions were finalized during the Antimonopoly Office's first year of existence.[40] According to a representative of the Antimonopoly Office, the Office was consulted on some 500 privatization cases during the first half of 1991, but only objected to six or seven of these.[41] Another observer argues that, during the 1991-1993 period, "de-monopolization proceedings" were only initiated in four sectors: grain-milling, wood, seed, and meat processing.[42]

To be sure, these figures understate the impact of the Office's structural policies in some important respects. First, neither the "conditional approval of transformations" issued by the Office, nor the large number of cases in which no formal ruling was issued, necessarily connotes passivity towards the formation of anticompetitive structures. Many state firms, at times voluntarily, at times at the behest of the privatization authorities, divested themselves of assets and activities prior to and during privatization—even without the Antimonopoly Office's formal intervention. More generally, the above figures do not convey the influence of the Office's informal pressures and activities. And because some of the Office's rulings serve as precedents, they may have affected the number (and type) of "structural" cases brought before the Office. Still, whether good or bad, competition policy in Poland since 1990 can hardly be described as either structuralist or activist.

The absence of such activism produced predictable charges that the Antimonopoly Office was too willing to permit state-owned "dominant firms" to pass into the private sector essentially untouched.[43] Perhaps for this reason, the Office began to assume a more active stance vis-à-vis privatization after mid-1991. Opposition to the inclusion of some two dozen dominant firms in the list of state enterprises slated for mass privatization in mid-1991 subsequently led to these firms' removal from the program.[44] In 1992, the Office was apparently successful in removing virtually all the wood-products firms slated for inclusion in mass privatization from this program.[45] And, according to the law creating the 15 national investment funds that are to act as owners of the enterprises privatized through this program, no fund may own more than 30 percent of the assets of firms in a given industrial branch.[46] The Antimonopoly Office has generally ensured that the investment funds around whom the program is based would not be able to obtain monopoly (or monopsony) power by acquiring firms located in the same (or closely related) industry(s), or in a given geographical area.

Regulation of Dominant Firms

The Antimonopoly Office's relatively passive structural posture, combined with the emphasis on dominant-firm regulation in EU competition policy, make the treatment of firms classified as "dominant" a question of central importance in Polish competition policy. According to a report issued in April 1991 by the Antimonopoly Office, for example, dominant firms (then defined as having more than 30 percent of total branch sales) were present in 516 of the 825 industrial product markets examined (see Table 5.5).[47]

Policy towards dominant firms in Poland has relied almost exclusively upon regulation of price and output, with sanctions for firms that abuse their "dominance." The strategy is not so much to prohibit *a priori* undesirable conduct by dominant firms, but rather to closely supervise their activities, applying in practice a rule of reason standard to practices which may injure consumers or competitors.

Following Pittman, judgment of Polish treatment of dominant firms issue can be broken down into three separate questions:[48]

- How easily (and arbitrarily) can a firm be classified as "dominant" by the Antimonopoly Office?
- To what extent are vertical restraints by dominant firms permitted?

Table 5.5   Distribution of Polish Dominant Firms by Market Share, 1991

Market Share	*Number of Firms*
30 - 40 percent	131
40 - 50 percent	96
50 - 60 percent	81
60 - 70 percent	39
70 - 80 percent	43
80 - 90 percent	40
90 - 100 percent	86
TOTALS	516

Source: *Informacje o stanie zmonopolizowania gospodarki polskiej* 1991:7.

- To what extent are other firms protected from "innocent, pro-competitive behavior" by dominant firms?

The definition of what constitutes dominance is perhaps the most important and problematic aspect of this area of competition policy. In theory, the application of a rule of reason is certainly preferable to the use of quantitative market-share criteria. Otherwise, firms with large market share may by penalized for being successful, even if their success is of a transient nature. The statistical and methodological problems of determining market share discussed above also argue strongly against the use of such quantitative measures. On the other hand, relying solely on qualitative criteria to determine dominant-firm status could endow the Antimonopoly Office with excessive discretion, with attendant public choice problems. While these problems would seem to have been minimal in Polish practice to date, this may not always be the case.

Under Polish competition law, the Antimonopoly Office can rely on such qualitative criteria as a perceived "lack of competition" in making the determination of dominance, although these factors are to be supplemented by quantitative measures, such as the rule that firms with market shares of 40 percent or more may be classified as dominant firms.[49] (A register of firms with market shares in excess of 80 percent is kept by the Antimonopoly Office.) Activities that would not be prohibited when conducted by smaller firms are prohibited when undertaken by dominant firms. These include tying contracts, reducing output (or purchases), price discrimination, "excessive" price increases, creating "artificial shortages," and restricting access to a market.

According to the legislation, then, Polish treatment of the dominant firm issue seems to be relatively consistent with the rule of reason approach advocated by Pittman and others.[50] Since problems of rent-seeking behavior induced by excessive discretion on the part of competition policy makers do not seem to be significant in Poland, the Polish approach to the dominant-firm issue may indeed be preferable. On the other hand, an obvious tension is present between the outright prohibition of the above-mentioned forms of dominant-firm conduct and the expectation that the Antimonopoly Office will examine individual dominant-firm cases on their merits, under the rule of reason. This is apparent in the Office's treatment of "excessive" price increases introduced by dominant firms, for example. Strong inflationary pressures during 1989-1991,[51] combined with the fact that much of its personnel came from the Pricing Office, pushed the Antimonopoly Office in the direction of more aggressive regulation of dominant-firm pricing than might otherwise have been the case.

For example, the Antimonopoly Office in October 1990 attempted to force the state-owned FSO automobile maker to retract a price increase, basing its argument on FSO's dominant position on the Polish automobile market. If successful, this argument could have established the precedent of allowing the Antimonopoly Office to veto "excessive" price increases by firms with "dominant" market shares, even though numerous factors besides market power could have been responsible for the price increase. Such an arrangement would hearken back to the supervision of enterprise pricing policies by the Price Office (and other central organs) during the 1980s, and would be difficult to reconcile with the logic of a market economy or Western competition policy. In any case, the Antimonopoly Office's ruling in the FSO case was overturned by the Antimonopoly Court upon appeal in December 1990, and the Supreme Court upheld the Antimonopoly Court's reversal in May 1991. This apparently precipitated something of a reappraisal of dominant-firm regulation in Poland.[52] It did not, however, mark the end of the Antimonopoly Office's efforts at regulating price increases by dominant firms. In 1993, for example, the Antimonopoly Office forced Polish Telecom (the monopoly provider of local telephone service for much of Poland) to reduce a planned 50-percent rate increase to 30 percent.[53] However, by helping to curb some of the Office's more interventionist instincts, the FSO case may have prevented the extensive (and arguably counterproductive) regulation of dominant firms apparent in Russian competition policy during 1992-1993.[54]

Three potential solutions to the problems of dominant-firm regulation seem apparent in Poland. First, workable *de facto* regulatory standards may ultimately emerge from practice and precedents established via case law. Second, as Poland's market infrastructure continues to develop and as Poland becomes further integrated into the international economy, entry by actual and potential competitors will become more likely, so that even highly concentrated markets will become more contestable. All this will create more market checks upon dominant firms.

Third, as the data in Table 5.5 suggest, a significant share of the enterprises classified as dominant firms should more properly be regarded as natural monopolies. This is certainly the case for many local utilities, water companies, and parts of the national energy and electricity networks. However, although legislation defining and regulating natural monopolies in the energy sector was submitted to the parliament in 1993, opposition by the energy (and other) industrial lobby(s) has prevented its passage. This has meant that responsibilities for natural monopoly regulation have been divided in a somewhat haphazard fashion between the Antimonopoly Office's central and local branches, and the central and local administrative organs that discharge the functions of ownership vis-à-vis these firms. This state of affairs is widely regarded in Poland as unsatisfactory; presumably it will be changed at some point in the (hopefully not-too-distant) future. Addressing the natural monopoly problem will simultaneously mean a new approach to regulating at least some of the firms now handled by the Antimonopoly Office within the dominant-firm framework. Whether natural monopolies will be regulated by the Antimonopoly Office (and its local divisions) or by specialized regulatory commissions remains to be seen.[55]

Monopolization

The treatment of monopolization issues is arguably one of the weakest elements of Polish competition policy. The basic law of January 1990 provides an "exhaustive list"[56] of monopolistic behaviors that are generally regarded as culpable, unless it can be shown that such behavior is necessary to conduct economic activity, or does not "significantly" restrain competition. Various horizontal and vertical agreements are on this list, including tying contracts, imposition of onerous terms, interlocking directorates, anti-competitive share and asset acquisitions, restrictions on market access, and collusion (discussed below). Crucially, these acts are prohibited regardless of the market share held by the firm(s) in question.[57]

On the one hand, this approach can be defended by pointing to the extensive difficulties that appear in defining relevant product and geographic markets in the post-communist context. If an activity can unambiguously be viewed as anti-competitive, why not ban it outright, instead of having to worry about calculating a critical market share? The problem with this argument is that none of the activities on this "exhaustive list" can be viewed as unambiguous evidence of effective anti-competitive behavior, unless they are undertaken by firms with market power.[58] This is one of the reasons why most of these practices are judged under a rule of reason in Western countries. Moreover, the fact that the legislation itself permits such activities if they do not "significantly" restrain competition, or if economic activity can not occur without them, can itself be seen as recognition of this fact. Nevertheless, the 1990 law allows Polish competition policy makers to persecute firms on workably-competitive markets for actions that can only be regarded as anti-competitive when conducted by firms with market power. This problem is especially likely to appear in the case of vertical agreements, such as franchising, which almost inevitably involve restrictions on choices for some market participants.[59]

This ambiguous treatment of monopolization mirrors to some extent the problems of dominant-firm regulation; policy in both areas displays a relatively unsophisticated (from a Western vantage point) static view of competition and monopoly. To be sure, this perspective was dictated by the initial conditions facing Polish competition policy makers, especially the existence of numerous dominant state-owned firms and the legal and administrative problems inherent in attempting to restrict their potentially anti-competitive behavior. This perspective may have been perfectly justified during 1990-1991. As the forces of market competition mature, however, this justification becomes weaker. Indeed, the amendments awaiting parliamentary approval in early 1995 would, among other things, apparently prescribe a more flexible approach in monopolization questions.[60]

Preventing Collusion

While Polish competition law emphasizes prohibiting (or at least discouraging) price fixing and other anti-competitive horizontal agreements, this prohibition is not subject to a *per se* standard. As described above, horizontal agreements are explicitly permitted when cooperation does not reduce competition, or where cooperation is necessary to conduct economic activity. In addition to this legislative enumeration of the appropriate criteria for cartelization, cartels can also be sanctioned (with proper notification) by administrative decision. The Polish coal industry was effectively permitted to cartelize itself during 1993, for example, in the hopes that this would help the industry resolves its perpetual crises of excess capacity and unprofitable mines.

Still, policy towards collusion is broadly consistent with the EU framework, and the Antimonopoly Office obtained two well-publicized collusion convictions (against the insurance and sugar refining industries) in 1992, and against chemical fertilizer producers in 1994.[61]

The real questions concern the effectiveness of Polish anti-cartel policies. Not only are traditions of business rivalry generally absent from East European corporate culture; there is instead a legacy of enterprise cooperation against the central authorities associated with the bargaining processes typical of Soviet-type economies. This is especially apparent in Poland, where the intermediate-layer *zrzeszenia* (producer associations) through the late 1980s often promoted (and enforced) price-fixing and other collusive activities by "their" enterprises.[62] The probable retention of informal, collusion-promoting links between enterprises created through spontaneous de-monopolization could also be a significant factor. Finally, it should be added that the sorry financial condition of the insurance and sugar refining firms convicted of collusion in 1992 prevented the execution of fines upon the colluders, as specified under Polish law. Likewise, the metallurgical firms who were damaged by the coal industry's alleged price fixing conspiracy in 1993 refused to press charges,[63] probably in order to avoid antagonizing one of Poland's most powerful industries. Finally, as former President Fornalczyk told the Polish press in mid-1993, the Antimonopoly Office does not possess the resources needed to fund the detective work required by price-fixing investigations.[64] Thus, in addition to the problems that competition agencies everywhere face in ferreting out price fixing, the presence of these other factors specific to the post-communist transition raise further doubts about the Antimonopoly Office's abilities to make much of a dent in what has to be an extensive problem.

Competition Advocacy

Perhaps the Antimonopoly Office's most important (and least-discussed) function has been the advocacy of liberal, pro-competitive solutions to economic policy problems during the Polish transition. By all accounts, the Antimonopoly Office has been a consistent advocate of market and trade liberalization,[65] the development of market infrastructure, and making Poland's legal system more consistent with the European Union's. Over time, however, successive cabinets have shown themselves to be less and less interested in pro-competitive solutions, so that the Office increasingly found itself isolated within the Polish government. Because the Antimonopoly Office is itself subordinated to the government, it increasingly had to fight rear-guard actions to secure what compromises were possible within anti-competitive policy frameworks.

This problem sharpened considerably after the September 1993 parliamentary elections, which were won decisively by parties descended from the pre-1990 communist political order.[66] The governments of Prime Minister Waldemar Pawlak (October 1993 - February 1995) and then Prime Minister Józef Oleksy (March 1995 -) have demonstrated a much more ambiguous attitude towards Poland's transition to capitalism than that shown by its Solidarity-based predecessors.[67] However, Poland's most influential industrial (and agricultural) lobbies at times proved too strong for the Solidarity governments in power during 1990-1993 as well. This was apparent in trade policy, as the above-mentioned tripling of nominal tariff rates August 1991 shows. In May 1992, the government of then Prime Minister Jan Olszewski approved the merger of most of Poland's coal mines into a small number of monopolistic holding companies, whose creation was justified by the imperative of being "strong enough to handle market competition."[68] These holding companies were authorized to supervise restructuring within the coal industry, "coordinate inter-firm cooperation in matters of production and sales," and oversee the liquidation of those mines unable to survive market forces. Not surprisingly, the resulting increases in industrial concentration were followed in 1993 by allegations of price-fixing among the holding companies, although purchasers apparently refused to press the issue if it meant risking the coal lobby's displeasure.[69]

While such anti-competitive tendencies were hardly insignificant prior to the formation of the Pawlak government in October 1993, they strengthened considerably thereafter. Most of the attention focused on the Pawlak (and then Oleksy) governments' ambiguous attitude towards privatization. The Pawlak government delayed the start of Poland's long-suffering mass privatization program by up to 12 months (during 1993-1994); while the Oleksy government further politicized privatization policy in general by passing legislation (in mid-1995) requiring parliamentary approval for the sale of state firms in the energy, banking, telecommunications, and other sectors.[70]

The Pawlak government's fondness for state monopolies, particularly in the sugar and tobacco industries, was perhaps even more unsettling.[71] The battle for "Polish Sugar" began when the Sugar Council (a lobby for Polish sugar refiners), supported by the Ownership Transformation Commission in the Sejm, convinced the Ministry of Agriculture that the amalgamation of Poland's 80 refineries into a single state monopoly ("Polski Cukier") was the answer to the industry's problems. As a result of protests from the Antimonopoly Office, other government agencies, and the press, a compromise solution was adopted in mid-1994, according to which 70 of the 80 refineries were grouped into four geographically-based holding companies. Sugar prices would be set by the Ministry of Agriculture, while the holding companies were to ensure the maintenance of price discipline, finance the refineries' restructuring, and promote sugar exports. Equally unsettling was the legislation approved by the Sejm in the second half of 1994 that effectively provided cooperative enterprises immunity from Polish competition law.

The regression in Poland's open trade regime apparent since mid-1991 continued, if not accelerated, under the post-communist governments. The was apparent, for example, in the 160-percent increase in maximum tariff rates on agricultural imports introduced on July 1, 1995. On the one hand, this increase was part of an effort at making the Polish trade regime more transparent, since quantitative barriers and other variable levies were to be reduced to compensate for the higher tariff rates. Still, the tariff increases were also difficult to square with the spirit (if not the letter) of Poland's 1991 association agreement with the European Union, which envisions reductions, rather than increases, in agricultural tariffs.[72] By that time, however, Fornalczyk had already resigned as head of the Antimonopoly Office.[73] Her departure in January 1995 was followed by the appointment of Andrzej Sopoćko, one of the founders of the Antimonopoly Office's precursor within the Ministry of Finance during 1988-1989.

On the Effectiveness of Competition Policy in Poland

How effective has competition policy in Poland been? The Antimonopoly Office has certainly not conducted a dramatic dissolution of a socialist mega-monopoly along the lines of the *Standard Oil* or *Alcoa* cases in the US. While the Office has been more active than some other competition agencies in the region, this hardly constitutes proof of greater efficiency in the battle for post-communist competitive markets. In any case, a verdict on the desirability of the relatively minimalist approach adopted by the Antimonopoly Office depends on the degree to which: (1) pre-existing levels of structural concentration constitute significant impediments to the development of competitive markets; and (2) the Office is capable of conducting welfare-improving dissolutions and divestitures of large firms. Instead, the Antimonopoly Office has been largely preoccupied with dominant-firm regulation, monopolization, preventing collusion, and competition advocacy. So while it is difficult to ascribe any great successes to Polish competition policy, it is also difficult to know what such success might look like.

Further progress in de-monopolization in Poland now revolves around two issues. First, the presence of state-owned natural monopolies that function without well-defined regulatory frameworks is probably the largest challenge now facing competition policy. Their positions as (at least partially) natural monopolies means that competitive pressures are unlikely to force them to become more efficient, and their political power has delayed or prevented the construction of the appropriate regulatory frameworks, especially in the energy sector. Second, Poland may well be governed for the foreseeable future by parties descended from the pre-1990 communist political system. While the post-communist Pawlak and Oleksy governments during 1994-1995 did not deviate dramatically from the macroeconomic stabilization framework inherited from its Solidarity-based predecessors, their commitment to maintaining open and competitive markets is somewhat questionable. The danger is not of an immanent return to central planning: it is that economic policy is increasingly being made by powerful sectoral lobbies, against whom the Antimonopoly Office is simply overmatched.

Conclusions

Significant progress in industrial de-monopolization in Poland has undoubtedly occurred. However, the precise degree and causes of this progress are difficult to ascertain, especially in the area of structural deconcentration. Although statistical yearbook data indicate that significant declines in industrial concentration have occurred since 1987-1988, problems with data quality, consistency, and comparability make interpreting the extent of structural change rather difficult.

It is clear, however, that the structural deconcentration that has occurred has largely been a spontaneous derivative of other aspects of the post-communist transition. This outcome lends support the "privatize first" view. However, it is also clear that progress in de-monopolization has been greater in effecting change in enterprise conduct, due to the effects of privatization, increased import competition (although this has largely been confined to manufacturing), the liberalization of prices and entrepreneurship, and the virtual eradication of shortage pressures. Correspondingly, the significance of competition policies in overall transition has been relatively minor. Priority has instead been given in Poland to privatization and other industrial-policy concerns. The "de-monopolization before privatization" approach has definitely not been attempted.

The Polish experience does not support the view that *ex ante* structural deconcentration is a general prerequisite for effective privatization and systemic transformation. On the other hand, large, unprofitable, state-owned industrial firms ("dinosaurs") have been the microeconomic bane of the transition in Poland (and not only in Poland!). These firms have often resisted the efficiency-inducing market pressures associated with market liberalization and stabilization; they are at the heart of the "bad debts" that pose such a burden on the Polish financial system;[74] and their large size and poor financial status limit their prospects for privatization. In such a situation, dissolving some of these large firms into smaller units may be desirable in terms of both privatization and competition policy. While this may involve short-run technical efficiency losses, a dissolution policy could promote the component-wise (decentralized) privatization of these large firms, while simultaneously reducing structural concentration and improving dynamic efficiency.

In any case, Polish competition policy has been able to avoid the worst aspects of the privatization/de-monopolization trade-off, because privatization and liberalization have in and of themselves produced important increases in market competition. Poland has also been able to avoid some of the excesses in regulating dominant firms that have appeared in competition policy elsewhere. These are advantages that other post-communist economies may not be able to replicate, since they stem in part from the relatively advanced state of Poland's market reforms at the start of the 1990s. Firms in the former Soviet Union and the Balkan economies, by contrast, are generally less (often much less) prepared for the rigors of market competition, and their reactions to market pressures are more likely to be perverse. These economies have often been unable to introduce the current-account convertibility and exchange-rate stability needed for sustained import competition; the private (and genuine cooperative) sectors are less able to generate effective competition for state firms; and price liberalization and the abolition of supply rationing have occurred in a more limited fashion.

Despite the problems it has encountered, competition policy in Poland has found its place within the overall economic policy framework. Barring unexpected reversals, revising Polish competition law and policy in line with EU standards by the end of the century would now seem to constitute the largest challenge.[75]

APPENDIX: CASE STUDY

The Polish Antimonopoly Office versus the Dairy Cooperative "Spomlek"[76]

Ben Slay

Vertical agreements between two parties, one of which possesses market power, frequently raise contentious competition-policy issues in developed market economies. These issues are made more difficult in transitional economies by the emphasis on "dominant" firm regulation, and by the many firms with dominant market positions inherited from the old system. Competition agencies are frequently predisposed in such situations to take the side of small firms who claim to be damaged by the dominant competitor's "abusive" conduct. While the underlying intent of providing all competitors with a level playing field is certainly laudable, the end results can be less sanguine.

Many of these issues appeared in the "Spomlek" case. On December 2, 1990, the management of Spomlek, a dairy cooperative located in Radzyń Podlaski (in Poland's Biała Podlaska *województwo*, near the Belarussian border), issued a new pricing policy to its milk suppliers. As a result of the new policy, higher prices (in the form of a 15-percent price supplement) were paid for milk purchased from the cooperative's members, as opposed to milk purchased from non-members. These higher prices were described as (among other things) a mechanism for supplying its members with working capital. (During 1990-1992, many farmers found that bank credit was either prohibitively expensive or downright unobtainable.) In return, Spomlek required that its members conclude exclusive-dealing contracts with the cooperative. By guaranteeing a pre-arranged supply of raw milk of an agreed-upon quality, Spomlek contended that these arrangements helped keep the dairy's costs down, as well as maintain the high quality of its milk products.

Spomlek's price supplement raised the ire of the local council of the "Rural Solidarity" farmers' union, who in 1991 demanded that the Antimonopoly Office determine whether the dairy's pricing policies were consistent with the law of February 24, 1990 on "Combating Monopolistic Practices." The Office agreed, and upon the conclusion of its investigation, ruled that Spomlek was in fact in violation of the law. Specifically, the Office found that, by requiring its members to conclude exclusive-dealing agreements with the dairy, and by offering members more advantageous purchase prices than those offered to non-members, Spomlek was abusing its dominant position as a milk purchaser in some 31 local townships in the *województwo* (county).[77] On May 5, 1992, the Antimonopoly Office ordered the dairy to rescind the price supplement.

Spomlek appealed this decision to the Antimonopoly Court in Warsaw. In its appeal, the dairy did not dispute that, in the 31 Biała Podlaska townships in question, its market share was well above the 40-percent threshold needed to prove dominance. Nor was the definition of the appropriate product market–the purchase of raw milk–contested. Instead, Spomlek argued, neither the exclusive contracts nor the price supplement should be taken as evidence of abuse of dominant position. Instead, the dairy contended, its activities actually promoted the development of market competition.

Spomlek supported its position with two arguments. First, the exclusive contracts with the cooperative's members did not preclude entry to the dairy. During the second half of 1991, for example, 1,438 new members had in fact joined the cooperative. Non-members who found themselves disadvantaged by the dairy's pricing policy could therefore join the cooperative and avail themselves of the supplement, just as members who wanted to sell their raw milk to other dairies were free to leave the cooperative and do so. Second, by forcing the dairy to offer the same prices to members and non-members alike, the Antimonopoly Office's ruling challenged the *raison d'être* of the dairy and, by implication, all Polish cooperatives who supplied their members with price-related benefits and services. Spomlek was supported in this argument by the Warsaw-based National Association of Dairy Cooperatives, which filed a friend-of-the-court brief on behalf of the dairy.

On December 10, 1992, the Antimonopoly Court accepted Spomlek's arguments, and reversed the Antimonopoly Office's decision. The Court found that the ease with which farmers could become members of the cooperative blunted the anti-competitive effects of the dairy's exclusive-dealing agreements. "Economic criteria" the Court ruled "determine the form of [seller] participation in the milk market, not pressure posed by the coop." The Court also found that "uniform milk purchase prices would result in unjustified privileges for suppliers who are not members of the coop. Eventually, dairy cooperatives would lose both members and funds." This, the court felt, was the more serious threat to competition. "The differentiation of milk purchase prices stimulates here entrepreneurship of farmers, induces development of competition and, as a result, helps enforce the objectives of the Act [on Combating

Monopolistic Practices]." Spomlek was permitted to reinstate the price supplement for its members, and the Antimonopoly Office was ordered to cover the dairy's court costs.

The Spomlek case did not end there. On the basis of an appeal filed by Poland's national ombudsperson, Spomlek became one of the first competition-law cases to be beard by the Polish Supreme Court. The Supreme Court's Civil Law Chamber on June 23, 1993 sided with the Antimonopoly Office and returned the case to the Antimonopoly Court but did so on something of a technicality. Specifically, the Supreme Court found that the Antimonopoly Court, in its decision overturning the Antimonopoly Office's ruling, had not fully investigated the "additional reasons for [the Coop's] subsidizing prices of milk, especially the services rendered by members of the Coop which could justify increased prices for milk." In its subsequent reconsideration of the case, the Antimonopoly Court upheld its original verdict.

An explanation for the Antimonopoly Court's reaffirmation of its original decision is not provided in the source materials for this case. However, it would seem that, had Spomlek used its monopsony power to in effect overcharge its members for services rendered, it is the members who would have been likely to complain to the Antimonopoly Office. (Or, they would have left the cooperative.) The fact that the complaint about the dairy's behavior originated instead with the competition indicates that the coop's membership was relatively happy with this state of affairs. While non-members may have in a sense been damaged by the lower purchasing prices Spomlek paid for their raw milk, non-members did not have to pay for the services the dairy provided for its members. Moreover, as long as membership in the cooperative was essentially open to all (qualified) farmers, the value added the dairy provided for its members is likely to have consisted largely in the services themselves, rather than in the cooperative's ability to monopsonize the purchase of raw milk.

The Spomlek case is of interest primarily for two reasons. First, it demonstrates some of the practical difficulties inherent in attempting to apply dominant-firm regulation in the post-communist context. Despite the fact that Spomlek's dominant position on the relevant market was not seriously contested, and even though Spomlek employed exclusive-dealing arrangements and practiced price discrimination with its suppliers, a reasoned, balanced application of economic analysis to this case did not produce a verdict that many would regard as consistent with the "dominant firm" approach. Instead, the Antimonopoly Court's broader view of the pro- and anti-competitive effects of Spomlek's behavior produced the opposite result.

Second, "Spomlek" was one of the first cases in Polish competition law dealing with price discrimination, a topic which, as the Antimonopoly Court's decision put it, is afforded only "marginal" treatment in the relevant legislation. Conscious of the fact that its "Spomlek" decision could serve as a precedent in the adjudication of future price-discrimination cases, the Court ruled that: "price discrimination agreements do not infringe on the Act [on Combating Monopolistic Practices] provided that they are the result of a legal relationship between the parties, are economically justified, and are based on the provision of equivalent services." Likewise, "economic relations between participants of an agreement...that do not restrain market mechanisms and are based on equal rights for other participants justify differentiated prices, depending upon the [economic] entity." Future price-discrimination cases could certainly be adjudicated under a less sensible precedent.

Notes

1. This chapter does not focus in a comprehensive manner on natural monopoly regulation in Poland. For more on natural monopoly regulation in the post-communist context, see Chapters 6 and 7.

2. This does not mean that activist deconcentration policies by competition agencies are required outside of Central Europe. It only means that the pace of spontaneous demonopolization is likely to be slower elsewhere.

3. *Polska 1918-1988* 1989:122.

4. Åslund 1985:235.

5. Parkot 1989:3.

6. For more on the WOG reform, see Rychard 1980, Wojciechowska 1978, and Wanless 1980.

7. Employment in the *zrzeszenia* rarely exceeded 30 percent of the levels in the *zjednoczenia* (Cylwik 1985:1-2). For more on the organizational dimensions of reforms in the 1980s, see Slay 1994a (chapter 2), 1990.

8. According to one remarkably candid *zrzeszenie* (enterprise association) officer, his greatest accomplishments in 1982 (the initial year of Poland's "first stage" of economic reform) were: (1) the elimination of competition, both among the enterprises within the association's purview and between "his" firms and other firms; and (2) the development of a cooperative supply network among firms within the association. The latter "helps in the battle for central supply requisitioning...as well as obtaining the most favorable systemic parameters" (Grelik 1984:4). See also Fornalczyk and Kasperkiewicz 1988:73-74.

9. The *Wspólnota Węgla Kamiennego* was an amalgamation of 48 enterprises, and employed more than 600,000 workers (Szwarc 1987).

10. See, for example, Fornalczyk and Kasperkiewicz 1988, and Jakóbik 1988.

11. For more on spontaneous privatization in Poland, see Staniszkis 1991, and Levitas and Strzalkowski 1990.

12. In the short run, however, this organizational diversification meant new monopoly problems, in that many of the disbanded *zrzeszenia* attempted to reconstitute themselves as holding companies with controlling interests in the firms that had previously been subordinated to them (Matusiak 1989).

13. While the Antimonopoly Office is able to generate better-quality data on concentration levels, these data are generally assembled on a case-by-case basis, and are not made available to the public.

14. The extent to which concentration is overestimated depends upon the degree to which extra-branch sales are concentrated in the hands of the branch's largest firms. If a disproportionately large share of the largest firms' total sales occurs outside the branch, this methodology will overstate the extent of actual market concentration. On the other hand, if a disproportionately large share of the largest firms' total sales occurs within the branch, this methodology will understate actual market concentration.

15. According to the Polish statistics, for example, national concentration levels in production of electrical energy are relatively low. Since, however, suppliers of electricity are frequently monopolies in a given locality, this measure of concentration is quite misleading.

16. For more on the evolution of the Polish private sector during the 1980s, see Slay 1993a.

17. The large decline in the aggregate Gini coefficient between 1987 and 1989 is deceptive, for reasons explained in Table 5.2, note d.

18. Only five of the 23 industrial branches reported Gini coefficients greater than the aggregate figure in 1984; and only two of the branches reported Gini coefficients greater than the aggregate figure in 1987.

19. See, for example, Fallenbuchl 1988.

20. "Statystyka Polski" 1994b:III.

21. The total number of state enterprises (not just in industry) increased from approximately 8,000 to 10,231 during this time (Fallenbuchl 1991:11-12, "Statystyka Polski" 1992:IV).

22. The use of Herfindahl-Hirschman indices as measures of concentration would clearly be preferred to concentration-ratio and Gini-coefficient data.

23. This figure, taken from *Rocznik Statystyczny: Przemysł* 1993:2, refers to the so-called "new private sector," which includes the 2,341 co-operatives officially reported for 1992.

24. "Statystyka Polski" 1995:II.

25. *Rocznik Statystyczny Przemysłu* 1986:3.

26. See, for example, Dziewulski 1992, Gács 1993, Slay 1993b:33.

27. The opposing hypothesis was put forward by (among others) Newbery and Kattuman, who argued that: "The difficulty of introducing competition should not be underestimated–it will not happen naturally, but will need the active encouragement of the state..." (Newbery and Kattuman 1992:332).

28. This was the "Ustawa z dnia 28 stycznia 1987 r. o przeciwdziałaniu praktykom monopolistycznym" ("Law of January 28, 1987 on Combating Monopolistic Practices").

29. This was the "Ustawa z dnia 24 lutego 1990 r. o przeciwdziałaniu praktykom monopolistycznym" ("Law of February 24, 1990 on Combating Monopolistic Practices").

30. See Skoczny 1992, Reynolds 1991.

31. Andziak 1995. Other important elements of Polish competition law include: (1) the Act on Publicly-Traded Securities of March 22, 1991; and (2) the Act on Combating Unfair Competition of April 16, 1993. See Antimonopoly Office 1994.

32. These data come from Antimonopoly Office 1994:16-17.

33. Brzezinski 1994:1144.

34. In reality, the roughly 17 percent decline in Polish GDP during 1990-1991 was the smallest recorded for any of the post-communist economies of Eastern Europe and the former Soviet Union since 1989; and Poland since 1992 has been one of the most rapidly-growing economies in Europe. Likewise, Polish inflation rates during the early 1990s, though high by Western and Central European standards, are well below those recorded in the Commonwealth of Independent States. The point here is that, regardless of how Poland's inflation and declines in incomes and output are now viewed in an historical or regional context, the *perception* of unprecedented economic instability almost certainly had a strong influence on economic actors and policy makers during 1990-1991.

35. See "Wniosek do Urzędu Antymonopolowego" for more information on the privatization-antitrust nexus.

36. See Brzezinski (1994:1142-43) for a comparison of the Polish, Czech, Slovak, and Hungarian offices' competencies in this area.

37. As Brzezinski points out (Brzezinski 1994:1140-41), the Antimonopoly Office's ability to supervise the privatization process is also limited by the fact that the Office is only authorized to intervene in privatizations taking the form of a sale (or transfer) of shares. When privatization takes the form of the sale (or transfer) of physical assets–so-called "liquidation privatization"–the Office is not authorized to intervene. While liquidation privatization is by and large confined to small and medium-sized firms, these firms could possess market power on local or regional markets.

38. *Urząd Antymonopolowy* 1993:12.

39. Fornalczyk 1993:37.

40. Modzelewski 1991. The dissolution of cartel-like producer cooperatives (and their associations) conducted in 1990 by the Antimonopoly Office was a partial exception to this statement. However, this dissolution was authorized by special legislation, and was something of a "one-shot" deal.

41. Based on an interview conducted in the Antimonopoly Office in Warsaw, June 18, 1991.

42. Brzezinski 1994:1146.

43. See, for example, Modzelewski 1991.

44. Slay 1991.

45. *Urząd Antymonopolowy* 1993:8.

46. This provision was added to the law creating the national investment funds (passed April 16, 1993) at the insistence of the Antimonopoly Office (*Urząd Antymonopolowy* 1994: 12-13). See also Pokojska 1995:21.

47. *Informacje o stanie zmonopolizowania gospodarki polskiej* 1991:7.

48. Pittman 1992:495-96.

49. The market share originally specified in the 1990 legislation was 30 percent; this was raised to 40 per cent by the June 1991 amendment.

50. See Pittman 1992:495-96, and Brzezinski 1994:1134.

51. Consumer price inflation rates in Poland were 251 percent, 586 percent, and 70 percent for 1989, 1990, and 1991, respectively (*Mały Rocznik Statystyczny* 1993:124).

52. According to the Supreme Court ruling, "The Antimonopoly Law could not be a hidden mechanism for controlling prices" (*Bulletin of the Antimonopoly Office of Poland* 1994:48).

53. See Mozolski 1993, Waleńcik 1993.

54. For more on this, see Chapter 3.

55. See Chapter 6 for the significance of this distinction.

56. Brzezinski 1994:1134.

57. Brzezinski 1994:1134.

58. Although collusion and interlocking directorates are *per se* illegal under US antitrust law, neither is likely to be anti-competitive–and collusion is unlikely to occur–if the firms in question do not themselves possess, either singly or jointly, market power.

59. See Brzezinski 1994:1136-37 for some real-world examples.

60. Andziak 1995.

61. See Andziak 1994, Szot 1994a.

62. Grelik 1984:4.

63. Wrabec *et al.* 1993.

64. Grzegorzewski 1993.

65. Representatives of the Antimonopoly Office sit on the Inter-Ministerial Commission for Updating and Modifying Customs Duties, for example, as well as other foreign trade committees (Brzezinski 1994:1164-65).

66. "Various industrial lobbies, which were silent for four years (after the fall of communism in 1989), have begun to press for privileges," Fornalczyk told the press in late 1994. (This quotation was picked up by *Reuters*, December 22, 1994.) According to the then President of the Antimonopoly Office, the mining, energy, telecommunications, milk, and sugar industries were among the most insistent lobbies.

67. See, for example, Slay 1994b.

68. The coal industry, according to Polish press reports, had recorded a 3.6 trillion zloty (approximately \$260 million) loss in 1991, and losses on the order of 12.5 trillion zloty (almost \$900 million) were anticipated in 1992. More than 11 million tons of coal had accumulated in inventories by June 1992, while total coal output in 1991 was only 507,000 tons ("Górnictwo" 1992).

69. Wrabec *et al.* 1993.

70. This law was ruled unconstitutional by Poland's Constitutional Tribunal in late 1995.

71. For more on the battles for "Polish Sugar" and "Polish Tobacco," see Zybała 1994, Szot 1994b, Mejssner and Możdżyński 1994, and Mac 1994.

72. See, for example, "Food Duties Spark Fears of Inflation" 1995.

73. For more on Fornalczyk's resignation, see Zagrodzka 1995 and Lipszyc 1994.

74. For more on this, see Vinton and Slay 1994.

75. For more on this, see Skoczny 1993, and Brzezinski 1994:1149-56, 1169-72.

76. The source for this case is the *Bulletin of the Antimonopoly Office* 1994. 1: 44-51.

77. An allegation of market division was also made, but this was apparently of secondary importance.

References

Andziak, R. 1995. "Competition is Pivotal." *Rzeczpospolita* (February 21): 1.

_____. 1994. "Miliardy od kartelu nawozowego" (Billions from the Fertilizer Cartel). *Rzeczpospolita* (September 10-11).

Antimonopoly Office. 1994. *Competition Law and Policy in Poland (1990-1993)*. Warsaw: Antimonopoly Office (January).

Åslund, A. 1985. *Private Enterprise in Eastern Europe*. London: McMillan.

Brown, A.W., B.W. Ickes, and R. Ryterman. 1993. "The Myth of Monopoly: A New View of Industrial Structure in Russia." Policy Research Working Paper No. 1331. Washington D.C.: World Bank.

Brzezinski, C. 1994. "Competition and Antitrust Law in Central Europe: Poland, the Czech Republic, Slovakia, and Hungary." *Michigan Journal of International Law* 15: 1129-78.

Bulletin of the Antimonopoly Office of Poland. 1994 0: 46-48.

Chajęcki, A. 1985. *Zmiany w strukturach organizacyjnych spółdzielczości: ewolucja form koncentracji* (Changes in Organizational Structures within the Cooperative Sector: Evolution of Forms of Concentration). Warsaw: Institute of Organization, Management, and Personnel Training.

Cylwik, A. 1985. *Zrzeszenia przedsiębiorstw państwowych: ocena i prognoza rozwoju* (State Enterprise Associations: An Evaluation and Developmental Prognosis). Warsaw: Institute of Organization, Management, and Personnel Training.

_____. 1984. *Ogólna charakterystyka zrzeszeń przedsiębiorstw* (A General Description of Enterprise Associations). Warsaw: Institute of Organization, Management, and Personnel Training.

Dymkowski, R. 1991. "W sidłach ustawy" (In the Snares of the Law). *Rzeczpospolita* (April 11).

Dziewulski, K. 1992. "Kogo protegować?" (Whom to Protect?). *Życie Gospodarcze* (February 12).

Fallenbuchl, Z.M. 1991. "Poland: The New Government and Privatization." *Radio Free Europe Report on Eastern Europe*. 12: 11-16.

_____. 1988. "Present State of the Economic Reform", in Marer, P., and W. Siwiński, eds. *Creditworthiness and Reform in Poland*. Pp. 115-30. Bloomington: Indiana University Press.

"Food Duties Spark Fears of Inflation." 1995. *Weekly Capital* (31 May-6 June): 1, 16.

Fornalczyk, A. 1993. "Competition Policy in the Polish Economy in Transition," in Estrin, S., and M. Cave, eds., *Competition and Competition Policy: A Comparative Analysis of Central and Eastern Europe*. Pp. 28-43. London: Pinter Publishers.

Fornalczyk, A. and W. Kasperkiewicz. 1988. "Demonopolizacja polskiej gospodarki: Założenia i praktyki lat 1981-84" (The De-monopolization of the Polish Economy: Principles and Practice during 1981-84), in W. Caban, *System ekonomiczny w procesie przemian* (The Economic System in the Process of Change). Warsaw: Państwowe Wydawnictwo Ekonomiczne.

Gács, J., 1993, "A külkereskedelem liberalizálása Kelet Európában: gyors reformok és újraértékelés" (Foreign Trade Liberalization in Eastern Europe: Rapid Reforms and a Reappraisal). *Külgazdaság* 12: 12-33.

"Górnictwo" (Mining). 1992. *Trybuna Śląska* (July 17).

Grelik, M. 1984. *Reakcje przedsiębiorstw na zmiany systemowe* (Enterprise Reactions to Systemic Change). Warsaw: Institute of Organization, Management, and Personnel Training.

Grzegorzewski, Z. 1993. "Gra w Monopole" (Playing Monopoly). *Życie Gospodarcze* (July 11).

Informacje o stanie zmonopolizowania gospodarki polskiej (Information about the State of Monopolization of the Polish Economy). 1991. Warsaw: Urząd Antymonopolowy (April).

Jakóbik, W. 1988. *Monopol na rynku polskim* (Monopoly on the Polish Market). Warsaw: Państwowe Wydawnictwo Ekonomiczne.

Levitas, A. and P. Strzalkowski 1990. "What Does 'uwlaszczenie nomenklatury' ('Propertisation of the nomenklatura') Really Mean?". *Communist Economies* 3: 413-16.

Lipszyc, J.B. 1994. "Nie jesteśmy urzędem cen" (We Are Not the Price Office). *Rzeczpospolita* (July 27).

Mac, J.S. 1994. "Układ czworokątowy" (A Four-sided Structure). *Wprost* (July 17).

Mały Rocznik Statystyczny 1993 (1993 Pocket Statistical Handbook) 1993. Warsaw: Główny Urząd Statystyczny.

Matusiak, M. 1989. "W owczej skórze" (In Sheep's Clothing). *Gazeta Bankowa* 23: 6.

Mejssner, M., and B. Możdżyński. 1994. "Przeciąganie tytoniu" (Stretching Out the Tobacco). *Życie Warszawy* (July 12).

Modzelewski, W. 1991. "Nowelizacja ustawy antymonopolowej: niektóre wątpliwości" (Amending the Antimonopoly Law: Some Doubts). *Rzeczpospolita* (September 16).

Mozolski, A. 1993. "Wrzuć monetę, wrzuć monetę..." (More Coins, Please). *Polityka* (July 24).

Newbery, D.M., and P. Kattuman. 1992. "Market Concentration and Competition in Eastern Europe." *The World Today* 2: 315-334.

Parkot, M. 1989. *Raport na temat stanu koncentracji i zmonopolizowania struktur w gospodarce polskiej*. (Report on the State of Concentration and Monopolization in the Polish Economy). Warsaw: Ministry of Finance (April).

Pittman, R. 1992. "Some Critical Provisions in the Antimonopoly Laws of Central and Eastern Europe." *International Lawyer* 2: 485-503.

Pokojska, M. 1995. "Brzydkie kaczątko" (The Ugly Duckling). *Gazeta Bankowa* (May 14): 21.

Polska 1918-1988 (Poland 1918-1988). 1989. Warsaw: Główny Urząd Statystyczny.

Pryor, F.L. 1973. *Property and Industrial Organization in Communist and Capitalist Nations*. Bloomington, Indiana: Indiana University Press.

Przepisy w sprawach antymonopolowych (Regulations in Antimonopoly Matters). 1990. Warsaw: Antimonopoly Office.

Reynolds, M. 1991. "Enforcing Anti-trust Law in Central Europe." *Financial Times* (September 26).

Rychard, A. 1980. *Reforma gospodarcza: Socjologiczna analiza związków polityki i gospodarki* (Economic Reform: A Sociological Analysis of the Links Between Politics and Economics). Warsaw: Wydawnictwo Polskiej Akademii Nauk.

Roczniki Statystyczne: Przemysł (Statistical Yearbooks: Industry). Various years. Warsaw: Główny Urząd Statystyczny.

Skoczny, T. 1993. *Zakres i kierunki dostosowywania polskiego prawa antymonopolowego do europejskich reguł konkurencji* (Extent and Principles of Adapting Polish Antimonopoly Law to European Rules of Competition). Warsaw: Friedrich Ebert Stiftung.

_____. 1992. *Competition Legislation in Post-Socialist Countries*. Warsaw: Friedrich Ebert Stiftung.

_____. 1991. "Competition Acts of the Post-Socialist Countries: Czecho-Slovakia, Poland, Hungary. (some comparative remarks)." Paper presented to the OECD seminar in Brno, Czechoslovakia (December 5-6).

Slay, B. 1994a. *The Polish Economy: Crisis, Reform, and Transformation*. Princeton, New Jersey: Princeton University Press.

_____. 1994b. "The Polish Economy under the Post-Communists." *Radio Free Europe/Radio Liberty Research Report* 33: 66-76.

_____. 1994c. Bad Debts and the Polish Restructuring Program" (with Louisa Vinton). *Most* 4: 85-108.

_____. 1993a. "The Indigenous Private Sector in Poland," in P.L. Patterson, ed., *Capitalist Goals, Socialist Past: The Rise of the Private Sector in Command Economies* Pp. 19-40. Boulder, Colorado: Westview Press.

_____. 1993b. "The Political Economy of External Transformation," in Brabant, J.M. van. ed. *Eastern Europe in the World Economy*. Pp. 13-36. Boulder, Colorado: Westview Press.

_____. 1991. "Poland: The 'Mass Privatization' Program Unravels." *Radio Free Europe Report on Eastern Europe* 44: 13-18.

_____. 1990. "Monopoly and Marketization in Polish Industry." *Jahrbuch der Wirtschaft Osteuropas* 1: 58-84.

Staniszkis, J. 1991. "'Political Capitalism' in Poland." *East European Politics and Societies* 1: 127-141.

"Statystyka Polski" (Statistics of Poland). 1995. Supplement to *Rzeczpospolita* (February 9).

_____. 1994a. Supplement to *Rzeczpospolita* (August 4).

_____. 1994b. Supplement to *Rzeczpospolita* (February 7).

_____. 1992. Supplement to *Rzeczpospolita* (August 4).

Szot, E. 1994a. "Przeciwko podwyżkom cen nawozów" (Against Price Increases for Fertilizers). *Rzeczpospolita* (September 10-11).

_____. 1994b. "Przyszłość polskiego cukrownictwa" (The Future of Polish Sugar). *Rzeczpospolita* (March 16).

Szwarc. K. 1987. "Reforma centrum" (Reform of the Center). *Życie Gospodarcze* (October 25).

Urząd Antymonopolowy. 1993. *Annual Report on Activity of the Polish AntiMonopoly Office 1992*. Warsaw: Urząd Antymonopolowy.

Waleńcik, I. 1993. "Urząd Antymonopolowy obniża podwyżkę" (The Antimonopoly Office Reduces the Price Increase). *Rzeczpospolita* (July 31-August 1).

Wanless, P.T. 1980. "Economic Reform in Poland: 1973-79." *Soviet Studies* 1: 28-57.

"Wniosek do Urzędu antymonopolowego" (A Petition to the Antimonopoly Office). 1991. *Prywatyzacja* (March).

Wojciechowska, U. 1978. *Studia nad systemem wielkich organizacji gospodarczych 1973-75* (Studies of the Large Economic Organization System, 1973-75). Warsaw: Państwowe Wydawnictwo Ekonomiczne.

Wrabec P., B. Warpechowska, and M. Dreszer. 1993. "Zmowa węglowa" (The Coal Conspiracy). *Gazeta Wyborcza* (August 3).

Zagrodzka, D. 1995. "Rząd czekania i gadania" (A Government of Waiting and Talking). *Gazeta Wyborcza* (January 12): 12.

Zybała, A. 1994. "Gorzko" (Bitter). *Wprost* (July 3).

Żychowicz, E. 1991. "Konkurencja nade wszystko." (Competition Above All). *Rzeczpospolita* (February 16-17).

6

Competition Policy for Natural Monopolies in a Developing Market Economy[1]

*Janusz A. Ordover, Russell W. Pittman,
and Paul Clyde*[2]

Introduction

Policy-makers in the post-socialist countries of Eastern Europe face the challenging task of designing appropriate competition policies for the key infrastructure sectors of their economies—energy, transport, and communications—sectors whose efficient functioning is vital to sustained economic development in these countries.

The task facing the policy-makers is especially difficult for several reasons. First, state-owned enterprises (SOEs) operating in these sectors were often heavily subsidized by the socialist governments in order to keep the prices of their products and services artificially low. Consequently, price liberalization in these sectors is likely to have, and in fact already has had, serious economic impacts on buyers.

Second, these sectors are often characterized by production technologies, and concomitant cost relationships, that favor high concentration. (And this is on top of the fact that industries in formerly planned economies are already overly concentrated and excessively vertically integrated.) Consequently, competitive forces cannot readily be relied upon to ensure that SOEs in these sectors, even if they are privatized, will keep prices close to costs and will have incentives to keep costs low.

Third, these sectors as a rule produce and sell goods and services that are non-tradable internationally. Consequently, international trade cannot be relied upon to create the needed competitive pressures.

Fourth, and perhaps most importantly, SOEs in these sectors often employ extremely outdated technologies.[3] Consequently, competition policy in these sectors must create incentives for investment in new technologies.

There are several broad types of competition policy that might be applied to these "infrastructure" sectors. First, post-socialist countries may continue with public ownership of SOEs coupled with non-transparent price setting, a policy which combines both economic and other objectives and includes the potential for subsidies for both current operations and future investments from the state budget. In our view, this option carries great risks. In particular, as we argue below, it is likely to impose significant burdens on state budgets, something that these countries can ill afford. Moreover, it is likely to discourage direct foreign investment. This type of policy has, however, been used frequently in Western Europe (and other market economies).

The next two policy options presuppose that enterprises in the relevant sectors are motivated primarily by the profit motive. This is because they have been either privatized or converted into joint-stock companies (perhaps owned by the Treasury) and have been effectively cut off from subsidies that enabled them virtually to ignore market signals.

The behavior of the "marketized" enterprises in the relevant sectors can be influenced either by regulation of prices (or output) or by application of antitrust statutes aimed at restraining abuse of market dominance.

In this paper, we argue that during the transition period to market economies, antitrust scrutiny may in some circumstances offer an effective and reasonably low-cost method of restraining undue exercise of market power by firms in the "infrastructure" sectors. In this regard, it must be noted that the antimonopoly statutes of post-socialist countries tend to follow European Union law more closely than U.S. law in their emphasis on preventing "abuses" by "dominant" firms. U.S. law seeks to prevent mergers that are likely to facilitate or enhance the exercise of market power (Section 7 of the Clayton Act) and unfair or anticompetitive behavior by firms with large market shares (Section 2 of the Sherman Act), but firms which achieve large market shares through lawful means are granted wide latitude in their actions. EU law is more restrictive with regard to actions by firms with large market shares that may create a disadvantage for suppliers, customers, or less efficient competitors.[4] We also argue that if antitrust scrutiny is deemed undesirable on an ongoing basis, independent regulatory agencies should be established.

We suggest that, with the assistance of international agencies, incentive regulation is preferable when world prices are available. However, because of the unsettled economic situation in economies in transition and other factors, in other cases traditional rate-of-return regulation is likely to be preferable to incentive regulation.

In short, there are few microeconomic issues of greater importance now in the post-socialist countries than those surrounding the privatization and the design of competition policies for infrastructure sectors. In this paper, we address four aspects of this issue, focusing on the lessons learned from the U.S. regulatory experience and their relevance in the Eastern European context. These aspects are the following:

- privatization;
- the appropriate sectors for regulation;
- the appropriate treatment of unregulated subsidiaries of regulated firms, and
- the appropriate regulatory regime for regulated sectors.

We begin with a brief discussion of Eastern European economies in which we highlight some of the differences from developed economies that are relevant to the analysis of this topic.

The Economic Environment in Eastern Europe

Policy analysis for infrastructure industries in former socialist countries will differ from policy analysis for those industries in developed countries because of the current economic condition of former socialist countries. The absence of a profit motive has led to a number of distortions (from a market perspective) in former socialist countries.

These distortions create some problems that do not exist in developed economies and exacerbate some problems that do exist. Perhaps the most important problem is that prices in some sectors of former socialist countries do not reflect the cost of the product to society. This results in an inefficient input mix and, often, overuse of costly resources. Public utilities, in particular, generally charge rates that are too low to cover resource costs.[5]

Another important problem is that the capital needs of infra-structure industries are proportionately greater in former socialist countries than in those sectors of developed economies. An operating profit earned by a public utility in former socialist countries went directly to the Finance Ministry, and the enterprise had no particular claim on it for maintenance and depreciation expenses, much less for modernization and expansion.[6] Public utilities will therefore require substantial investment to narrow the gap between their often obsolete physical assets and state-of-the-art technology.[7] This need for capital is amplified by the dramatic increase in capacity of public utilities these countries will need as their economies develop.[8]

The problem of raising capital will be exacerbated by the lack of developed financial markets. In the past few years, Hungary, Poland, Slovakia and the Czech Republic have opened exchanges of some sort. However, even in these countries, capital markets are in their infancy, with relatively low levels of liquidity and a great deal of uncertainty as to regulation of the exchanges in the future. All of this leads to higher transaction costs in countries in which private savings will not be substantial to begin with, and, thus, to a limitation on the role of private domestic investment.

Rigorous accounting procedures and accepted accounting principles are also lacking in most post-socialist countries. As a result there are limited historical accounts of value, and a lack of professionals trained to develop and analyze such records.[9]

At this early stage in the development of these economies, laws that clearly articulate property rights are lagging behind. In some Eastern European countries, ownership rights on assets as basic as land are not yet known.[10] In the extreme, the lack of well-defined property rights alone can be sufficient to strangle any development attempts. While the situation is not that bleak in most post-socialist countries, the lack of well-defined property rights does increase the cost of operating a business in these countries, dramatically so in some cases.

Finally, the ability of the governments to commit to a given set of property rights is likely to be much more limited in former socialist countries than in economies with a longer history of a free market. This increased uncertainty raises the cost of operating a business in these countries and therefore increases the required return. The cost of the inability to commit will vary across industries and, in the area of natural monopoly, across types of regulation. In industries characterized by natural monopoly where technology tends to be capital intensive and investments tend to be largely "sunk", the result of this inability to commit can be both severely suboptimal investment levels and a channelling of the investment that does take place toward inappropriate, less appropriable technologies.[11]

Should Public Utilities in
Post-socialist Countries Be Privatized?

The empirical evidence concerning the relative efficiency of publicly owned and privately owned enterprises does not seem to support the notion that, in a developed market economy, the privatization of infrastructure industries will necessarily yield significant public benefits. Kay and Thompson (1986) and Vickers and Yarrow (1988, 1991) summarize the findings of this literature in similar ways:

- Privately owned firms tend, on average, to be the more internally efficient when competition in product markets is effective.[12]
- Privatization will tend to improve performance in a company only if supported by liberalization; and if the two conflict, liberalization is decidedly to be preferred.[13]

Vickers and Yarrow (1988:40) address specifically the issue of the infrastructure sector:

> Subject to the...condition about competition and provided that other allocative inefficiencies associated with market failures are not substantial, we would argue that the available evidence supports a presumption in favor of private enterprise. However, when market power is significant, and particularly when company behavior is subject to detailed regulation, there is little empirical justification for a general presumption in favor of either type of ownership, and case-by-case evaluation of the various trade-offs is therefore in order.

However, the empirical evidence upon which these statements are based concerns almost exclusively the US, the UK, and Canada. The "case-by-case evaluation" called for by Vickers and Yarrow suggests a reformulation of the question that forms the title of this section: Is there something special about the public utility sectors of the post-socialist countries that makes their privatization more likely to lead to improvements in efficiency than has been the experience in the West?

We believe that the answer is yes. One of the most important advantages of privatization is that, by placing both residual control rights and residual cash flow rights in the hands of private shareholders rather than the government, it renders short-term political intervention in the day-to-day operations of the enterprise more costly and so allows the enterprise to focus on long-term economic efficiency.[14] Put another way, privatization represents a commitment by government—a commitment made credible both by these transfers of rights and by the prospect of future privatizations—not to overturn or otherwise interfere with the basic operational decisions of management. We believe that the gap between the current and efficient levels of operation has been so large in the infrastructure sectors of the post-socialist countries—and so much larger than in Western countries—that this "constitutional" change may be especially powerful in this setting. We discuss here four areas in which we believe a strong case can be made that private ownership will result in dramatic improvements in the performance of the infrastructure sector in these countries. These areas are the following:

- ability and incentive to raise rates;
- ability and incentive to raise capital;
- ability and incentive to utilize the efficient mix of inputs; and
- adaptability to change in the future;

Ability and Incentive to Raise Rates

As discussed above, public utilities in the post-socialist countries charge rates that are too low. They are below average cost and below marginal cost, sometimes dramatically so.

It is a standard result of welfare economics that, in general, this sort of income redistribution policy would be effected more efficiently through direct transfers of purchasing power or targeted subsidies than through broad subsidization of the price of particular goods. The direct result of this policy has been and will continue to be shortages and the overuse of inputs that are, in fact, costly to society (especially energy); a less direct result has been and will continue to be a lack of funds for capital upkeep and modernization; a still less direct (but ultimately very important) result will be that new businesses will hesitate to invest if they require dependable utility service.

Can and will these utilities raise rates to more efficient levels if they remain under direct government management? Certainly, this has occurred in some instances (as noted above), but it seems doubtful that it will occur systematically. The redistributive effects of increases in utility rates will sometimes be large, and there will always be a strong temptation—where "constitutional" provisions do not impede—for politicians to prevent them.[15] Furthermore, so long as utility managers are employees of the state who earn no residual income streams from profitable operation, they will have the incentive not to raise prices to market-clearing levels but rather to maximize their side payments (either explicit or from so-called "secondary [barter] markets") by maintaining prices below those levels.[16] On the other hand, the process of privatization of a particular enterprise may provide a propitious time for a simultaneous institutional restructuring, in which management is replaced, price controls are removed (perhaps gradually), and a regulatory mechanism (where necessary: see below) is set in place.[17] New private management, allowed a degree of freedom from interference in day-to-day operations unavailable to public management, will raise prices to a level at least sufficient to cover costs. Robinson (1992a) summarizes the British experience with electricity privatization:

> Despite the good intentions of the founding fathers..., it proved impossible to have "arms-length" relationships between the nationalized corporations and government. Instead, governments of both major parties found irresistible the temptation to interfere with the decisions of state-owned industries so that, in practice, the corporations had little control over pricing and investment decisions ...An independent regulatory body is capable of providing the industry with a much clearer set of ground rules which avoids much of the confusion between commercial and political objectives associated with nationalization.[18]

Ability and Incentive to Raise Capital

Infrastructure industries are among the most capital-intensive industries in a modern economy. The need to replace the decrepit and obsolete physical plants and the need to provide for dramatic increases in demand as the transforming economies expand raise an important question for former socialist countries: Where will the money for expansion and modernization come from?

If the enterprises remain in public hands, there does not seem to be a likely source for the massive funds that will be required. Rate increases by the enterprises would be helpful in this regard, but, as argued above, they do not seem likely to be forthcoming. Most of the post-socialist countries have serious government budget deficits resulting from badly underdeveloped systems of public finance.[19] Expansion of these deficits, even if desired by the government, is typically constrained by agreements with international lending bodies. And this gap in funding is, for reasons described earlier, unlikely to be filled by domestic private investments.[20]

This suggests that the enterprises must be privatized, and that if they are to attract the investment funds required, they must be open to foreign investment.[21] Certainly the issue of foreign investment in infrastructure industries is a controversial one politically, and there will be differences between countries in the feasibility of this outcome and the volumes of investment that are politically acceptable. Still, as has been demonstrated in both the UK and France, it is quite possible for the government to privatize an enterprise and open it to foreign investment while still maintaining some discretion over its ownership structure.[22] Indeed, Tenenbaum, Lock, and Barker (1992:1135) argue that the "special" nature of infrastructure enterprises—used in the past as a rationale for nationalization—may now be the best reason for privatization:

> One of the major factors that drove many electric system nationalizations earlier in this century, the industry's central or infrastructural role in the country's economy, now mandates its privatization in debt ridden countries if economic growth is to continue.

Along these lines, the *Financial Times* reports that "Hungary is set to open up infrastructure development to western investors." At his parliamentary confirmation hearings, finance minister Iván Szabo said that "foreign companies could finance the construction of motorways, airports, railways, and eventually mines."[23] A decree of the Hungarian government permits private (including foreign) acquisition of partial ownership interests in various infrastructure enterprises—up to 49 percent in electricity, broadcasting, and telecommunications, up to 74 percent in gas distribution.[24] Foreigners have invested heavily in the modernization and expansion of Poland's telecommunications network.[25] And in a pilot project in cooperation with the World Bank, two Scandinavian power generating utilities have announced a commitment to invest $25 million each in the modernization of a heat and power station in Kraków, Poland.[26]

Ability and Incentive to Utilize
the Efficient Mix of Inputs

Publicly owned firms operate under constant political pressure to utilize input mixes that would not be chosen by profit-maximizing managers. Such firms have demonstrated repeatedly a tendency toward bloated labor forces,[27] but they may be forced by political considerations to favor other inputs as well.[28] Boycko, Shleifer, and Vishny (1992:4), may well be correct in arguing that "the greatest reason for the inefficiency of state firms is not managerial problems, but rather the insistence by the state that the firms produce inefficiently." Private management, responding both to its own direct incentives and to the profit-maximization dictum of capital markets, and insulated from government intervention in its day-to-day operations, would be expected to produce its output at significantly lower cost to society— though, to be sure, a fundamental challenge facing those designing regulatory institutions for transforming economies will be to ensure that regulation does not blunt these incentives for efficiency. (We discuss this issue below.)

Along this line, a *Warsaw Voice* report on the process of partial privatization of the Polish airline LOT concludes that:

> The most visible result has been streamlined employment. At the end of 1990, LOT employed more than 7,300 people. Currently, employment stands at about 4,800.[29]

Indeed, the report quotes an officer of the company on the rationale for this partial privatization (in which 49 percent of the firm's stock will be placed in private hands, probably those of a large western air carrier): "The company doesn't need capital or a change of strategy as much as it needs joint work with a partner to improve, for example, corporate management."[30]

Adaptability to Change in the Future

Many infrastructure industries change in important ways over time. Two important kinds of changes may be noted here: change in the technology of production and distribution of a particular sector, and change in the competitive conditions facing producers in a particular sector. (The first kind of change may lead to the second.) Both kinds of changes—perhaps especially the first—may have such large welfare impacts over time that a policy that facilitates and enables dynamic efficiency has much to recommend it, even if it is not the policy that reaches the highest level of static efficiency.[31] In this case, we believe that the post-socialist countries are in the fortunate situation where the same policy encourages both static and dynamic efficiency.

The case of technological change offers perhaps the most striking example. Assume that there are innovations in the process of production that would dramatically lower costs but would also entail some risk of failure. Assume further that this risk, or the consequences of failure, are small enough that a social welfare maximizing enterprise would adopt the innovation. Which form of ownership, public or private, is more likely to result in adoption?

The answer seems clear. It is true that private managers may face inadequate incentives to innovate if regulators tax away part of the benefit of successful innovation. (Again, we shall discuss this issue below.) But at least with private ownership there is an important constituency—the shareholders—favoring innovation that increases profits by reducing costs. On the contrary, the only incentive that public managers face for successful innovation stems from the desire of the sponsoring ministry for a smaller budget deficit—likely a decidedly less powerful stimulus.[32]

A change in competitive conditions facing an infrastructure industry may also have important welfare implications. As we will discuss below, several sectors in the U.S. that were once regulated were later substantially deregulated as a result of the appearance of competition. (Long-distance telecommunications and railways are two good examples.) Privately-owned, regulated firms may resist this competition, to be sure, and may seek to use the regulatory process to impede it (as was the case in both of the sectors just cited), but it seems clear that an enterprise owned by the state will be able to resist more strongly and use the force of government more successfully in doing so.[33]

Conclusion

We believe that all of the factors just discussed—rate levels, capitalization, static operating efficiency, and dynamic allocative efficiency—argue in favor of the privatization of infrastructure industries in the post-socialist countries. We have not addressed the issue of what form the privatization should take; there are many possibilities, and it may be feasible in some circumstances for a less-than-complete privatization (like the Hungarian plan noted above) to address public concerns while still achieving the goals discussed here.[34]

We have also not yet addressed the issue of whether and how to regulate such enterprises following privatization. It is to this important issue that we now turn. First, how does one decide which sectors need regulation? Second, if part of the operations of a privatized infrastructure firm may be deregulated but part must be regulated, should ownership of the two parts be separated? Finally, what kind of regulatory regime seems most appropriate in post-socialist economies?

The Appropriate Sectors for Regulation

It is by now commonly recognized that direct regulation of prices should be confined to those sectors of the economy that exhibit natural monopoly characteristics.

A natural monopoly may be defined, semi-technically, as a firm that employs a given technology for which the output demanded can be produced most cheaply by a single firm. Often this occurs because the average total cost for a firm using this technology declines continuously over the existing range of demand. The problem, of course, is that this one firm with lowest costs, if not regulated, may be expected to act as a monopolist and to increase its profits by reducing output in order to raise prices. An efficient regulatory regime seeks to ensure that output is maintained at or near the competitive level at the same time that single-firm operation allows the highest level of technical efficiency to be reached.

It is important to note, however, that just because a firm is a natural monopoly, it does not follow that government regulation is either appropriate or necessary. This is so for two principal reasons.

First, regulation imposes costs upon regulated firms. The firms must hire attorneys and experts to interact with the regulators. They must delay taking actions while they consider their regulatory implications and await regulatory reaction. They must optimize under the constraints imposed by the regulators—some of which may not be well understood at the time of their imposition, and some of which may reflect bureaucratic interest rather than public interest. Such burdens can be justified on a welfare basis only where the costs to the economy of the firm acting in an unregulated manner would be large.[35]

Second, a natural monopoly may not, in fact, be a monopoly in a sense that matters for prices (and levels of output). That is, even if a firm operates as a natural monopoly in producing a certain product with a certain technology at a certain location, it may face competition from firms producing competing products, or the same product with a different technology, or the same product at a different location, and, thus, not require regulation.[36] Recent U.S. examples of this phenomenon include the following:

- There has been a general consensus in the United States that both the local distribution of electricity and the long-distance transmission of electricity from one point to another are natural monopolies. However, technological change has made possible the economical construction of large and small generators of electricity (including as a byproduct of industrial processes).[37] This means that there may be situations where rates for wholesale energy[38] need not be regulated.[39] But it means more than that: if a particular location is served by more than one long-distance line from more than one generating location, then it may be that the transmission service no longer needs rate regulation, either.
- Similarly, the long-distance transmission by pipeline of petroleum between two points may well be a natural monopoly. However, in the United States the Department of Justice has argued for years that certain pipeline destinations

that have multiple sources of petroleum—say, from a pipeline from another origin or from water or truck transportation—do not require regulation to protect them from monopoly pricing.[40] Similar considerations may hold for some natural gas pipelines.

- The operation of a railway from a particular origin to a particular destination may sometimes be a natural monopoly, especially in locations where the density of traffic between the two points is low.[41] However, it is widely accepted in the United States that government regulation of this natural monopoly is unnecessary in those situations where the transport of the commodities via road or water is an economic substitute for their transport by rail, and in those situations where the origin is served by other railways (to other destinations) and the destination is served by other railways (from other origins), so that shippers and customers have access to competitive sources of supply or demand.[42]

To summarize: each of these is an example of a sector which is arguably a natural monopoly but where some form of competition from another product, from another technology, from another location —makes government regulation unnecessary. This may occur because natural monopolies are defined with respect to technologies, not with respect to consumer preferences. The latter are relevant to market definition but not to natural monopoly characterization.

The Appropriate Treatment for Unregulated Subsidiaries of Regulated Firms

One of the most controversial issues in the regulatory arena in the United States is the degree to which regulated firms should be allowed to compete in unregulated markets. Many people fear that if a regulated firm is allowed to compete in unregulated markets it will be able to divert a portion of costs directly attributable to activities in these markets onto the customers of its regulated operations, thus, "cross-subsidizing" its unregulated customers and unfairly and inefficiently putting its competitors in unregulated markets at a disadvantage.[43] This may be especially harmful in those situations where the unregulated sector offers the only competition, however imperfect, to the regulated sector. Others point to the cost advantages that will accrue to society if a regulated firm takes advantage of economies of scope by producing and competing in both kinds of markets.[44]

Because of the economically irrational industry structures inherited from the socialist economies, some of these decisions are not difficult ones. It requires no econometric study to conclude that there are probably no important economies of scope in the simultaneous operation of a local telephone company and a vacation resort, or a railway and a local vegetable distributor. If the telephone company and the railway are to be regulated as natural monopolies, the separation of the vacation resort and the vegetable distributor from their common ownership will eliminate the necessity of carefully ensuring that the firms are not using profits from their regulated operations to subsidize their unregulated operations, to the harm of competitors there.

But there is no evading the fact that sometimes the trade-offs involved are difficult. In fact, there is a certain inherent difficulty to the trade-off, since it is in precisely those areas where there are economies of scope between the provision of regulated and unregulated services that the separation of the costs of the provision of regulated and unregulated services may be the most complex task (or may be, in fact, logically impossible). Few in the United States would deny that there would be real economies of scope to the provision of information services by regulated providers of either local telephone or local cable television service, but few would deny also that this is a situation in which the possibility of cross-subsidies—and hence unfair competition to other providers of information services—is a matter of real concern, in the absence of regulatory safeguards. In a variety of circumstances, policy-makers in the United States are seeking to balance these considerations just now.

If cross-subsidization is a matter of concern in market economies, it may be even more of a danger in the post-socialist economies. This is so for two reasons.

First, the prevention of cross-subsidization requires that firms keep careful accounts according to well-accepted accounting principles and that regulators be well-trained in the interpretation of these accounts. Since none of these preconditions exist in the post-socialist countries (nor are they likely to for many years to come), the accounts of regulated firms are likely to be kept in such a way as to make the detection of cross subsidies difficult.

Second, the careful interpretation of firm accounts to prevent cross-subsidization, inevitably, requires important judgments to be made by individual regulators. Whenever such judgments are required, there is the possibility of corruption and conflict of interest on the part of regulators—what is sometimes termed "regulatory capture". Economists have noted an unfortunate tendency in the West for regulatory bodies to protect regulated firms from competition as much as they protect the public from the abuses of monopoly.[45] As Tirole (1991) notes, the post-socialist economies may be especially susceptible to this problem:

> Strong safeguards must be put in place to prevent governments from serving the interests of specific groups. Many of these safeguards did not exist under the previous regimes and will take time to install: organization and rotation in the civil service, administrative procedures and regulatory hearings, independent administrative courts, checks and balances in government, development of a tradition of investigative reporting by the media, etc.[46]

For these two reasons, it seems likely to be especially difficult in the post-socialist countries for regulators to prevent firms from subsidizing unregulated operations from regulated operations, and, thus, it seems appropriate to hold a strong bias in these economies toward the separation of ownership of regulated and unregulated businesses. The most likely exception may be when the regulated service and the unregulated service are the identical service offered in different markets—for example, the cases of deregulation described in the previous section, or the cases of expanding existing service to new customers described below.

Early developments in this area do not appear especially promising. Both Poland and Hungary have chosen to allow their monopoly providers of local telephone service to enter into the provision of related services that may not be natural monopolies, such as mobile radio, cellular telephone, paging, packet data transmission, and electronic mail. Since these kinds of services provide the only likely competition to local telephone service in the near future; since there is little chance that in the near future demand in either country can support more than one or two providers of these services; and since regulation to prevent cross-subsidization is likely to prove ineffective—indeed as of this writing it is contemplated that Hungary will privatize local telecommunications with no regulation—this joint ownership raises the likelihood that cross-subsidization will be used as an entry deterrent, to the detriment of competition and consumers.[47]

The Appropriate Competition Regime
for Natural Monopoly Sectors

Background

For the last hundred years, the predominant form of regulation in the United States has been "rate of return" regulation. This form of regulation operates in the following manner. At a particular point in time, the regulated firm estimates the value of its capital stock. For a particular period of time (perhaps one year), the firm estimates the quantity of its products that will be demanded by customers. It then estimates the costs that it will incur in satisfying this demand, including the cost of depreciation of its capital stock. The regulatory body calculates the amount of surplus, net of both operating costs and depreciation, that must be allowed the firm if it is to earn a "normal" rate of return, or profit. The body then permits the firm to set such prices as the body calculates will yield that return.

Critics of this system of regulation have charged that it is both costly and inefficient. It may be costly because there is a sufficiently large number of difficult judgments required of regulators in administering the system that a particular decision may result in expensive and time-consuming lobbying, deliberation, and litigation. It may be inefficient because some of the principles involved may provide poor behavioral incentives to the profit-maximizing firm.

Examples of the difficult judgments required include the following:

1. What is the exact value of the capital stock of the firm? (Those who have studied Marxist economics will have a special understanding of the difficulties involved here.) Exactly how much of that capital stock depreciates in a single year? Natural monopoly sectors tend to be among the most capital-intensive sectors of the economy, so that small changes in the answers to these questions may make large differences in the prices charged by and return earned by firms.

2. What is the "normal" rate of return to capital that should be allowed by regulators? This rate—which is the rate that the firm must be allowed to earn if it is to attract funds from investors—should be determined in a particular industry largely by the riskiness of investing there. But exactly how risky is investing in a particular natural monopoly sector? Again, the capital-intensity of the typical natural-monopoly sector makes this a very important question.

3. The capital intensity of many natural monopoly firms is accompanied by the problem of "common costs": a significant portion of the capital costs incurred by the regulated firm is not sensitive to the level of output, or to the output mix, of the firm. Thus, while these costs may be large in magnitude and must be recovered if the firm is to earn a return on its capital, it is logically and operationally impossible to assign them to

particular units of output of the firm. How they are recovered then may become as much a matter of "fairness"—hence of lengthy discussion and persuasion—as of economics.

Examples of poor incentives provided by the terms of the system include the following:

1. If the firm reduces its costs, the regulatory body will respond in the next period by reducing the prices that the firm is allowed to charge, since less revenues will be required to cover operating costs and still allow the normal rate of return. Conversely, the firm knows that if its costs increase, the regulatory body will allow its prices to increase as well. Thus, the incentives of the regulated firm to seek to operate more efficiently are attenuated.

2. The higher the level of capital intensity of the firm, the higher the level of surplus that must be allowed by the regulator to achieve the normal rate of return on capital. Thus, firms may have an incentive to increase their capital intensity beyond the most efficient level.

The widespread perception of these kinds of problems with rate-of-return regulation has—besides supporting the arguments in favor of the sectoral deregulation discussed earlier in this paper—stimulated a search for new forms of regulation that do not impose the costs and inefficiencies that may accompany rate-of-return regulation. In some sectors of U.S. and other Western economies, regulated firms have been allowed to set their prices in such a way that a particular long-term revenue path is not exceeded, without regard (in principle, at least) to the costs incurred by the firm in a particular year. For example, the firm may be told that its revenues may increase each year at the same rate as the rate of inflation in the economy, minus a predetermined allowance for increased operating efficiency. These kinds of regulatory regimes have been labelled "incentive" regulation, because—again, in principle—they do not penalize a firm for lowering its costs by forcing it to lower its prices as well.

The Appropriate Regulatory Mechanism

For those firms in the post-socialist countries that require government regulation, what is the appropriate regulatory mechanism? At least three broad categories of mechanisms would seem to be candidates:

- dominant-firm oversight under an antimonopoly statute;
- cost-of-service regulation, as traditionally used in the United States; and
- incentive regulation.

Government oversight under the first category would simply treat the natural monopoly firm as one more firm with market power whose possible "abuse of dominance" is to be guarded against by the antimonopoly authorities. (The defined abuses typically include price discrimination, tying, charging "excessive" prices or earning "excessive" profits, and withholding output to increase prices.)[48] Under the second category, a regulatory authority would be created to set detailed prices for the firm, based principally upon the costs that it incurs, with an objective to ensure an adequate rate of return on the firm's assets. Under the third category, this regulatory authority would also set some prices—though perhaps in less detail than under cost-of-service regulation—but would base these prices upon some factors not tied directly to the past and present costs incurred by the firm.

Each of these types of mechanisms has advantages and disadvantages relative to the others, and some of these advantages and disadvantages take on a special importance in the context of the post-socialist economies of Central and Eastern Europe.[49] The World Bank has encouraged the use of incentive regulation schemes in many sectors in the post-socialist countries. As in the Western economies, different mechanisms may be more appropriate to one industry than to another; in addition, different mechanisms may be more appropriate at one point in the economic transition than at another. We suggest that the most important of these advantages and disadvantages may be included in one of three broad categories: the cost structure of the firm, changes in industry technology, and changes in industry demand.

Cost Structure of the Firm

As practiced in the West, cost-of-service regulation has been based upon detailed information and analysis concerning the costs already incurred by the regulated firm.[50] This has had the advantage of rendering rate-making an exercise of some predictability and routine, removing the scope for much regulatory discretion; it has had the disadvantage of requiring massive regulatory staffs to analyze massive volumes of data, and of tempering the incentive of the regulated firm to minimize cost. Incentive regulation schemes originated as a means of restoring the cost-minimizing incentive by severing the direct connection between a firm's costs and its prices, but they do so at the expense of requiring a prediction of the future costs facing the firm.[51]

Consider separately the issues of costs already incurred and costs to be incurred in the future. A full-information application of either dominant-firm scrutiny or cost-of-service regulation would require data on firm costs far more detailed and accurate than is available to enforcers in the post-socialist economies, with their lack of a tradition of cost accounting and capital budgeting. The President of the Polish Antimonopoly Office recently described the difficulties encountered by her office in trying to use the dominant-firm provisions of the Polish law to regulate prices charged by the automobile manufacturer FSO:

> In FSO case nothing could be done. It was even impossible to calculate the costs of one car—simply the FSO did not know them—and on this basis to reckon monopolistic profit that was earned by the Factory. Eventually the [Antimonopoly] Court decided the proof is not sufficient.[52]

Under these difficult circumstances, the practice of price regulation, where necessary, will likely focus on changes in prices as a function of changes in already-incurred costs. That is, the relevant authorities may take current prices as being reasonable and assess only increases from those prices. Thus, when the Competition Council of the Hungarian Office of Economic Competition recently judged a price increase for thermal water supplied by Budapest Swimming Pools Management to be excessive:

> While not pronouncing on the correctness of the prices the Jury decided that Defendant did offend the law when increasing their prices far beyond what would seem reasonable...[53]

All of this argues in favor of an inviting and arguably economically correct alternative: use world prices where available. Many of the inputs in public utilities are traded on a world market. Energy and capital equipment, for instance, are frequently traded across borders at world prices. For economies in transition, world prices have a number of advantages over domestic prices: (1) they are relatively stable; (2) they more accurately reflect the resource cost; and (3) the reduce the scope for regulatory capture, by establishing an independently determined yardstick.

Either an antimonopoly authority or a regulatory agency could use the available cost data to control prices. In cases where the bulk of firm costs are determined by the costs of one or a small group of inputs, an antimonopoly authority may well be able to monitor and interpret the cost increases and to ascertain whether price changes are indicative of the exercise of market power. In cases where the firm's cost function is more complex and not a function of such a small group of inputs, effective regulation might require the developing of industry-specific expertise by a specialized regulatory body.

Incentive regulation regimes seek to eliminate or minimize the necessity of detailed analysis of the cost experience of regulated firms, and to restore the incentive for firms to minimize their costs.[54] However, initial prices to which automatic price adjustments will be applied must still be determined. More importantly, all such regimes rely to some degree on the prediction of costs and productivity. For many industries, such predictions based on domestic data will be every bit as difficult in post-socialist economies as would be the detailed analysis of costs already incurred—first, because of rapid economy-wide inflation, second, because of the deregulation of the prices of important inputs.

As with cost regulation, these problems suggest incentive regulation would benefit from the use of world prices. World prices for tradables (e.g., electricity) would allow the regulatory authority to realize all of the advantages described above,[55] and, in contrast to cost-of-service regulation, there would be no need to rely on *any* domestic prices in the industries in which world prices are available.

Probably the most important detractor from incentive regulation is the ability of the government to commit to a give price path. That is not to say the ability to commit in cost-of-service regulation is unimportant (who is to say that the government will allow a pre-specified return after the investment has been made?[56]); it is simply that credible commitment is probably necessary for incentive regulation to have an advantage over cost-of-service regulation. The political pressure to renege on a commitment when firms are earning huge profits will be enormous. This pressure can be expected to be particularly pronounced in a country in which the population is still waiting for the fruits of capitalism to accrue to them.[57] Conversely, the pressure from the regulated enterprise to increase the allowed price when there are sizable losses will be significant.

These pressures combined with the post-socialist governments' already limited ability to commit would seem to handicap incentive regulation beyond serious consideration. However, organizations like the World Bank may help post-socialist countries deal with this problem. Financial aid from these organizations which is conditional upon the government adhering to the commitment may be sufficient to alleviate any fears of potential investors. The World Bank's independence from domestic political pressures and special interest group pressures puts them and organizations like them (including IMF, European Bank, and USAID) in a potentially useful position.

Burden of Regulation

We mentioned earlier the costs the regulation imposes upon regulated firms and upon the economy in general. These costs may be greater under cost-of-service regulation than under incentive regulation, but the latter can not eliminate them entirely.

In this regards, reliance on dominant-firm provisions in anti-monopoly statutes by the antimonopoly authorities may be an acceptable "middle way" in some circumstances.[58] These authorities lack the large staffs necessary to impose upon firms the kinds of large, day-to-day burdens just described. Just as important, they may have less of a will to do so. Both the Polish and the Hungarian antimonopoly authorities have stated publicly their distaste for heavy involvement in price regulation:

> Price control would hinder the transition from a command economy to a market one. In practice, we react only to the most aggressive price behavior of our monopolists.[59]

> We...sensed an illusory expectation that the Competition Office would, in the course of its investigations, determine "proper" prices for monopolistic or superiority situations. In fact, we have always done our best to resist such pressures. The Competition Law must not be allowed to reintroduce the *quasi*-official pricing of goods in areas which Parliament exempted in the price law. There may be—and in fact there were—cases when we were able to tell which part of a concrete price increase was justified and which was not, but these instances were exceptional.[60]

Dominant-firm regulation by the antimonopoly authorities institutionalizes price scrutiny with a body whose existence does not depend on regulating that industry; cost-of-service and incentive regulation institutionalize regulation with a body created, staffed, and dedicated to that purpose. It seems likely that the former will impose the smaller burden.[61]

Furthermore, a generalized enforcement agency, such as an antimonopoly authority, will be less susceptible to regulatory "capture" than a regulatory agency; the staff and management of the former must deal with a variety of industries and interests on a day-to-day basis and are likely to develop neither the rapport nor the institutionalized interdependence with the regulated industry that may develop under the latter.[62]

There are responses to these arguments in favor of the use of the antimonopoly authority as regulatory agency. If the antimonopoly authority lacks the resources to impose a long-term regulatory burden, it also lacks the resources to develop the extensive industry expertise required of a regulator. If a generalized antimonopoly authority may be to some degree protected from "capture" by a particular industry, so may be a generalized regulatory agency; one need not create a regulatory agency for each regulated sector. There may be spillover costs from using the antimonopoly authority as a price regulator in natural monopoly industries if the authority thereby develops expertise in the science of price regulation and begins to favor that remedy over remedies that create or promote the process of competition in its antimonopoly enforcement regarding the unregulated sectors of the economy. And the existence of a competition authority free of any regulatory power ensures that there is an advocate for efficiency within the government which is free of special interest group pressure.[63]

These factors suggest that the most appropriate circumstances for the use of the antimonopoly authority as regulatory agency will be not only where regulation is relatively straightforward (as discussed above) but also where regulation is deemed necessary on only a short-term basis as competitive forces develop in a particular sector. Where long-term regulation is contemplated, an agency dedicated only to regulation is probably in order.

Changes in Industry Technology

The transformation of the post-socialist economies will result in large, discontinuous changes in the technologies used in virtually every natural-monopoly industry. The issues discussed in the previous two sections—the cost structure of the regulated firm and the burden of regulation—are especially important in the presence or anticipation of such technological changes.

The likelihood of such changes increases the importance of firms facing the proper incentives to use the appropriate production technology at all times. It increases the advantage of incentive regulation over rate-of-return regulation, which responds to a lowering of the firm's costs by a lowering of its allowed price.

Furthermore, such changes increase the importance of regulatory decisions, at the same time that they increase the scope of regulatory discretion, and, thus, may significantly increase the likelihood of regulatory capture. A regulator faced with large, discontinuous technological changes must make decisions on a variety of issues with far reaching implications: how the regulated firm is to adopt the new technology, the cost treatment of obsolete capital, whether the new technology changes the optimum number of firms in the industry (i.e., whether and to what extent entry may be permitted), whether the new technology removes the need for government regulation.

In industries in which final product world prices are available, and assuming the commitment problem can be solved by an international agency, incentive regulation seems to be the clear choice. In addition to its direct incentive advantages, incentive regulation may take some judgments out of the hands of the regulator, thereby reducing the problems associated with regulatory capture.

If final product world prices are not available or if international agencies are unwilling or unable to mitigate the commitment problem, the prediction and commitment problem would seem to hold trump over the incentive problem. Incentive rates will, rightly, not be taken seriously if likely changes in industry structure mean that a commitment to announced rates could lead to either huge profits or ruinous losses for the regulated firm. The capture problem serves to strengthen the argument for mechanisms to control regulatory discretion in these economies—through more explicit legislative direction where that is feasible, in general through a strengthening of safeguards against the use of government agencies to further the interests of particular groups.[64] It also serves, on the basis of the argument that generalized agencies are less susceptible to capture than are specialized agencies, to strengthen the argument for reliance on antitrust provisions in those sectors where the structure of cost and production is not so complex as to definitively require a specialized agency, or a generalized rather than a specialized regulatory agency. The "burden of regulation" argument also points toward the use of the antimonopoly agency (though with the same caveats noted above): an antimonopoly authority may be less inclined to micro-manage the evolution of the infrastructure sectors of the economy.

Changes in Industry Demand

If the transformations of the post-socialist economies are to be successful, changes at the micro level will be as sweeping and dramatic as changes at the macro level. New plants and shops will be built. Old plants and shops will go out of business or will change their input requirements. Managers, old or new, will require a new dimension of service flexibility as they seek to satisfy customers rather than the requirements of a long-term plan. The success of all of this will depend in part upon the owners and managers of infrastructure industries facing the correct incentives to provide these new services and new packages of services.

What kinds of regulatory structures will be most effective at providing these incentives? Clearly this is another example, like that of the previous section, where the incentive properties of incentive mechanisms—the fact that firms and managers are rewarded directly, monetarily, for performing in a socially beneficial way—seem well suited to solving the problem at hand. (Cost-of-service regulation, and to a lesser extent dominant-firm scrutiny by antimonopoly authorities, could discourage such innovative behavior by seeking to remove any "excess" profits received.) But what about cases in which incentive regulation will not work? Is there a way to use the incentive properties of such regulation without requiring overall government commitments that cannot be made credible?

The answer is yes. The solution—not applicable in all settings, but promising in some—is first, to require the regulated firms to maintain their current service offerings, presumably under continuing regulation, while second, allowing the regulated firms to contract with customers to provide new services at mutually agreed upon, unregulated prices and terms. The first half of this proposal ensures that existing customers continue to be protected from monopolistic abuses by the regulated firm, while the second provides the regulated firm with the profit incentive to offer new services and attract new customers as the economic transformation progresses.

How might this work in practice? Consider the three industry settings discussed in the first section of this paper.

- Owners of electrical transmission lines would continue to face regulation in their service to locations without competing sources of generation and/or transmission (or without enough competing sources that rate deregulation would be in order). They would be required to continue to offer the same level of service—perhaps an increasing level as population and the economy grow—under rates and terms regulated by an electricity regulating authority or—less likely in this complex sector—the antimonopoly authority. However, subject to their satisfying these requirements, they would be free to contract to provide new service to new industrial locations or towns that they had not previously sewed, under terms to be mutually agreed upon by customer and supplier and subject only to the regulatory requirement that they not interfere with the duty of the firm to supply its existing customers.[65]

- Owners of oil pipelines would continue to face regulation in their service to locations without competing sources of oil. They would be required to offer the same or an appropriately improving level of service under terms regulated by the appropriate authority. However, subject to their satisfying these requirements, they would be free to contract to provide new service to new industrial locations or towns that they had not previously served, under terms to be mutually agreed upon by customer and supplier and subject only to the regulatory requirement that they not interfere with the duty of the firm to supply its existing customers.

- Owners of railways would continue to face regulation in their service to locations without sufficient competing transport options. They would be required to offer the same or an appropriately improving level of service under terms regulated by the appropriate authority. However, subject to their satisfying these requirements, they would be free to contract to provide new service to new industrial locations or towns that they had not previously served, under terms to be mutually agreed upon by customer and supplier and subject only to the regulatory requirement that they not interfere with the duty of the firm to supply its existing customers.

Note that in all three of these situations the provision of service to new customers may require major capital expenditures. This proposal would require that such expenditures be accounted for separately from the capital and improvements serving the "core" customers, so as to avoid artificially inflating the rate base under rate regulation.[66] For that matter, by allowing firms to offer services in both regulated and unregulated markets, this proposal raises the problems of potential cross-subsidization discussed above. As noted in that section, it will not do to be doctrinaire in seeking to prevent or eliminate all such potential problem situations; circumstances in which the regulated service and the unregulated service are the same service (but in different locations) seem especially likely to be those circumstances where the economies of joint service provision will outweigh the costs of possible regulatory evasion. The policy described here would in many cases provide the correct incentives for important new capital expenditures to be made, and could, thus, make an important contribution to the economic transformation and development of the post-socialist countries.

Conclusion

Privatization can be an important component of the restructuring and modernization of the public utility sectors in post-socialist countries. In order that the forces of competition may work in as powerful a way as possible in furthering the economic transformation, government policy-makers should set up economic regulatory schemes in only those industries where competition clearly cannot work: those industries that both have the production structure of a natural monopoly and do not face significant competition from other producers or industries. Policy-makers can protect against the inefficient, anticompetitive, and unfair use of the regulatory process to subsidize unregulated operations by requiring that regulated firms sell off unregulated operations in those instances where this would not entail a huge sacrifice of scale or scope economies. In those sectors where regulation is necessary, the use of the existing antimonopoly authority as regulator may in some situations have advantages over the creation of a new regulatory authority, especially where regulation is likely to be necessary only temporarily. Where formal regulatory mechanisms are created, the new incentive schemes are preferable if international agencies can make the government commitment to price paths credible. If the commitment problem cannot be overcome, cost-of-service regulation may be preferable. However, even in these cases, regulated firms can be provided with the proper incentives to provide important new services by deregulating such services, subject to the firm's continuing to satisfy its "core" responsibilities.

Notes

1. This chapter was published in *Economics of Transition*, Volume 2(3), 1994, and is reprinted here by Permission of Oxford University Press.

2. The authors are grateful for helpful comments from Cindy Alexander, Timothy J. Brennan, Paul T. Denis, Michael Einhorn, Mary E. Fitzpatrick, Clive Gray, Gary Hewitt, Richard P. O'Neill, Robert D. Willig, and two anonymous referees. The views expressed are those of the authors and do not necessarily represent the views of the Department of Justice.

3. This is especially true in telecommunications where, for political reasons, socialist governments tried to restrict the public's access to the means of production and dissemination of information.

4. See, e.g., Hawk (1985:565-658).

5. "The communist systems preferred to keep the prices of these services at artificially low levels....The governments concerned must spare no time to readjust the price scales" (Vissi 1992b:3). Evidence that prices in infrastructure industries have been too low is abundant. In Slovakia, the authorities

considered shutting down the railroad at the end of 1993 because of a lack of funds (August 5, 1993). At this same time, prices for electricity were to rise 48 per cent as a step toward liberalization; natural gas prices were to rise 25 per cent (October 20, and December 30, 1993, respectively). In Hungary, passenger train fares covered about one-third of costs (August 26, 1993). In Poland, passenger train fares covered 20 per cent of the costs for local and suburban trips and 70 per cent of the costs for longer trips (January 17, 1994). In early 1992, prices for natural gas, electricity, and heating rose 70 per cent in Poland. Some prices have had to rise even further since then (January 8, 1992). In the Czech Republic, electricity prices were to rise 35 per cent to "further approach the levels of expenditures" (Oct. 18, 1993). And in Bulgaria, heating prices covered only one-half of costs, while rail fares covered about one-third of costs (November 11, 1993, and February 15, 1994, respectively). All information can be found in *Reuter Textline* on the date in parentheses.

6. "By the early 1990s, the backwardness of the infrastructure in most public service sectors had become a major obstacle to the development of the economy in general...Catching these services up will require sizeable investments." (Vissi 1992b:2). *The Washington Post* describes the situation in the former East Germany: "The infrastructure demands are staggering...Three-quarters of the east's highway system was built before 1950; half its...coal-fired power plants need refurbishing; most canals are too narrow and shallow for modem European barges, and a majority of locks are at least 80 years old; railways and bridges need wholesale renovation" ("E. Germans Update the Party Line: Fixing the Phone System A Slow, Massive Task," August 18, 1993, p.A23). *The Financial Times* reports that "Western Europe has an average of 43 telephone lines per 100 people. In Eastern Europe, only the Baltic states and Bulgaria have more than 20, while most of the region has between 10 and 15" ("The West rings the changes in Eastern Europe," October 1, 1993, p. 21).

7. Alois Ruta from the communications and safety division of the Czech railway admits that the large sections of unusable railway track are the fault of 40 years of neglect. Maintenance equipment built in the 1930s is common, and there is some equipment in place from 1897 (April 20, 1993). Janos Csaradi, managing director of the Hungarian railway, says that 1993 was the first year in fifteen that important investments were made in the Hungarian railways (January, 8, 1994). Polish authorities anticipate that they will need between $800 million and $1 billion investment per year for eight years in order to modernize and develop the country's telecommunications sector (December 17, 1993). All information can be found in *Reuter Textline* on the date in parentheses.

8. Polish authorities hope to increase telecommunications service from the current ratio of 9 lines per 100 citizens to 30-35 per 100 citizens by the year 2000. The Czechs hope to increase that ratio from 17 per 100 in 1994 to 36 per 100 in 2000 (*Reuters Textline*, Nov. 15, 1993). See also Šip (1992).

9. Evidence of this can be found in Bulgaria, where electricity sector losses for 1993 were $96 million according to the accounts of the National Electricity Company and $197 million according to international accounting standards as estimated by Arthur Anderson (*Reuters Textline*, January 20, 1994).

10. For a brief summary, see "Property Laws in Central and Eastern Europe," *Central European Business Weekly*, March 4-10, 1994; for a more thorough survey, see Gray (1993). Rental rates in Bratislava, Slovakia are as high as they are in Washington, D.C. This is in part due to uncertainty regarding a landlord's freedom to charge a rate he or she pleases. Potential investors in housing are justifiably concerned that they will not be allowed to receive a sufficient return on their investment and are therefore hesitant to increase the supply of housing.

11. For an excellent discussion, see Spiller (1993).

12. Vickers and Yarrow (1988:40).

13. Kay and Thompson (1986:25).

14. "The important difference between public and private ownership, in our view, involves the residual rights of intervention. Under public enterprise, the government retains some authority to intervene directly in the delegated production arrangements and implement major policy changes when it is deemed necessary to do so. Under private ownership, special rights of intervention are afforded creditors (in the event of bankruptcy) and major financial interests (who can gather the resources necessary to finance a takeover of the private firm); but the government's right to intervene is more limited than under public ownership" (Sappington and Stiglitz 1987:568). Boyko, Shleifer, and Vishny (1992, 1993) make essentially the same argument, while Shapiro and Willig (1990) base this difference in the costs of government intervention on "an informational barrier between...the regulator and the owners and managers of the enterprise."

15. See, for example, "Hungarian Utility Expects Losses," *Central European Business Weekly*, August 27-September 2, 1993: "MVM cannot currently raise the price of district heating energy due to government limitations. And with elections next spring, a hard-pressed government is unlikely to allow any increases in domestic heating [prices] during the next six months."

16. Wiseman (1991); Shleifer and Vishny (1992).

17. Indeed, Robinson (1992a) argues that "the main argument for privatization is that it provides the quickest and most effective means of liberalization in many markets."

18. See also George (1991). Bös (1993) is less optimistic: "A priori it is not clear why the state, failing to run the firms as owner, should now suddenly have become an efficient regulator."

19. See, e.g., Bolton and Roland (1992); Kornai (1992); Tenenbaum, Lock, and Barker (1992); Hussain and Stern (1993); Newbery (1993); and "Tax Evasion: An Auditor's Nightmare," *Warsaw Voice*, Financial Voice, December 1992, p. 1.

20. See, for example, Hare (1991); Heald (1992).

21. This has become a commonplace observation in the post-socialist countries. The *Warsaw Voice* quotes a private consultant on telecommunications to the Polish Ministry of Ownership Change: "The industry does not have the money for either research or to buy new technology, which means it needs foreign capital to modernize" ("Poland's Telephone Network: Uncrossing the Wires," March 7, 1993, p. B8). Similarly, "what is needed to modernize Eastern Europe's power plants is money...The former Eastern Bloc countries simply do

not have the money. Assistance from the West is needed, not only financially but also technically" ("Nuclear Energy in Eastern Europe: Poison Power?" *Warsaw Voice*, March 7, 1993, p. B4). "The question for managers of water supply and sewage installation companies is where to find the money to improve water systems. Polish water users are reluctant to foot the bill, while municipal and state coffers are nearly empty" ("Water in Poland: Crystal Clear Crisis," *Warsaw Voice*, January 31, 1993, pp. 12-13).

22. The British "golden share" and the French "hard core" have both served especially to prevent the purchase of a controlling interest in the privatized firm by a party unacceptable to the government. See Graham and Prosser (1991:138-174).

23. See also "Foreigners may buy Hungarian power," *Financial Times*, February 24, 1994, p. 17, and "Hungary awards phone contracts," *Financial Times*, March 1, 1994, p. 4; "Gas companies now ready to join privatization queue," *Central European Business Weekly*, April 15-21, 1994, p .7.

24. Hungarian Governmental Decree 126.1992 [August 28], "Decree on the Enterprises Remaining Partly or Completely in the Possession of the State on a Long-Term Basis."

25. "Expanding the Telephone Network: Dial C for Chaos." *Warsaw Voice*, April 12, 1992, p. B4.

26. "Two Scandinavian utilities give backing for Polish power station," *Financial Times*, March 9, 1993, p. 5.

27. See, e.g., Pint (1991); Zank (1991); Tenenbaum, Lock, and Barker (1992). The latter authors cite a report that the UK's National Power cut staff by 47 percent following privatization.

28. For example, such considerations have led electrical generation in the UK to use both more coal and more nuclear energy than cost minimization would dictate (Robinson 1992:124-128). "Public enterprises are inefficient. They employ too many people, produce goods that consumers do not want, locate in economically inefficient places, do not upgrade their capital stock, and so on. While these problems are particularly severe in Eastern Europe, public enterprises throughout the world are conspicuous for their inefficiency, as well. This observation is no longer controversial" (Boyko, Shleifer, and Vishny, 1993:141-142).

29. "Prelude to Privatization: New Legal Status for LOT." *Warsaw Voice*, January 17, 1993, p. B1. Skeptics might note that this reduction in employment has occurred simultaneously with the spin-off from LOT of some "peripheral" businesses. One may answer that: (1) such concentration on core businesses likely represents an efficiency gain in itself; and (2) in any case LOT is in the process of reducing employment still further through the introduction of operating efficiencies.

30. *Ibid.*

31. Of course, this is an idea most closely associated with Joseph Schumpeter, especially Schumpeter (1942).

32. "In recent decades, many economists have returned to the Schumpeterian view that the advantage of the market economy (relative to its alternatives) lies more in its facilitation of innovative activity than in its

allocative efficiency. The system of central planning is surely deficient in both respects, but its shortcomings seem to be much greater in the area of innovation than in allocative efficiency...Innovative activity usually carries a high risk of failure, and bureaucracies normally are incapable of providing the high-powered incentives...that induce some people to become entrepreneurs in market economies" (Clague 1992:3).

33. "Public enterprises have a comparative advantage relative to private enterprises in regulatory capture, in which the industry captures those parts of the legislative process that can protect it against competition" (Newbery 1992 :18).

34. Sappington and Stiglitz (1987:579-580); Bös (1991:192-193); Hussain and Stern (1993:66).

35. For a discussion in the context of developing economies, see Bradburd (1992). For a more general discussion of the costs of regulation, see Coase (1960, 1989a).

36. This consideration will play an important role in the decision about the form privatization should take—that is, whether to privatize the enterprise in parts or as a whole.

37. Robinson (1992a:8, 1992b:118-124).

38. These are the rates that the producer of energy charges the retail distributor.

39. Tenenbaum, Lock, and Barker (1992:1139); Bös (1993:8, 14); and Hammond (1992).

40. U.S. Department of Justice (1986); Untiet (1987).

41. See, for example, Keeler (1983), or Caves, *et al.* (1985). John Stuart Mill reached the same conclusion nearly 150 years ago: "In the case of railways...no one can desire to see the enormous waste of capital and land (not to speak of increased nuisance) involved in the construction of a second railway to connect the same places already united by an existing one" (Mill, 1848, Vol. 2:142).

42. Friedlaender and Spady (1981); Pittman (1990); Winston, et al. (1990); Ordover and Pittman (1994). Irwin (1992) conjectures that the telecommunications sector may be an example of this phenomenon at some point in the future: How long will the premise of price cap regulation remain valid? If wireless telecom, digital packet switching, fibre optics, satellite relay and a cornucopia of information appliances are on the horizon, then is it possible that scale economies and the concept of franchise exclusivity will be rendered obsolete? Will, in short, price cap regulation be superseded by the open market?

43. It is not a simple matter to ascertain whether such cross-subsidization exists. Another complication ensues when buyers of the regulated service benefit from quality-improving investments made because of competitive conditions in the unregulated service.

44. For an interesting treatment of the trade-off between cross-subsidization and economies of scope, see Brennan and Palmer (1991); see also Brennan (1987, 1990). Special problems ensue if the regulated product is an essential input into the unregulated product (discrimination) or if the unregulated product is an input into the regulated product (inflated pricing). An example of potential

discrimination especially dangerous in a transforming economy would be the refusal of the firm to sell the regulated product to its rivals in the unregulated market. See Pittman (1992:497-498).

45. Stigler (1971), Posner (1974), Peltzman (1976). A useful review of recent developments in this literature is provided by Noll (1991).

46. Tirole (1991:240). One example of the problem is complaints that advisors to the Czech Ministry of Privatization will be able to use confidential information for their personal gain (Tereza Nemessanyi, "Privatization's Loopholes May Allow Future Abuses," *Prague Post*, August 25-31, 1992).

47. An ironic related development: electricity privatization in the former German Democratic Republic resulted in the ownership integration of previously separate enterprises for power generation and power distribution (Bös 1991:185).

48. See, for example, Fox and Ordover (1992), Pittman (1992), and Slay (1994).

49. There is a broad literature comparing cost-of-service with incentive regulation. Recent examples include Brennan (1989), Schmalensee (1989), Brown, *et al.* (1991), Pint (1992), and Liston (1993). Tirole (1991) makes the comparison in the context of Central and Eastern Europe. One advantage of incentive regulation not discussed in the current paper is that it is designed to reduce or eliminate the incentive for the regulated firm to engage in cross-subsidization (Brown *et al.* 1991:331); one disadvantage is that it creates an incentive for the regulated firm to reduce service quality (Brown, *et al.* 1991:332).

50. See generally Kahn (1971).

51. See, for example, Beesley and Littlechild (1989); Schmalensee (1989).

52. Poland, Antimonopoly Office (1992a).

53. Hungarian Office of Economic Competition, case Vj-74/1991/17, National Sports Swimming Pool v. Budapest Swimming Pools Management. See also Vissi (1992a:70). More recently, the Polish Antimonopoly Office limited the percentage price increase planned by the Polish Telecommunications Company ("Telephone Rate Hikes on Hold," *Central European Business Weekly*, August 13-19, 1993).

54. Lewis and Sappington (1989), Sibley (1989), and Brown *et al.* (1991).

55. Price stability is particularly important with incentive regulation: "Without uncertainty, price caps are generally optimal; with uncertainty they almost never are" (Schmalensee 1989:418).

56. Levy and Spiller (1993), Spiller (1993).

57. "The failure to recapture efficiency gains for consumers can seriously reduce the desirability of an incentive mechanism" (Brown *et al.* 1991:328).

58. Obviously, other types of conduct by dominant firms, e.g., exclusionary practices, fall readily within the purview of antitrust authorities and are not discussed here.

59. Fornalczyk (1991:8).

60. Hungary, Economic Competition Office (1992a), § 15.

61. Nor should the general prejudice against setting up a new government regulatory body at a time of overall deregulatory transformation be ignored. "The public is highly suspicious about the newly established authorities. For

obvious reasons, the first impression tends to be 'uh, another bureaucratic body'" (Vissi 1992a:11).

62. Stigler (1975:166).

63. It should be recalled that in the United States the Federal Communications Commission resisted the opening of telecommunications to competitive forces from new entry, while the Department of Justice was taking steps to ensure that competition prevailed.

64. Levy and Spiller (1993) offer an extensive and valuable discussion of this broad issue.

65. Tenenbaum, Lock, and Barker discuss a similar proposal (1992:1141).

66. Under some circumstances it would increase the importance of the monitoring of product quality by a regulatory body. This proposal may give some firms an incentive to degrade product quality on their existing regulated service and offer a high quality substitute unregulated service at a higher price.

References

Baron, D.P. 1991. "Information, Incentives, and Commitment in Regulatory Mechanisms: Regulatory Innovation in Telecommunications," in Einhorn, M., ed., *Price Caps and Incentive Regulation in Telecommunications*. Boston: Kluwer Academic Publishers.

Beesley, M.E., and S.C. Littlechild. 1989. "The Regulation of Privatized Monopolies in the United Kingdom." *RAND Journal of Economics* 20: 454-472.

Bolton, P., and G. Roland. 1992. "Privatization policies in Central and Eastern Europe." *Economic Policy* 15: 275-309.

Bös, D. 1993. "Privatization in Europe: A Comparison of Approaches." *Oxford Review of Economic Policy* 9, forthcoming.

_____. 1991. "Privatization and the Transition from Planned to Market Economies: Some Thoughts About Germany 1991." *Annals of Public and Cooperative Economics* 62: 183-194.

Boycko, M., A. Shleifer, and R.W. Vishny. 1993. "Privatizing Russia." *Brookings Papers on Economic Activity* 2: 139-192.

_____. 1992. "Property Rights, Soft Budget Constraints, and Privatization." Unpublished paper, Harvard University and University of Chicago.

Bradburd, R. 1992. "Privatization of Natural Monopoly Public Enterprises: The Regulation Issue." World Bank, Country Economics Department, Policy Research Working Papers, WPS 864 (revised).

Brennan, T.J. 1990. "Cross-Subsidization and Discrimination by Regulated Monopolists." *Journal of Regulatory Economics* 2: 37-51.

_____. 1989. "Regulating by Capping Prices." *Journal of Regulatory Economics* 1: 133-148.

_____. 1987. "Regulated Firms in Unregulated Markets: Understanding the Divestiture in U.S. v. AT&T." *Antitrust Bulletin.* 32: 749-793.

Brennan, T.J., and K. Palmer. 1991. "Comparing the Costs and Benefits of Diversification by Regulated Firms." Presented at Telecommunications Policy Research Conference, Solomons Island, MD.

Brown, L., M. Einhorn, and I. Vogelsang. 1991. "Toward Improved and Practical Incentive Regulation." *Journal of Regulatory Economics* 3: 323-338.

Caves, D.W., L.R. Christensen, M.W. Tretheway, and R.J. Windle. 1985. "Network Effects and the Measurement of Returns to Scale and Density for U.S. Railroads," in A.F. Daughety, ed., *Analytical Studies in Transport Economics.* New York: Cambridge University Press.

Clague, C. 1992. "Introduction: The Journey to a Market Economy," in Clague, C. and G.C. Rausser, eds., *The Emergence of Market Economies in Eastern Europe.* Cambridge, Mass.: Blackwell.

Coase, R.H. 1989a. *The Firm, the Market, and the Law.* Chicago: University of Chicago Press.

_____. 1989b. "Notes on the Problem of Social Cost," in R.H. Coase, *The Firm, the Market, and the Law.*

_____. 1960. "The Problem of Social Cost." *Journal of Law and Economics* 3: 1-44.

Einhorn, M.A. 1991. *Price Caps and Incentive Regulation in Telecommunications.* Boston: Kluwer Academic Publishers.

Fox, E.M., and J.A. Ordover. 1992. "Free Enterprise and Competition Policy for Central and Eastern Europe and the Soviet Union," in Rayner, S.A., ed., *Privatization in Central and Eastern Europe.* London: Butterworths.

Friedlaender, A.F., and R.H. Spady. 1981. *Freight Transport Regulation: Equity, Efficiency, and Competition in the Rail and Trucking Industries.* Cambridge, Mass.: MIT Press.

George, K. 1991. "Public Ownership versus Privatization," in de Wolf, P., ed., *Competition in Europe: Essays in Honor of Henk W. de Jong.* Boston: Kluwer.

Graham, C., and T. Prosser. 1991. *Privatizing Public Enterprises: Constitutions, the State, and Regulation in Comparative Perspective.* Oxford: Clarendon Press.

Gray, C. 1993. "Evolving Legal Frameworks for Private Sector Development in Central and Eastern Europe." World Bank Discussion Paper #209.

Hammond, C.J. 1992. "Privatization and the Efficiency of Decentralised Electricity Generation: Some Evidence from Inter-War Britain." *Economic Journal* 102: 538-553.

Hare, P.G. 1991. "Privatization in Eastern Europe: Some Theoretical Issues." Unpublished paper, Centre for Economic Reform and Transformation, Heriot-Watt University.

Hawk, B.E. 1985. *United States, Common Market, and International Antitrust: A Comparative Guide.* 2nd ed. New York: Harcourt.

Heald, D. 1992. "How Much Privatization Should There Be in Developing Countries?" *Annals of Public and Cooperative Economics* 63: 229-269.

Hungary, Economic Competition Office. 1992a. *Report to Parliament on the Activities of the Economic Competition Office in 1991 and the Experiences of the Office in Implementing the Law on Competition.* Budapest.

_____. 1992b. *Experience on Law Application of Business Competition Supervisory Procedures in 1991.* Budapest.

Hussain, A., and N. Stern. 1993. "The Role of the State, Ownership and Taxation in Transitional Economies." *Economics of Transition* 1: 61-87.

Irwin, M.R. 1992. "Review of Einhorn (1991)." *Review of Industrial Organization* 7: 255-257.

Kahn, A.E. 1971. *The Economics of Regulation: Principles and Institutions.* New York: Wiley.

Kay, J.A., and D.J. Thompson. 1986. "Privatization: A Policy in Search Of a Rationale." *Economic Journal* 96: 18-32.

Keeler, T.E. 1983. *Railroads, Freight, and Public Policy.* Washington, DC: Brookings Institution, Studies in the Regulation of Economic Activity.

Kornai, J. 1992. "The Postsocialist Transition and the State: Reflections in the Light of Hungarian Fiscal Problems." *American Economic Review* 82: 1-21.

Levy, B., and P.T. Spiller. 1993. "Regulation, Institutions, and Commitment in Telecommunications: A Comparative Analysis of Five Country Studies." *Proceedings of the World Bank Conference on Development Economics 1993*, pp. 215-252.

Lewis, T.R., and D.E.M. Sappington. 1989. "Regulatory Options and Price-Cap Regulation." *RAND Journal of Economics* 20: 405-416.

Liston, C. 1993. "Price-Cap versus Rate-of-Return Regulation." *Journal of Regulatory Economics* 5: 25-48.

Mill, J.S. 1848 (reprinted 1965). *Principles of Political Economy with Some of their Application to Social Philosophy.* Toronto.

Newbery, D.M. 1993. "Tax and Expenditure Policies in Hungary." *Economics of Transition* 2: 245-272.

_____. 1992. "The Role of Public Enterprises in the National Economy." Cambridge, England: University of Cambridge, Department of Applied Economics Working Paper No. 9209.

Noll, R.E. 1991. "Economic Perspectives on the Politics of Regulation," in Schmalensee, R., and R. Willig, *Handbook of Industrial Organization.* North Holland.

O'Neill, R.P., and A. Brown. 1992. "Privatization and Regulation of the Oil, Natural Gas, and Electric Industries of Hungary." *Energy Law Journal* 13: 25-43.

Ordover, J., and R. Pittman. 1994. "Restructuring the Railway for Competition." Presented at OECD/World Bank Conference on Competition and Regulation in Network Infrastructure Industries, Budapest, June 1994. (Previous versions issued as Discussion Paper 93-10, U.S. Department of Justice, Antitrust Division, Economic Analysis Group, and published in *Przegląd Organizacji* (Warsaw), January 1994.

Ott, A.F., and K. Hartley. 1991. *Privatization and Economic Efficiency: A Comparative Analysis of Developed and Developing Countries.* Aldershot: Edward Elgar.

Peltzman, S. 1976. "Toward a More General Theory of Regulation." *Journal of Law and Economics* 19: 211-240.

Pint, E.M. 1992. "Price-Cap versus Rate-of-Return Regulation in a Stochastic-Cost Model." *RAND Journal of Economics* 23: 564-578.

_____. 1991. "Nationalization vs. Regulation of Monopolies: The Effects of Ownership on Efficiency." *Journal of Public Economics* 44: 131-164.

Pittman, R. 1992. "Some Critical Provisions in the Antimonopoly Laws of Central and Eastern Europe." *International Lawyer* 26: 485-503. Reprinted (in Czech) in *Narodni Hospodarstvi*, August 1992, and (in Russian) in *USA: Economics, Politics, Ideology*, August 1992.

_____. 1990. "Railroads and Competition: The Santa Fe/Southern Pacific Merger Proposal." *Journal of Industrial Economics* 39: 25-46.

Poland, Antimonopoly Office. 1992. *Press Conference of the President of the Antimonopoly Office*. Warsaw, February 24, 1992.

Posner, R. 1974. "Theories of Economic Regulation." *Bell Journal of Economics* 5: 335-358.

Rayner, S.A., ed. 1992. *Privatization in Central and Eastern Europe*. London: Butterworths.

Robinson, C. 1992a. "The Results of UK Electricity Privatization." unpublished paper, University of Surrey.

_____. 1992b. "Privatizing the British Energy Industries: The Lessons to Be Learned." *Metroeconomica* 43: 103-129.

Sappington, D.E.M., and J.E. Stiglitz. 1987. "Privatization, Information and Incentives." *Journal of Policy Analysis and Management* 6: 567-582.

Schmalensee, R. 1989. "Good Regulatory Regimes." *RAND Journal of Economics* 20: 417-436.

Schumpeter, J.A. 1942. *Capitalism, Socialism and Democracy*. New York: Harper.

Shapiro, C., and R.D. Willig. 1990. "Economic Rationales for the Scope of Privatization," in Saleiman, E. and J. Waterbury, eds., *The Political Economy of Public Sector Reform and Privatization*. Boulder: Westview Press.

Shleifer, A., and R.W. Vishny. 1992. "Pervasive Shortages Under Socialism." *RAND Journal of Economics* 23: 237-246.

Sibley, D. 1989. "Asymmetric Information, Incentives and Price-Cap Regulation." *RAND Journal of Economics* 20: 392-404.

Šip, E. 1992. "Evaporation of Natural Monopoly: Another Idea for East Europe Telecommunications?" Presented at conference, Financing and Investments for Telecommunications Development in Central and Eastern Europe, Budapest, October 1992.

Slay, B. 1994. "Industrial Demonopolization and Competition Policy in Poland and Hungary." Presented at meetings of Eastern Economics Association, Boston, March 1994.

Spiller, P. 1993. "Institutions and Regulatory Commitment in Utilities' Privatization." *Industrial and Corporate Change* 2: 387-450.

Stigler, G.J. 1975. *The Citizen and The State: Essays on Regulation*. Chicago: University of Chicago Press.

_____. 1971. "The Theory of Economic Regulation." *Bell Journal of Economics* 2: 3-21.

Tenenbaum, B., R. Lock, and J. Barker. 1992. "Electricity Privatization: Structural, Competitive and Regulatory Options." *Energy Policy* pp. 1134-1160.

Tirole, J. 1991. "Privatization in Eastern Europe: Incentives and the Economics of Transition," in: Blanchard, O. and S. Fischer, eds., *The NBER Macroeconomics Annual 1991*. Cambridge: MIT Press and National Bureau of Economic Research.

U.S. Department of Justice. 1986. *Oil Pipeline Deregulation*. Washington DC: Government Printing Office.

Untiet, C. 1987. "The Economics of Oil Pipeline Deregulation: A Review and Extension of the DOJ Report." U.S. Department of Justice, Economic Analysis Group Discussion Paper 87-3, May 22.

Vickers, J. and G. Yarrow. 1991. "Economic Perspectives on Privatization." *Journal of Economic Perspectives* 5: 111-132.

_____. 1988. *Privatization: An Economic Analysis*. Cambridge, Mass.: MIT Press.

Vissi, F. 1992a. "The Role of Anti-trust in Hungary," in S.A. Rayner, ed., *Privatisation in Central and Eastern Europe*. Pp. 112-122. London: Butterworths.

_____. 1992b. "The Peculiarities of Regulating the Monopolies in the Economies in Transition in General, and in Hungary in Particular." Remarks at World Bank Conference on Natural Monopolies in Eastern Europe, Vienna.

Winston, C., T.M. Corsi, C.M. Grimm, and C.A. Evans. 1990. *The Economic Effects of Surface Freight Deregulation*. Washington DC: Brookings Institution.

Wiseman, J. 1991. "Privatization in the Command Economy," in Ott, A.F., and K. Hartley, *Privatization and Economic Efficiency: A Comparative Analysis of Developed and Developing Countries*. Aldershot: Edward Elgar.

Zank, N.S. 1991. "Perspectives on Privatization in LDCs: Encouraging Economic Growth and Efficiency," in Ott, A.F., and K. Hartley, *Privatization and Economic Efficiency: A Comparative Analysis of Developed and Developing Countries*. Aldershot: Edward Elgar.

7

Natural Monopoly Regulation: A Comparison of Hungarian and Russian Telecommunications

Erik Whitlock

Introduction

This chapter presents an overview of Hungarian and Russian telecommunications policy as a case study in natural monopoly regulation in transitional economies. As discussed in Chapter 6, industries that are recognized as natural monopolies will be subject to a much different policy regime than other monopolies during the transition to a market economy. But what constitutes the best policy approach is far from unambiguous. Answers to questions of which industries and services constitute natural monopolies in practice and what particular forms of regulation will be required during and after the completion of the transition are diverse, particularly in telecommunications services.

The characteristics of telecommunications service in transitional economies pose a number of special challenges for regulatory policy. As with other infrastructure sectors of Eastern Europe, telecommunications are seriously underdeveloped given the levels and types of demands that now exist or can be expected as the economies grow and return to conditions of full employment. Indicative are the low telephone densities which, at the beginning of the 1990s, ranged from about 10 (Poland) to 25 (Bulgaria) phones per hundred inhabitants, as well as the forty-year lag found in most of the existing exchange and transmission technologies. Inefficiencies, as evinced *inter alia* by excessive staffing, are another handicap common to the region's infrastructure services.

In the area of finance and investment, we find that, although public telecommunications service as a whole is profit-making in the region, cross subsidization across services is widespread. These cross-subsidies are often economically unjustified, a legacy of pricing based on political objectives. Costs associated with the provision of local services greatly exceed their revenues, requiring the maintenance of very high tariffs for long distance services. Prices for business access in some cases completely cover the cost of installing lines, while new residential subscribers pay a paltry sum for network access. Moreover, despite an available supply of domestic and foreign funds for the development of certain telecom services, the needs are tremendous. Consultants to the European Bank for Reconstruction and Development (EBRD) estimated in 1993 that Russia, for example, would need to invest $65 billion to achieve a telephone density equal to that of the OECD countries. New regulatory tools and ownership reform must be designed to maintain pre-existing incentives for investment while encouraging a level of investment dramatically higher than in the past and directed at all parts of the telecom system.

Finally, the formulation of regulatory policy must be carried out in a dynamic, if not chaotic, legal and political environment. Most of these countries had to begin the task of regulating service providers without relevant sector-specific legislation, and general legislation concerning basic structural questions of each industry (e.g., privatization, taxation, etc.) has been in a constant state of change. Inadequate and unstable legislation is only one by-product of the political transition occurring in these countries. The inherent uncertainty involved in the process has prevented the development of a framework for reasonable regulatory policy.

This chapter begins with an examination of how the telecommunications service industry was managed before the transition began. It describes a generalized set of institutional characteristics of the industry in the region. Although the assumption that the previous economic regimes can be described by a single set of institutional arrangements obscures important differences in their structure and performance, the commonalities are sufficient to make developing and applying a single model unavoidable.

Those who are familiar with how these economies operated will find much similarity between planners' organizational approach to telecommunications services and other sectors. This should not be too surprising as the essence of central planning—supplanting competitive market mechanisms with administrative institutions, replacing consumer sovereignty with planners' preferences, and marginalizing the role of prices—requires organizational uniformity across sectors. Subtlety or variation in monitoring or control across sectors would have imposed extra costs on central planners whose informational and administrative resources were scarce enough given the scale of their task.

Some of the countries of the region began significant economic reforms before the revolutionary developments of the late 1980s. These reforms generally incorporated attempts at shifting towards indirect forms of regulating enterprise activity (e.g., through taxes and subsidies), the introduction of profit-related incentive schemes for management, and the liberalization of prices. As a result of such reforms, Hungary and Poland were increasingly classified in the economic literature as "modified" centrally-planned economies. Telecommunications were largely unaffected by these reforms, however. In Hungary, for example, as opposed to agriculture, light industry, and trade, in which liberalization policies were carried furthest, telecommunications remained under firm central control. For these reasons, the provision of telecommunications service until the late 1980s, even in these more reform-oriented countries, can be captured in a single organizational model of its core elements—relations between the enterprise and the state, network planning, and price setting.

The subsequent sections of the chapter focus on the two very different paths Hungary and Russia have taken to restructuring telecommunications service provision. To be sure, policy makers in both countries are sensitive to the special problems of the sector, and favor a higher degree of government activism than would be considered appropriate in most economies with mature telecommunications networks. The opinion that the state should play a regulatory role that goes beyond preventing abuse of monopoly power and deciding which markets should be open to competitive entry is commonly shared, for example, among policy-makers in these countries. The Hungarian and Russian approaches also share the inclination to maintain a mixture public and private ownership in the sector. However, concerning the central issues of the role of the state in network development, the use of licensing, and approach to tariff and interconnection regulation, the Hungarian and Russian experiences have been very different.

Telecommunications Under Central Planning

In the centrally-planned economy (CPE), public telecommunications service was managed through a monopoly enterprise and developed at the discretion of national political entities. This general attribute was, of course, not unique to the CPE case, as most states of the world have at one time or another chosen to regulate the service through various forms of public ownership and management. It is the instruments and the extent of state intervention that distinguish the public authority-operator relationship in the CPE from other economies. In particular, we may list the following specific characteristics of telecommunications provision in CPEs:

- the functions of service provision and regulation are dispersed across many state bureaucracies;
- a simplified and inertial price structure that plays a passive role in service development and rationing demand; and
- the determination of the size and structure of investment is beyond the control of the network operator, and network development is based on non-economic principles.

Indeed, under such circumstances, regulation is not an appropriate word to use to describe the relationship between operator and state. In the traditional CPE, whether we speak of local or long-distance operators, we find entities of extraordinarily limited autonomy. The operator's activities were governed by a plan drawn up by the ministry responsible for communications (hereafter MC) on the basis of information provided by the enterprise. Given sector objectives and resource constraints worked out in conjunction with a national planning office, the MC set a list of input and output targets which largely predetermined all financial flows in and out of the operator. The maneuverability the operator acquired by manipulating the flow of information sent to the MC notwithstanding, the constraints placed upon enterprise management were very tight.

In Hungary, after reforms in 1968, the role of the ministry in operating telecommunications service was limited to endorsing overall telecommunications development plans (which were, in turn, submitted to the government for approval), proposing state budget allocations for telecommunications development, drafting laws for the sector, endorsing basic tariff changes, and approving/limiting cross-subsidization among communications services. Yet, although the state no longer intervened directly in production decisions, the financial flows in and out of the firm were highly dependent on government policy, and so reflected political considerations rather than purely economic ones.

Dispersion of Decision-making

The above clearly indicates that governmental organs were directly involved in questions of operator management. The number of organs responsible for supervising the activities of the operator was large, and interactions were complex and unwieldy. In addition to the MC, these organs included the national price office, national planning office, the ministry of finance, the ministry of labor, and others. Interestingly, just as dozens of agencies were making decisions directly concerning the provision of telecommunications services in the country, the enterprise was often burdened with tasks generally associated with state regulatory authorities, such as monitoring and enforcing technical standards.

Moreover, decision-making within the firm was highly dispersed. The Hungarian service provider, Magyar Posta, combined all communications functions into one organization in a standard Post, Telegraph and Telephone profile until 1989; the Russian communications service industry was similarly organized until 1993. This "amalgamation" facilitated cross-subsidization from telecommunications to low-profit postal services, and dissipated management focus and resources.

Before 1985, there were 33 middle-level units directly subordinate to Magyar Posta's head office in Budapest. These units included both regional and functional directorates, and they played the executive role in the implementation of the enterprise's policies and programs. The territorial directorates (comprising only eight out of the 33) were operating divisions providing all communications services (post, telegraph, telephone, and broadcasting) within a specific geographic area. The other 24 directorates were either functional organizations (e.g., the materials office, the reporting and information office, the central periodical office, the central telegraph office, the construction and maintenance divisions, etc.), or directorates that served needs specific to a branch of the PTT (e.g., the radio and television technical directorate, or the long distance telephone directorate). Although this structure was changed somewhat in the mid-1980s to achieve a more divisional structure and thereby sharpen the focus of decision-making and upgrade incentive schemes, residual attributes of the old system rendered the reforms ineffective. A similar set of institutions and maladies could be found in Russia.

Tariff Setting

Pricing played a minor role in resource allocation in the CPE. In contrast to Western experience, where pricing and associated welfare issues lie at the center of much telecommunications policy and analysis,[1] tariff setting was a dead issue in the East. Before the years of significant open inflation in the mid-1980s (Hungary, Poland) and 1990s (the former Soviet Union), nominal tariffs were virtually fixed. In the economic literature of the region during the period of central planning one reads that wholesale and producer goods' prices were to be set on the basis of average costs plus planned profit for any given industry, including telecommunications provision; retail prices included marketing costs and arbitrary turnover taxes. However, the fact that in the Soviet Union, for example, telecommunications tariffs had not been significantly changed for more than thirty years before a price revision in 1991 illustrates that cost had little to do with pricing in practice.

As extreme examples of divergence of costs from prices, we note that, before the revision of 1991, the charge for channel leasing was some five times higher than its cost of operation. The charge for servicing lines on the rural network was one-fourth its cost.[2] An analogous observation can be made for the profitability of each branch of telecommunications. Comparing 1978 and 1989 profitability rates, we find that the profitability (profit to operating cost) of the long-distance networks rose from 33.2 to 60.7 percent, and the urban local networks from 1.3 to 6.52 percent, while the rural networks remained significantly loss-makers at -12 and -7.1 percent.[3] (While Western methodology for allocating costs for these services may differ from the Soviet approach, this does not undermine the basic conclusion.)

As a result of this fixity, in the Soviet case, the level and structure in comparison with purchasing power (measured in Table 7.1 in working hours for a constant mix of telephone usage) steadily dropped. In Hungary, the experience before the mid-1980s was slightly, but not fundamentally, different. Hungarian tariffs did show some movement over time (see Table 7.2). Usage rates doubled between 1978 and 1986. Local rates jumped from 1 forint to 2 forints per three minutes; domestic long distance rates (for three minutes) rose from 4.5 to 9 forints, 9 to 18, and 12 to 24 forints, depending on the distance.[4] However, with regard to other rates, monthly subscription fees and installation fees and revenues per line remained more or less fixed despite rising costs (see Table 7.3) until the second half of the 1980s.

Sharpening budgetary tensions and increasing inflation made more substantial price hikes both necessary and feasible politically. Open inflation occurred in Hungary much earlier than in the former Soviet Union, and large jumps in nominal Hungarian telecom rates occurred already in the 1980s. In order to stem the growth in excess demand and minimize the opposition to tariff hikes, the authorities raised installation fees much more than other tariffs. Connection fees therefore became among the highest in Europe in relative terms. After a fall from 107.16 hours in 1975 to 100.84 hours in 1980 (see Table 7.1), the average state sector employee had to work 116.48 hours in 1986 for a fixed basket of telecommunications services. Still, compared to an aggregate consumer

Table 7.1 Sample Russian and Hungarian Telephone Bills in Equivalent Working Hours,[a] 1970, 1980, 1985, 1990

Year	Russian	Hungarian
1970	106.50	n.a.
1980	76.96	100.84
1985	68.38	116.48[b]
1990	54.00	89.94

[a]Based on officially-reported average wages and the following mix of telephone charges for one year: 700 local calls; 100 long-distance calls at peak traffic time, 100 off-peak; subscriber charge; and the 1/10 payment of the installation fee per year for ten years. (Although the installation fee is in fact a one-time payment, it is assumed here to be paid over time to avoid distorting the index.)
[b]1986 data.

Source: Whitlock 1993.

price index, overall real telephone tariff rates fell throughout the period.[5] Moreover in the latter half of the 1980s the tariffs were falling again in terms of labor-hours. By 1990, the average state sector employee had to work only 84.94 hours to pay for yearly telephone service.

Network Planning

In any telecommunications service, levels of output (e.g., the number of telephone lines, the volume of telephone traffic, and the level of traffic quality) are codetermined by the facilities, location, and overall configuration of the networks making up the telecommunications system. The first step in planning any network can be thought of as determining who is going to be given access to a phone and to the network beyond his local switching facility or exchange. This will govern the customer calling patterns the network must accommodate. It is in this basic consideration, allocation of subscriber access, that telecommunications network design in the CPE differs most significantly from the West.

The network designers used a "normative" method (which contrasts with an approach based on first meeting the demand of those users most willing to pay, or demand estimation based on income distribution) for planning the local network.[6] This method effectively

Table 7.2   Prices for Basic Telecommunications Services[a] in Hungary, 1978-1994

Type of service	1978-81	1981-82	1982-85	1986-88	1989	1990	1991-92	1993	1994
Subscriber charges[b] (forints per month):									
Businesses:									
Main line	40	120	120	120	240	240	420	500	600
Party line	30	80	80	80	220	220	370	440	530
Residential:									
Main line	40	40	40	40	120	120	270	350	420
Party line	30	30	30	30	100	100	240	300	360
Call charges (forints per three minutes):									
Local	1	1.5	1.5	2	2	2	5	5	6
Long distance (peak):									
Within 1 zone	4.5	7.5	7.5	9	9	12	15	15	18
Within 2 zones	9	13.5	13.5	18	18	30	45	45	50
Within 3 zones	12	21	21	24	24	40	60	60	60
Long distance (off peak):									
Within 1 zone	3	4.5	4.5	6	6	6	7.5	7.5	9
Within 2 zones	6	9	9	12	12	18	22.5	22.5	24.3
Within 3 zones	9	13.5	13.5	18	18	24	30	30	30
Connection fee (thousands of forints):									
Business:									
Main line	30	45	45	90	90	90	90	90	90
Party line	20	30	30	60	60	60	60	60	60
Residential:									
Main line	6	6	6	12	12	12	12	12	12
Party line	4	4	4	8	8	8	8	8	8

[a]Switched by automatic exchange.
[b]Includes rental of phone from service provider.
Source: Matáv 1995.

represented a decision rule for rationing. Once actual or offered demand ("absolute demand for services") for the period was estimated, a level of demand that could be met given investment constraints ("relative current demand") for any locality was determined according to "norms of demand satisfaction."

Table 7.3   Revenues and Costs of Existing and New Line Service in Hungary

Time period	Subscriber charges (from Table 7.1)	Line operating costs	Annual connection fee (weighted average)	Cost of installing new line
1976-1980	120/40	136	19,100	65,700
1981-1985	120/40	145	23,100	65,700
1986-1990	120/40	215	72,300	89,900

Source: Whitlock 1993.

The norms of demand satisfaction for the urban network were differentiated by type of residential and business customers.[7] For residential customers, the norm was expressed as the number of phones per 100 apartments, pay phones on the city network, and hotels. For businesses, the norms were defined by the number of phones per 100 employees in business and government organizations. The disaggregated subscriber categories were summed to determine the phone density for the entire locality. Thus, the amount of access to be installed in a planned period t for any given locality could be expressed as:

$$P^t = \sum_{i=1}^{n} w_i R_i^t + \sum_{j=1}^{n} w_j B_j^t$$

where P^t is the number of phones or mainlines planned for period t; w_i is the chosen density (norm of demand satisfaction) for the number of residential customers, R, of type i (e.g., apartments, inhabitants); and w_j is the chosen density of business customers, B, of type j (e.g., employees in industry, government).

As alluded to previously, investment levels in telecommunications in CPEs followed directly from the top political authorities' desired levels of output or service. The top political authorities would thus select the w's that corresponded to their preferences within their investment constraint, determining the number of residential lines, business main lines, connections to office exchanges (PBXs), and pay phone lines for the urban networks. Once these levels and ratios of access were decided upon, the local operator was then relatively free to choose among investment projects[8] to meet the implied traffic patterns. A normative method corresponding to the number of calls that were expected to originate from a given quantity and mix of subscriber types was used to plan the transmission and switching capacity for the urban and rural telephone networks, as well as for accommodating outgoing intra-regional long-distance traffic. In a similar manner, increases in local network access were supposed to translate into increases in capacity for carrying inter-regional traffic.

We, of course, do not exclude the possibility that political authorities used their influence to arrange access for favored groups or individuals beyond this planning methodology described above; nor do we deny that special consideration was given to the military and internal security organizations. The important point here is that network planning was based on demographic (residences and business) attributes of the locality coupled with the preferences of political authorities. Economic considerations were not foremost, if present at all, in the purpose of the planners. This approach can be referred to as the "locality strategy" of network development, since localities or districts were the focus of planning and were expanded individually to meet a chosen level of local aggregate demand.

The Birth of "Regulatable" Entities

Again, it would be improper to refer to telecommunications under centrally planning as a regulated industry, since the state dominated all aspects of service from price setting to investment levels to output choice. Very little decision making was left to service enterprise managers. In 1989-1990 this situation began to change significantly in Eastern Europe and the former Soviet Union. By 1992, the old structure had disappeared, and the state found itself confronting an entirely new set of policy issues in the sector.

The Creation of the Matáv Monopoly

In Hungary by 1988 there was already a broad consensus among telecommunications specialists and policy-makers that telecommunications development had to become a national priority; and simply devoting greater amounts of capital to service expansion coupled with marginal institutional change would not be adequate for a serious modernization effort. What was needed was deeper restructuring and liberalization of the industry. The first major policy moves came in 1990. On January 1, the postal, broadcasting and telecommunications branches of Magyar Posta[9] were separated into independent firms— Magyar Posta Vállalat, Magyar Müsorszóró Vállalat, and Magyar

Távközlés Vállalat, respectively. Assets and staff were divided up, general financial transfers between these divisions ended, and joint services, jointly-run assets, and other transactions were converted to a strictly contractual basis. From here on, we consider only the monopoly services of Magyar Távközlés Vállalat (or Matáv), the telecommunications provider.

As part of the break-up, Matáv was internally reorganized along more commercially-oriented lines. Its divisions numbered eleven, only two of which now were functional departments (the materials supply center and the investment office). The rest were regional telecom directorates or service divisions. Many of the less profitable departments were spun off as limited liability companies over the course of 1990 and 1991. For example, two companies were set up to service PBXs (COMEX in Budapest and CENTROPHONE in Pécs). EMTEL and TELEÉP were made into self-standing construction companies. PLEASE Ltd. and VIDEOTEX Service and Development Ltd. handle the more advanced telecommunications services. All these new separate entities were profitable in their first years of existence.[10]

Hungarian telecommunications now had a more focused entity for its public services. Alongside this important organizational restructuring, Magyar Posta and the Ministry of Transport, Communications, and Water Management (hereafter, MTC) had been formulating a detailed strategy of network development, which called for an enormous increase in the volume of telecommunications services by the year 2000, and a credible accompanying financial plan.

Magyar Posta had presented the MTC with its first proposal for network development already by the end of September 1989. It came in the form of two alternatives, both envisaged achieving a total of 2 to 3 million new phones lines (an increase in the existing number by over 200 percent) and the digitization of most of the public network by the millennium.[11] The MTC then drafted its own document, and in early December 1989 presented the two variants of the network development strategy to the members of the Parliament's Industrial Committee. One variant was based fundamentally on a traditional locality strategy with accelerated development targets.[12] The other strategy involved the construction of an overlay network.

The overlay strategy concentrates resources on building an entirely new digitized backbone network "over" or "around" the existing analog one.[13] Profitability would be greatly increased by expanding the system's capacity to handle a greater volume of higher priced (international and long-distance) traffic. Moreover, in order to ensure the best utilization of this capacity and minimize the problems of interconnection between analog and digitized networks, large-volume customers would be connected or transferred to the digital network first. These large-volume customers are generally those who conduct business with an international community which is already communicating via digitized networks.[14]

According to the original overlay concept outlined in the ten year development plan, local networks were to receive secondary consideration or were to be left to local enterprises to develop. In this manner, the technological leap forward and the massive increase in capacity would be supported by higher profits "up front" and would require less debt financing or state subsidization. The development of local and other less profitable networks would come into focus at a later stage. Ultimately the overlay strategy was, indeed, chosen because it offered a more convincing way of generating adequate reinvestable funds and attracting outside private investment to contribute to the 350-400 billion-forint bill (in 1990 prices) for achieving the millennium goals. The strategy, it was argued, would also introduce new technologies at lower cost over the long run.

When the overall concept was put into concrete development targets, the initial stage (1991-1993) involved expanding domestic and international digital exchange capacity six-fold. This included the completion of a large-capacity digital transit network connecting Budapest and the county seats (19 long-distance exchanges). By the end of 1993 or 1994, the system would link the county-seats and 37 other significant cities. Matáv would increase the number of main lines by some 400,000 lines, expand the mobile telephone network by 13,200 subscribers, and extend telex and data services to 11,800 subscribers.[15]

Table 7.4 gives the main targets and actual achievements for both this three-year period and goals for the longer ten-year time horizon. The initial planned trend in the ratio of business to residential and long-distance to local exchange capacity illustrates the basic thrust of Matáv's original overlay strategy. The growth of the these ratios in the first few years depicts the intended neglect of non-Budapest local networks. To a significant degree, local network expansion was left to the organization and financing of other companies or local communities, through which Matáv hoped to add some 350,000 more lines beyond what its own investment plans contained. Only after the most profitable markets were satisfied, in 1995, would Matáv shift its resources back to the less profitable ones.

Moreover, on the directorate level, under the original plan, installed capacity became positively correlated with economic factors. In particular, as opposed to the earlier period when access (as measured by the density of main lines or phones) development was unrelated to profitability or other economic attributes of the territorial directorates,

Table 7.4   Chief Indicators of the Hungarian 10-year Development Plan, 1990-
2000 (Main line figures in thousands. Targets actually achieved in parentheses.)

Type of service	1990	1991	1992	1993	1995	2000
Main lines	958	1042	1171	1351	1711	2807
	(996)	(1128)	(1291)	(1497)		
Residential	669	720	795	901	1152	2036
	(705)	(818)	(951)	(1135)		
(As percentage of total)	70%	69%	68%	67%	67%	73%
	(71%)	(73%)	(72%)	(76%)		
Business	263	296	348	416	518	705
	(265)	(283)	(311)	(332)		
(As percentage of total)	28%	28%	30%	31%	30%	25%
	(27%)	(25%)	(24%)	(22%)		
Local exchange capacity	1280	1341	1548	1770	2051	3469
	(1266)	(1383)	(1603)	(1970)		
Long dist. exchange capacity	106	106	212	274	332	476
	(n.a.)	(n.a.)	(n.a.)	(n.a.)		
(As percentage of total)	8%	8%	13%	16%	16%	14%
	(n.a.)	(n.a.)	(n.a.)	(n.a.)		
Density						
Main lines/100	9	10	11	13	16	27
	(10)	(11)	(13)	(15)		
Phones/100	17	18	20	22	23	38
	(18)	(19)	(20)	(21)		
Cellular Phones (thousands)	0	1	6.1	14.2	56.1	100
	(n.a.)	(n.a.)	(23)	(46)		
Telefax units (thousands)	2	3	4.2	5.6	9	24
	(n.a.)	(n.a.)	(24)	(19)		

The shares of residential and business main lines do not sum to 100 percent
because of the exclusion of pay phones.

Sources: Based on data in MTC 1990 (Appendix), and Matáv 1994.

the original plans for the 1990s implied that these economic attributes had become relevant. Comparing the number of mainlines existing in each directorate in 1988 to planned capacity in 1993, we find the growth rates by directorate ranged from 159 percent at the BUVI directorate to 215 percent at the Sopron directorate. The ranking closely matches (statistically significant using a Spearman rank coefficient at the .05 significance level) that of the telecom profitability of each directorate found in the late 1980s.[16]

Thus already by the end of 1990, Hungary had developed a self-standing national company for the provision of its basic public telecommunications services. Although the development program outlined above would be modified somewhat in 1991, it remained sensitive to economic considerations, commercially viable, and virtually independent of state financing. The next step to granting Matáv independence was its transformation into a wholly state-owned joint stock company. This occurred on December 31, 1991. The role of state ownership was key to the regulation of the firm and, as is explained below, the Hungarian state chose a cautious approach to altering this role.

The Emergence of Telecom Monopolies in Russia

In Russia, public telecommunications services found little gain in the gradual reforms under perestroika in the second half of 1980s. This was because the Ministry of Communications (MoC) continued to assert administrative control over state telecom firms, and because these firms were structurally not prepared to act in a commercially independent fashion. It was only the advent of more radical legislation, associated the economic program of acting Prime Minister Yegor Gaidar in 1992, that finally brought real change to telecom policy. In contrast with the Hungarian case, in which a certain amount of vision and care to particularities of the sector was displayed, in Russia significant reforms were introduced rapidly and came in the form of general legislation applicable to all state-owned enterprises in the economy, such as decrees on price liberalization, privatization, and antimonopoly policies.

The restructuring "from without," which prevented the articulation of a coherent set of regulatory and developmental policies for the telecom sector, is a legacy from which Russian telecommunications is still suffering. Worse still, this lack of direction in policy-making was compounded by the chaos caused by an economic crisis far more pronounced than in Hungary. The breakdown in supply networks, problems of interenterprise debt, and enormous rates of inflation came to a head during the 1991-1993 period. Thus, Russian telecom enterprises found themselves thrown into a most inauspicious business environment.

As was true in all sectors of the Russian economy, the price liberalization of 1992 was a watershed ridding state telecommunications operators of most of the institutional constraints of the past. In telecommunications, significant nominal increases in tariffs were first observed in 1990, but these changes were centrally determined. In January of 1992, when the prices for most goods and services in Russia were freed, tariffs for public telecommunications services remained under federal control. However, as inflation accelerated and financial crises grew, Minister of Communications Vladimir Bulgak had little choice but to request the government extend fundamental price liberalization to public telecommunications services as well. In April, the Gaidar government issued a decree empowering state telecommunications enterprises to set most of their own tariffs for local and domestic long-distance service. As a result, on 1 June charges soared. The installation fee for a residential line in Moscow, for example, jumped from 300 to 3,000 rubles, while the monthly service charge increased from 14 to 40 rubles. State telecommunications enterprises throughout Russia raised charges to different levels, but all by the same order of magnitude.

The next phase in the emergence of independent telecom monopolies in Russia resulted from presidential decrees concerning privatization in 1991 and 1992. Under these decrees, the MoC was required to produce a plan for modernizing the structure of the service industry and privatizing its enterprises. The MoC's first draft, which was circulated in mid-1992, envisioned a three-year process, in which most of the service enterprises would have been partially privatized, followed by what would have been forced mergers of high- and low-profit enterprises, and finally the dissolution of the enterprises' PTT structure. The program that was eventually published added to the Ministry's control of restructuring[17] by giving it the right to amend this process and even take particular enterprises out of the process if "change in the form of ownership would have a negative impact on the productive-commercial activity and its financial condition."

The strange sequencing of reform (i.e., partial privatization followed by state-implemented restructuring) envisaged in this plan proved to be short-lived. A presidential decree dated November 16, 1992 put the dissolution of the service industry's PTT structure ahead of privatization, so that on January 1, 1993 the postal services were separated from telecommunications. Moreover, the concept of merging the communication enterprises into larger entities disappeared entirely as the privatization program accelerated.

The first stage in restructuring began almost immediately following the issuance of the November decree. The eighty-odd regional enterprises set about separating their postal and telecommunications divisions and drafting privatization plans. All the regional service providers retained the same geographic markets, corresponding to regional political-administrative delineations. These regional operators, except for a handful of city networks, possess a two-level hierarchy of telecommunications networks, the local networks (*mestnye seti*) and the intra-regional networks (*vnutrizonovye seti*).[18] The former inter-regional communications operators under were organized under the umbrella of Intertelecom, later renamed Rostelecom.[19]

By mid-1993, 20 to 30 of these regional operators and Rostelecom had been transformed into 100 percent state-owned joint-stock companies. Privatization also proceeded apace. After an initial distribution of stocks among workers and managers, voucher auctions were held at many of these enterprises (discussed in the subsequent section). Between 10 and 15 regional providers had been restructured and partially privatized by the end of 1993, and the overwhelming majority had been restructured and partially privatized towards the end of 1994.

Tariff liberalization and the partial privatization of the public telecommunications service providers heralded their ability and power to act as rent-maximizing monopolies. By 1994, the MoC was a shadow of its former Soviet self; its role in the day-to-day operation of enterprises had been marginalized. What regulatory authority the ministry still possessed was not clearly formulated in the relevant legislation. Its responsibilities for issuing licenses, developing large-scale investment projects, and representing the state's interest in operators' boardrooms still afforded the Ministry some important influence, but there were bounds to its willingness and capability to wield these tools.

To be sure, the traditional operators face some competition in the areas of international voice and data transmission, as well as domestic cellular services. Indeed, by mid-1994, the MoC counted over 2,200 fully private firms offering various telecommunications services.[20] If one adds to this figure the enterprises subordinated to other ministries and state organizations, then the number approaches 2,500. Still, the newly-restructured partially-privatized enterprises possess virtual monopoly control over public local and domestic long-distance service, and therefore control dominant market shares in traditional telecommunications services. They seem to dispose of some 70-80 percent of the overall channel length of the telecommunications network in Russia, and provide between 85-95 percent of the volume of public telecommunications services.

Finally, with regard to network expansion, there was little in the way of comprehensive investment planning in Russia. Of the total funds invested in the expansion of existing public networks, most has gone to the construction of a cross-country digital network for carrying long-distance and international traffic. This much-touted project includes two lines originating in the West—one, a cable and microwave transmission line leading from Denmark to Sankt Petersburg and Moscow; the other, cable, from Italy across to Turkey and then into Russian territory to Novosibirsk and continuing up to Moscow. From Moscow, a digital microwave system now extends across to Khabarovsk and further as fiber optic cable to Nakhodka, where it continues to points in Korea and Japan.

More than half of the investment that took place in Russian telecommunications during 1993-1994 was in the form of bypass or parallel networks (in particular carrying international and mobile cellular services), according to the MoC. Plans and memoranda of understanding for the second stage of national network development, the so-called 50 by 50 project, have been initiated by the MoC. This project, if successful as presently conceived, would mean a reassertion of state-sponsored development. It foresees an overlay approach similar to the one adopted in Hungary, modernizing much of the regional public infrastructure and more than doubling the number of installed main lines by 2005. However, by the end of 1994, concrete business plans had not taken shape and the mode of financing was unclear. Thus, investment planning was another aspect of Russian telecommunications policy in which the state played a limited role until the mid-1990s.

Approaches to Regulation in the 1990s

Public Control of Basic Network Development

The future role of public ownership was essentially formulated in Hungary in 1989, during the wrangling over the technical and financial nature of Hungary's national network development program. At issue was the extent to which the public network should be opened to private sector entrants and, thus, the extent to which comparative rates of return would be permitted to determine the level and types of investment made in the sector. The alternative to such "decentralized" development was limiting the role of private and other non-state forms of capital to financing a state-approved development program, and permitting only minority private shares in the public network.

Perhaps the strongest domestic political interest pushing for decentralized development were communities seeking more rapid expansion of their local networks. Several of these communities, dissatisfied with Magyar Posta's general investment plans, successfully lobbied for additional network expansion projects in the second half of the 1980s. So-called "own resource" (*önerős*) projects were organized, in which Magyar Posta agreed to expand local networks, earlier than or in addition to what its general plan called for, in exchange for cost sharing. Local councils, whose constituents were willing to put up funds in advance, would sign a contract defining the terms of the cost sharing and collect the contributions. Under these arrangements, the local council was, in effect, merely a channel for transferring additional funds to Magyar Posta. Contributors received nothing beyond access to the telephone network sooner than they would have otherwise (within one or two years, instead of the average wait of over ten years).[21]

During the 1989-1991 period, a few localities used new legislation to try to move beyond this restricted form of local development. The legislation facilitating the attempt were the Company Law and an amendment to the 1964 Postal law, both passed in 1989. The Company Law was one of the first pieces of framework legislation in Eastern Europe delineating the rights and responsibilities of new types of companies, such as subsidiaries, joint ventures, joint-stock, and limited liability companies. The amendment to the 1964 Postal Law eliminated the requirement that public telecommunications service providers be 100 percent owned by the state. It required only that the state's equity share be 50 percent, and that Magyar Posta be a founding shareholder.

The first case to probe the boundaries of state control over the public network was the establishment of a local service provider in the small town of Nagykovácsi. Local officials opened negotiations with Magyar Posta and the MTC to create a joint-stock telecommunications company to develop and operate the local network. In March 1990 the MTC approved the founding of the First Domestic Telecommunications Company with 40 million-forint equity. As required by law, the state had 50 percent ownership (through a contribution of 47.5 percent from Magyar Posta's legal successor, Matáv, and the village council's of 2.5 percent). The non-state ownership was divided among West Germany's Unipharm (30 percent), Postabank (2.5 percent), and a Hungarian engineering firm (17.5 percent).[22]

The Nagykovácsi experience seemed to indicate that the state was prepared to be very flexible with new forms of ownership on the local public use network. However, Matáv soon began to co-opt this approach of creating separate local companies. In late 1991, for example, Matáv founded the First Pest Telephone Company together with

KONTRAX (a Hungarian telecommunications equipment manufacturer) and the local councils of three Budapest districts with starting capital of 2 billion forints.[23] This company promised to install nearly 100,000 telephones in the three southeastern districts of the capital by 1993, increasing the main line density from 22.4, 3.9 and 8.1, respectively, to an overall 35 per 100 inhabitants.[24] Matáv on its own initiative went on to found several more of these companies during the next few years, so that the option of local network development driven largely by private investment quietly lost relevance for the immediate future. While the interests of local communities hardly went unserved—indeed, more investment funds were being devoted to telecommunications in the 1990s than ever before—this trend did meet with some local resentment. Matáv's initial three year development plans emphasizing the digital trunk network did nothing to assuage this dissatisfaction.

Ultimately, in addition to forcing Matáv to become more entrepreneurial in the development of local public networks, criticism and complaints of local and regional groups were in part responsible for the subsequent modification of the national development program. In particular, as can be seen in Table 7.4, negative public reaction led Matáv to undertake a more aggressive strategy, in which the backbone network remained the central component, but density targets were raised and residential installation received more emphasis. Also, the state created a Telecommunications Fund for financing public telecommunications development in economically-backward and high-cost rural areas. It should be added that pressure from local interest groups and other de-monopolists was also a significant factor contributing to the acceptance of the liberal 1992 Law on Telecommunications which outlines a framework permitting broad opportunity for market entry and majority private ownership in public service provision.

In Russia, the MoC has held a view similar to that of the Hungarian MTC: in the interest of ensuring balanced network development and a unified telecommunications system, ownership of basic service providers should remain in the hands of the state. However, the nature of Russian privatization and the MoC's own approach to licensing has compromised the state's ability to achieve the goals sought through public control.

As mentioned above, virtually all state-owned telecommunications service providers have been transformed into joint-stock companies, and most had been partially privatized by the end of 1994. Although the process of privatization was outlined in general legislation, the MoC was able to ensure that more than 95 percent of these firms chose a pattern of initial stock distribution in which up to 35 percent of the total shares were transferred to workers and 5 per cent to management. With two thirds of the shares distributable to workers being non-voting, the state holding, set at 38 percent, was controlling. After this initial distribution, the residual 22 percent or so could be sold in voucher or money auctions. Rostelecom was one of the first to sell its residual at voucher auctions; its shares now play prominently on the Moscow stock market. The Moscow City Telephone Network and the Moscow Intercity and International Telephone Network plan to place their outstanding shares with strategic investors. Of course, the structure of ownership will continue to change as workers' and management's holdings, as well as the residual shares, are bought and sold on secondary markets. In many cases, management has succeeded in acquiring 30 to 35 percent of the voting shares in its company, and therefore commands strong influence on the board of directors.

As of late 1994, the "state's" interest was represented by MoC officials who were specially authorized for the purpose by the State Committee on Property. There is evidence, however, that the MoC has been incapable of exerting the control it would like over local development policy via the mechanism of board representation. The MoC, for example, from time to time issues warnings that investment guidelines are not being followed by regional operators, and has even reverted to old-style orders requiring enterprises to undertake or desist from certain commercial actions. One case that gained notoriety was the MoC's insistence that digital exchanges of only particular European manufacturers be installed in a local public network despite the fact that many more manufacturers have been certified for such use.

Indeed, the extent to which state ownership has been foregone entirely has been very significant for the near-term development trends in the sector. President Yeltsin issued a decree on June 31, 1992 permitting any state or private enterprise to set up and operate a telecommunications network in Russia. Operators are required to obtain a license from the MoC, and meet the technical norms of the national network. As we shall see, however, while the MoC has been somewhat careful to issue licenses to offer public network services, it has been very liberal in allowing the creation of by-pass networks.

To be sure, in many cases, the state-dominated telecommunications companies, the regional operators, and Rostelecom have maintained some control over new entry through equity participation. In Moscow, for example, most cellular telephone services are provided by joint ventures with the Moscow City Telephone Network. Still, by mid-1994, the MoC had granted several hundred licenses to alternative telecom providers, and except for the major transnational digital trunk project, most investment in telecom networks has been in these systems.

Regulation Through Contract

After years of debate, the Hungarian Parliament in 1992 passed a law on telecommunications. The law is a framework document outlining the mechanisms by which the sector is to be restructured and regulated, but it stops short of explicitly assigning a given market structure or forms of regulation for telecommunications services. With regard to public services, it simply states that fixed and mobile telephone services may be run by state-licensed private companies, or by enterprises founded and majority-owned by the state. It requires that in either case firms offer services through a concession or contract signed with the state regulatory authority. The law leaves to the MTC decisions concerning the number of potential service providers in any given market, specific regulatory tools, and the like.

Most of the document is devoted to the institutionalization of the concession. The concessions are to be granted on the basis of competitive bids, and are to be valid for a period established by the MTC (or local government if the concession covers a local network). The concession contract specifies the quality, quantity, and technical requirements of service, as well as the methodology for setting tariffs.

It took about a year for the MTC to design and implement the tender for the concession for providing basic public telecommunications service. In the process, outstanding issues of ownership and market structure for long-distance and local public telecommunications services were resolved for the next several years. The basic terms of the concessions for national and local fixed public networks are shown in Table 7.5.[25] In exchange for paying a multi-million dollar concession fee and accepting requirements concerning the ownership structure in the newly formed operating company, service maintenance and development, domestic equipment procurement, and employment of existing staff, the concession-holder would receive a 25-year concession (renewable for another 12.5 years without a new tender if deemed appropriate by the MTC) to run the given public network. The concession-holder is guaranteed a monopoly position for the first eight years of the concession.

The concession for the national long-distance monopoly involved the sale of a significant minority holding in Matáv and deciding voting power in operational management of the firm. The tender was announced at the end of September 1993 and consisted of a two-stage bidding process. The submission of initial bids was due on November 5, 1993. The competing consortia to submit bids included the Italian STET and the AT&T regional spin-off Bell Atlantic; Telefonica of Spain, the Dutch PTT, and the American GTE; France Telecom and another

Table 7.5   Attributes of the Hungarian Telecom Concession Tenders

Attribute	National Concession	Regional Concession	Both
Length of concession			25 years. Extendable for another 12.5 years without a new tender.
Exclusivity			Eight years.
Initial concession fee	40 billion forints in capital increase plus sum to obtain up to 30.2% ownership of concession.	55 to 17 million forints ($550,000 to $1.7 million).	
Annual concession fee			0.1% of gross revenues.
Hungarian ownership requirements	Hungarian state maintains 50%+1 ownership share.	Hungarian legal entity(s) maintain(s) at least 25%+1 ownership share.	
Service obligations	Maintain continuous, reliable, and improving operation of international and domestic long-distance services as well as local services not transferred to local concessions.	Maintain continuous, reliable, and improving operation of local service with systems that remain completely compatible with national service.	Minimum 15.5% annual increase in main line for 6 years, as long as demand warrants. From January 1, 1997, concession must meet 90% of phone installation applications within a 6-month period, and 100% within a 12-month period.
Procurement obligations		A minimum of 25% of the value of equipment and services procured for network development in the period immediately after the start of the concession (and 50% after January 1, 1997) should be of Hungarian origin.	Concession should procure from Hungarian sources whenever competitive offers are made. Concession bids must include planned % of Hungarian procurement in total.
Employment Obligations			Current staff must be kept for one year.

Source: MTC.

Baby Bell, US West; and Deutsche Telecom and a third former Bell operating company, Ameritech. As this list suggests, not just any firm could compete for the minority share in Matáv. To qualify for the competition, the consortia had to: (1) be operating public networks of at least one million subscribers; (2) have earned at least a billion dollars in income from such subscribers during the previous two years; and (3) have at least five years' experience in developing public telecom infrastructure. The short list contained only the last three consortia, which submitted final bids in mid-December 1993.

The selection from the short list was made on the basis of the following criteria: detailed business plan; the technical and commercial merit of the contestant's proposals for meeting the service obligations of the concession; the proportion of networking equipment to be sourced from Hungarian enterprises; and the total amount the contestant was willing to spend for the 30.2 percent ownership share.[26] The MTC ultimately chose Deutsche Telecom and Ameritech with their $875 million bid, over both the slightly lower French Telecom-US West proposal of $830 million, and the higher bid ($910 million) of the STET-Bell Atlantic consortium. This $875 million went to Matáv in the form a direct capital injection ($400 million),[27] the State Property Agency ($333.25 million), and the Telecommunications Fund ($133.25 million), while $6.5 million went to the consultants who had played advisory roles in the process.

Given the many uncertainties surrounding the sale, it may be said that the Hungarian state received a better-than-expected price for the minority holding in Matáv and the monopoly rights provided for under the concession. Matáv is heavily indebted, and its capital requirements are great. Moreover, at the time of the award, the share of the concession fee to be dedicated to network development had not been clarified. Upcoming elections had the potential of radically altering the concession's business environment. Finally, the total amount of assets that would remain with the national service provider was not yet determined, as a large number of local networks were up for tender in a process similar to the national concession sale.

Concerning the regional concessions, the decision of whether to put the local networks up for tender has generally been a matter of the local governments. Of the total 54 local networks (each containing several local exchanges), 25 were chosen for concession auction. The majority (15) of these local monopoly concessions were ultimately acquired by companies other than Matáv, which also was eligible to compete. The remaining 10 plus those local networks not auctioned off became concessions under Matáv's ownership and control. In terms of crude measures of market share, the 15 non-Matáv concessions service only

20 percent of the country's population, and possess 15 percent of total telephone lines. According to the Hungarian press, they command perhaps less than 10 percent of the total telecommunications service revenue.[28]

As a result of the tender outcomes, all but one of the new non-Matáv concession companies promised significant amounts of foreign capital and active foreign management. United Telecom Services, which won four of the local concessions, is dominated by American (US Telecom East) and Austrian (Alcatel-Austria) partners. Central European Telecom, which won two local networks, unites the Hungarian Microsystem Telecom Rt. with the American company Fail Telecommunications. The French-led (Compagnie Generale Des Eaux) venture won two networks, including the much coveted Szeged network. Digitel, CGE, and the Israeli Tal Giltek took over the Gödöllő and Vác networks. The Hungarian Telephone and Cable Corporation, an American firm, established several joint ventures in Hungary, two of which will be operating local networks as the result of successful concession bids. M.C.G., led by the Pennsylvania-based Denver Ephata Telephone and Telegraph, won the Monor local network. Finally, Papatel, originally established by Matáv and Microsystem Telecom Rt., has Central European Telecom, the International Finance Corporation, and others as foreign partners.

In Russia, contracts, in the form of licenses, play a very important role in telecommunications development. In fact, having divested itself of most of its control over tariffs and significantly reduced its ownership influence, the state must rely heavily on licensing as an instrument for regulating the conditions of service provision and market entry. This is not to say, however, that the Ministry has in practice developed a coherent and transparent policy towards licensing. Indeed, it was not until June 1994 that a set of guidelines on license issuing was formally enacted. At the end of 1994, the procedure for issuing licenses and determining their content remained very arbitrary.

Licenses have generally been issued on a first come, first served basis. The applicant supplies information concerning the firm and proposed service to the licensing department in the Ministry. The department generally approves the application if the proposal meets technical requirements and does not infringe on the MoC's development plans and its desired degree of control of the fixed public network. Bidding procedures are sometimes used in cases where applications are made for the same type of activity in the same region. For example, the MoC has auctioned off licenses for cellular services in more than forty localities.

The licensing fees themselves, which are approved by the Ministries of Finance and the Economy, have been quite minimal. Unable to determine license fees independently, the MoC has instead often required that the licensee contribute major investments into the public network to which it is connecting or, in some cases, bypassing. These investments can be very costly. Licenses may be granted for periods of three to ten years. Bypass service providers have generally been awarded three- to five-year licenses. The provisions of the licenses are monitored by Gossvyaz'nadzor, the Ministry's technical inspectorate.

It is difficult to make concrete judgments about the market-structure implications of licensing provisions, since these licenses are generally not published. Rostelecom's license has been made public, however, and may be suggestive. It gives Rostelecom the right to provide intercity and international public telecommunications services for ten years. What is most interesting about the document, however, is how little it says about Rostelecom's rights and responsibilities. Rostelecom has very little specific service or development obligations, for example. It is simply required to provide open access to all and expand the network in a manner technically consistent with government regulations and investment programs. There is no reference to either ownership structure or monopoly rights. It allows Rostelecom to set tariffs "independently" and does not refer at all to interconnection charges or revenue-sharing with local service providers.

Rostelecom and the 80-odd partially-privatized regional service providers received licenses for public services as soon as they became joint-stock companies. Most of the alternative service providers have been confined to operating by-pass networks. Although licenses are given to other enterprises allowing interconnection in order to provide public services in localities and across the nation, cross-ownership and informal restrictions limit serious competition to the traditional public service providers.

Price Regulation

In Hungary, the movement away from the inertial tariff setting of the earlier centrally-planned period began in the second half of the 1980s. In 1986, international long-distance rates were liberalized.[29] In 1990, the principle of maximum tariffs was adopted, affording Matáv the flexibility to price services under specific ceilings. Although adjustments of the ceilings on subscriber fees, domestic call charges, installation charges, and PBX services remained subject to case-by-case approval by the MTC, adjustments were indeed introduced. Matáv has been successful in justifying modifications on the basis of a number of standard, if sometime contradictory, criteria. In general, tariffs should: (1) cover the cost of providing the service, or at least move in line with cost changes; (2) reflect the relative value to the user (differing demand elasticities); and (3) facilitate the availability of local basic services to all citizens.

The general tariff restructuring that took place on February 1, 1991 shows how these general principles have been realized in practice. With regard to connection fees, owing to the introduction during the 1980s of bond programs and investment contributions associated with "own-resource" developments, up-front payments for installation had already increased significantly along with its rising costs. Thus, despite the fact that connection fees did not cover installation costs fully, Matáv did not lobby for a rise in connection fees, and the February restructuring left connection charges untouched. With regard to the low subscriber fees, which had remained unchanged for years, however, Matáv was successful in achieving its much desired increase vis-à-vis other charges. For individual business lines, for example, the monthly charge climbed from 240 to 400 forints; while for residential customers, the charge climbed from 120 to 250. For usage charges, Matáv had long wanted to restore their 1986 value, and in February, local charges did rise from 2 to 5 forints. Long distance rates were also raised by some 50 percent.

Despite these modifications, cross-subsidies remained significant and the bureaucratic nature of tariff adjustment has continued. Already in 1990, however, arguments were being heard in favor of introducing a simplified and flexible regulatory regime for basic services, in particular price-cap regulation. The price cap, as generally conceived, is a rule fixed for a multi-year period under which the company can make any changes it wishes provided that the average price of a specified basket of its goods and services does not increase faster than an economy-wide index of prices minus some constant specified by the regulator.[30] This constant is usually set equal to the productivity gains anticipated from higher than average technological progress, or from increasing returns to scale. There are many appealing qualities of the price cap. These include: (1) encouraging cost reduction; and (2) given the choice of an appropriate "constant," allowing the enterprise to maintain the real value of its revenues for financing its plans and profit generation.

Although the MTC had accepted the concept of the price cap for Matáv's basic services at the beginning of the decade, there was much delay in establishing its specific components, so that the new regime was introduced only on January 1, 1995. Its basic attributes are the following. An aggregate price-cap equal to the producer price index of the previous twelve-month period is imposed on the growth of a weighted average of three service basket indices. The three service baskets are: (1) the subscription fees for business/residential and main line/twin lines; (2) local and "shorter" long-distance charges;[31] and (3) other long distance and international call charges. The maximum growth in each basket index is limited to the change in the producer price index multiplied by a so-called "price rebalancing factor." These price rebalancing factors reflect not such much technological considerations as the intent to reduce the persistent cross-subsidization from long-distance to local service. The factors are set at 1.05, 1.07, and 0.96 respectively. The weight of any particular service or set of services in the aggregate (or sub-group) price cap is determined by its share in total revenues.

Another aspect of Hungarian price regulation reformed in the first half of the 1990s was the mechanism through which income from long-distance services is distributed within the public telecommunications system. The nature of long-distance service is such that traffic is generally settled by two or more separate organizations, but only one of these (the organization at which the call or other communication originates) receives payment. Some set of implicit or explicit charges are therefore required in order to cover the costs borne by all organizations involved. These costs are internalized in an fully integrated monopoly arrangement; however, once service provision is broken up, revenue sharing becomes a critical aspect of the economics of the industry.

With the advent of significant numbers of independent local operators, a change in the system of revenue distribution was essential. In addition to a list of fixed charges for interconnecting networks, a revenue-sharing scheme was therefore introduced on January 1, 1994. The basic attributes of the scheme are the following:

- All revenues from local and "shorter" long-distance calls remain with the local operators.
- For other long-distance calls, the long distance operator receives a third to a half of the revenue depending upon the distance of the call. The residual is then divided up between the originating and terminating local operator according to a 60:40 proportion.
- For international services, the local operators keep all revenues from international calls that originate with them. Matáv retains all revenues from incoming international calls (as determined by international agreements).

Based on current demand projections, total revenue from public telecommunications services is expected to be divided up between the local and the long-distance service provider in a 2:1 proportion.

Recent developments in Russia contrast sharply with the stable evolution of tariff regulation in Hungary. Russia, as mentioned previously, largely freed telecommunications tariffs in 1992 from central control. Formal control on tariff setting was initially established within the framework of antitrust policy soon after the general price liberalization of January 1992. The most consequential of this legislation for telecommunications were the "Rules on Price Regulation for Products of Monopoly Enterprises" (see Chapter 3), which authorized the supervision of monopoly pricing by local and federal pricing offices. When a monopoly planned to raise prices, it had to apply to the relevant office and provide extensive documentation to justify its application. This documentation included cost information on the product or service in question, the volume of output in the preceding year and the anticipated volume for the current year, the profits expected from the product or service, and the profitability (which, in the Russian context, means something resembling profit relative to operating cost) of the product or service after the price increase. The pricing office had one month to evaluate the proposal and the documentation. It could reject or modify the price increase if the resulting profitability of the enterprise exceeded a certain level. Because of the widely-held philosophy that a degree of cross-subsidization is socially beneficial, a profitability constraint (of 50 percent) was applied to overall enterprise activity rather than to individual services.

Tariffs for international calls provided by Rostelecom and domestic long-distance tariffs paid by state budget organizations are regulated by the MoC. Among local tariffs, only services provided on the public network to residential customers are regulated. Not surprisingly, local pricing authorities have used their power to keep these politically-sensitive tariffs low. The approach and attitude to the structure of tariffs have differed across regions, but it is clear that increases in residential connection and subscriber tariffs have been allowed to fall behind increases in costs. Moreover, in addition to the burden of low residential rates, local operators have general public service obligations to provide such services as rural telephony, telegraphic services, and wire radio transmission. Local operators must therefore raise unregulated local business and long-distance charges to cover these losses. According to OECD consultants, by the end of 1994, the ratio of business to residential installation charges, for example, ranged from 7:1 to 10:1.

As far as international and domestic long-distance revenue distribution is concerned, fees for interconnecting services are unregulated, and its license allows Rostelecom to set rates for its services. Formally, the distribution of international and domestic long-distance revenue between Rostelecom and the local public service operators is also unregulated. In practice, however, the MoC exerts significant control.

Revenue sharing for domestic long-distance service between Rostelecom and local service providers has been formally determined via contractual negotiations rather than on the basis of uniform national regulation. There does exist, however, an MoC-approved matrix of accounting rates for interregional traffic which forms the basis for this revenue sharing. Although data on revenues are extremely difficult to uncover, it appears that on average 60-70 percent of the revenues collected by regional operators for outgoing domestic long-distance calls are debited to Rostelecom. Rostelecom pockets about half and credits the remainder to the account of the regional operator terminating the call. In 1994, Rostelecom received 50 percent of the revenue from outgoing international traffic.

The resulting share of revenues from international and domestic long-distance traffic received by regional operators is quite low by international standards, and inadequate considering the investment required in the local network. The restrictive pricing and skewed revenue-sharing arrangements in Russia have thus reinforced the effects of the liberal licensing policy and approach to privatization in encouraging the blossoming of alternative networks. Comparatively few resources are made available for investment in local service, while regional operators are given strong incentive to work with outside investors to by-pass Rostelecom and obtain a greater share of long-distance and international revenues.

Conclusions

In telecommunications, as in any industry, ownership structure, investment financing, and price policy are intimately related. This overview has underscored the significance of a comprehensive approach to these enterprise foundations within the context of regulatory reform in Eastern European telecommunications services. Investment needs are tremendous in the region, but the absence of well-functioning credit markets, high inflation, and general uncertainty make debt very expensive in these countries. Increasing internally-generated investment resources (e.g., via a more commercially-oriented set of prices and a more commercially-oriented strategy of service development), as well as new capital injections from sales of equity, or forms of direct investment, will be of overriding importance. Tariffs vary significantly from costs, creating pressure to establish by-pass networks to exploit more profitable markets; this in turn undermines plans for more coherent, unified network development. In the absence of a pricing structure that provides incentives for more balanced development, arguments for maintaining state control over development or conservative licensing policies are strengthened.

Although the Hungarian approach may be faulted for its reliance on monopolies in all basic public services, its slowness to develop stable, transparent "rules of the game" in the form of delays in the law on telecommunications or its inability to rebalance the tariff structure, it reveals a sensitivity to the comprehensiveness necessary for effective reform. Hungarian telecommunications reform has been well-managed and effectively sequenced.

We traced the initial evolution from central planning to a more "arm's length" regulatory regime that relies heavily on maintaining public ownership and administrative pricing at the turn of the decade. By 1994, Hungarian telecommunications policy had moved beyond this restrictive regulatory approach, which in many ways differs little from that found in developed market economies. Competition for non-traditional telecommunications services was introduced, and Matáv's vertical monopoly on basic telephone service was broken up. Via concessions, the ministry in charge of telecommunications regulation captured the (perceived) efficiencies in maintaining a natural monopoly while ensuring acceptable levels of service provision. Perhaps more importantly, the policy has secured essential investment resources for national network development. Tariffs will be subjected to price-cap regulation which maintains the real value of tariffs, facilitates the reduction of cross subsidies, and obviates extensive cost analysis of Matáv's services.

In comparison, the Russian case appears chaotic. We should not be too quick to condemn policy makers, however, as economic and political circumstances in Russia were very different. This chapter is not the place to argue the relative merits of this or that pace and sequencing of general economic reform. The fact remains, however, that Russian policy makers did not have the luxury of the gradual price liberalization and closely managed privatization of its large enterprises from which Hungary's telecommunications regulatory policy seems to have benefited.

The Russian government had not, by early 1995, formulated a proper telecommunications policy. The regulatory environment for telecommunications service operators is defined by general legislation (concerning monopolies, mass privatization, and the like), the formulation of which rides roughshod over important particularities of the industry. The Russian parliament has long had drafts of a law on telecommunications before it, but had been unable by the end of 1994 to pass this legislation. Moreover, the law in its present form is too general to hold the promise of improving the situation. The most visible results of this absence of policy have been widely varying telecommunications prices and the blossoming of by-pass networks across the country. Although hard information on the cost of service provision is difficult to come by for Russian enterprises, the lack of stable and coherent regulation is also probably contributing to high operating and development costs for the overall system.

We should emphasize that, as of early 1995, the direction of Russia's future telecommunications policy was not at all clear. There is widespread dissatisfaction with the motley collection of price regulations. Russia could hold the course of a more liberal regulatory regime, or it may be compelled to reregulate tariffs for all basic public services in an attempt to more rationally manage cross subsidization and design financial plans for investment. Licensing will undoubtedly become more coherent as the MoC and other regulatory bodies more fully appreciate the value and necessity of transparent license procedures, as well as obtain a vision of what licensing policy is to achieve. But the market-structure implications of that vision are not yet known. The state's use of its ownership position is a similarly open question. However, it is already clear that the longer network development remains skewed as the result of price distortions, flawed licensing policy, and a general lack of investment, the costs of achieving well-functioning telecommunications public service will continue to rise.

Notes

1. Tariff setting in telecommunications has been a very fertile ground for applied microeconomic theory for over the last two decades in the West. Berg and Tschirhart 1988, and Mitchell and Vogelsang 1991, provide surveys of this research.

2. Srapyonov 1989:227.

3. Srapyonov 1982:309.

4. Domestic long distance rates in Hungary vary by distance from the where the call originates, measured in zones.

5. The consumer price index rose 96 percent from 1985 to 1990, while indexed telecommunications prices rose only 51 percent.

6. See Bakaleishchik 1977:49, Voronov 1982:55-62, Davydov 1985, Papp and Oprics 1988, Sallai *et alia* 1984:111-112, and Szitás 1988:173.

7. For the rural networks there was no division of subscribers into categories *per se*, rather there were targets for the length of lines and the number of units in collective- and state-farm networks.

8. Higher supervisory organs monitored expenditure on projects, but only through summary indicators. For example, there was a norm for the capital investment per unit of connection capacity created.

9. The directors of the three divisions signed the actual restructuring agreements in May 1990.

10. See Matáv 1991, 1992.

11. The anticipated tripling of subscribers by the year 2000, represents an annual increase in main lines of 12.2 percent. This compares to the 5.3 percent in the 7th Five Year Plan. Reductions in the waiting period for a phone to a maximum of one year by the millennium were also promised (Figyelő 1991).

12. As is described above, the localities or districts are the basic unit of planning in the locality strategy, and the level of demand is defined on the basis of demographic (residences and business) attributes, rather than economic ones.

13. There would be some transit points between the two, of course, but one of the objectives is to minimize the expense of integrating different signaling in the system.

14. The focus on the trunk network and large-volume customers constitutes a rejection of the old allegiance to demographic distribution of the locality strategy. It is however true that under both approaches preference is given to business subscribers. It also should be noted that this priority received formal legal backing by government decree in January 1991. See Magyar Közlöny 1991, and HVG 1991.

15. See MTC 1990, appendix 2. For another chronologies of the formulation of development programs in Hungary, see Ferenc 1990, and Bánhidi 1993.

16. For a more detailed analysis see Whitlock 1993.

17. See *Vestnik svyazi* 1994.

18. Srapyonov 1982:31-32, and Demina 1990:24.

19. There were a variety of other miscellaneous independent companies created during this period as well, including a wholly state-owned satellite communications enterprise, and those for other specialized services.

20. "Programma mer po demonopolizatsii otrasli 'svyazi' na 1994 i posleduyushiye gody" (MoC 1994).

21. See, for example, Korányi 1987, Szuly 1987:10, and Juhász 1986.

22. See Szabo 1991.

23. The company did not formally come into being until 1992, by which time the Helsinki Telephone Co. and some individual investors had become founding shareholders as well.

24. The company later became engulfed in scandal and financial trouble, and these targets were missed (*Figyelő* 1993).

25. Hungarian mobile cellular telecommunications are not dealt with in this chapter, as it is not a monopoly market.

26. Of course, political considerations were probably important as well, but their relative weight in the decision is difficult to measure.

27. As it turned out, the Hungarian Treasury took a big chunk (28 billion forints—approximately $280 million at the exchange rate then in effect) out of the 40 billion forint concession fee.

28. *Figyelő* 1994.

29. International call charges were reregulated under the 1992 Law on Telecommunications.

30. See, for example, Beesley and Littlechild 1989.

31. "Shorter" long-distance refers to interexchange calls within a single zone, or "Zone 1" in Table 7.3.

References

Bakaleishchik, F.B. 1977. "Nekotorye voprosy razrabotki general'nykh skhem razvitiya zonovykh telefonnykh setei" (Some Issues in the Development of Telephone Networks). *Elektrosvyaz'* 3 (March): 4-10.

Bánhidi, F. 1993. "With Special Regard to Privatization." *Magyar Távközlés* 10: 19-24.

Beesley, M.E., and S.C. Littlechild. 1989. "The Regulation of Privatized Monopolies in the United Kingdom." *RAND Journal of Economics* 3 (Autumn): 454-72.

Berg, S.V. and J. Tschirhart. 1988. *Natural Monopoly Regulation: Principles and Practice*. Cambridge: Cambridge University Press.

Cave, M. 1992. *Telecommunications Tariff Policy for Economies in Transition*. Paris: Organization for Economic Cooperation and Development.

Davydov, G.B. 1985. "Nekotorye problemy optimizatsii setei svyazi" (Some Problems of Optimizing Communications Networks). *Elektrosvyaz'* 12 (December): 1-5.

Demina, E.V. 1990. "Osnovy organizatsii sistemy elektrosvyazi" (Fundamentals of Organizing a Communications System), in R.P. Nekunde, ed., *Organizatsiya, planirovaniye i upravleniye predpriyatiyami elektricheskoi svyazi* (The Organization, Planning and Management of Communications Enterprises). Pp. 17-30. Moscow: Radio i svyaz'.

Ferenc, T. 1990. *A Távközlés új szabályozási rendszere Magyaroszágon az egységes Európa tükrében* (The New Telecommunications Regulatory System in the Context of a United Europe). Budapest: Kopint-Datorg.

Figyelő. 1991. "Pénz, Pénz, Pénz" (Money, Money, Money). December 12.

_____. 1993. November 18. (Tantusz supplement, p. 3).

_____. 1994. March 24. (Tantusz supplement, p. 1).

HVG. 1991. "Kultúrváró" (Waiting Room). October 26.

Juhász, G. 1986. "Kísérleteznek" (They Are Experimenting). *HVG*. November 1.

Korányi, T. 1987. "Tárcsaközi egyezmény" (An Interdialling Agreement). *HVG*. September 5.

Magyar Közlöny. 1991. A Kormány 12/1991 (I.18) Korm. rendelete. January 18, 293-4.

Matáv. 1991. *1990 Annual Report*. Budapest: Magyar Távközlési Vállalat Vezérigazgatóság.

_____. 1992. *1991 Annual Report*. Budapest: Magyar Távközlési Vállalat Vezérigazgatóság.

_____. 1993. *1992 Annual Report*. Budapest: Magyar Távközlési Vállalat Vezérigazgatóság.

_____. 1994. *1993 Annual Report*. Budapest: Magyar Távközlési Vállalat Vezérigazgatóság.

_____. 1995. *1994 Annual Report*. Budapest: Magyar Távközlési Vállalat Vezérigazgatóság.

Mitchell, B.M., and I. Vogelsang. 1991. *Telecommunications Pricing: Theory and Practice*. New York: Cambridge University Press.

MoC. 1994. *Programma mer po demonopolizatsii otrasli "Svyazi" na posleduyushiye gody* (Program for De-monopolizing the Communications Sector in the Next Years). Moscow. Photocopy.

Morgan, T.J. 1976. *Telecommunications Economics*. England: Technicopy Limited.

MTC. 1990. "Előterjesztés a Minisztertanácshoz a távközlés ezredfordulóigszóló programjáról" (Proposal to the Council of Ministers on the Millennium Telecommunications Program). Manuscript. Budapest: Ministry of Transport, Communications and Construction.

Nyevrikel, E. 1993. "Tarifaszabályozás az új távközlési törvény után (Rate Regulation After the New Telecommunications Law). *Transnational Data and Communications Report* (keleti európa kiadás). May: 27-29.

Papp, Z., and Gy. Oprics. 1988. "A müszaki tervezésben alkalmazott prognózis módszerek" (Forecasting Procedures Used in Technical Planning), in Posta Kísérleti, Intézet, ed., *Távközlés, gazdaság, társadalom* (Telecommunications, Economy, Society). Pp. 194-203. Budapest: KODEX Nyomdaipari Rt.

Sallai, G. *et al.* 1984. *Report on the Activities of the Research Institute of the Hungarian Post Office*. Budapest: Traffic Documentation Enterprise.

Srapyonov, O.O. 1989. "Planirovanie produktsii predpriyatii svyazi" (Planning the Production of Communications Enterprises), in N.V. Kopylova, ed., *Ekonomika, organizatsiya i planirovaniye na predpriyatiyakh svyazi* (The Economics, Organization, and Planning of Communications Enterprises). Pp. 231-37. Moscow: Radio i svyaz'.

Srapyonov, O.O. *et al.* 1982. *Ekonomika svyazi* (The Economics of Communications). Moscow: Radio i svyaz'.

Szabo, G. 1991. "Kábelpolitika" (Cable Policy). *HVG* (July 6).

Szitás, J. 1988. "Hosszutávú tervezés a Magyar Posta gyakorlatában" (Long-term Planning in the Practice of the Hungarian Post), in Posta Kísérleti Intézet, ed., *Távközlés, gazdaság, társadalom* (Telecommunications, Economy, Society). Pp. 173-81. Budapest: KODEX Nyomdaipari Rt.

Szuly, M. 1989. "Budapesti telefonok önerőből" (Budapest Telephones from Own Resources). *Posta*, 10-11.

Vestnik svyazi. 1992. "Programma aktsionirovaniya i privatizatsii" (The Corporatization and Privatization Program) 8: 8-11.

Voronov, B.A. 1982. *Razvitiye potreblenii produktsii svyazi i poryadok ego izucheniya* (The Development of the Demand for Telecommunications Production and the Order of Its Study). Moscow: Svyaz'.

Whitlock, E. 1993. "Hungarian Telecommunications." Bloomington: Indiana University. Unpublished Ph.D. dissertation.

_____. 1992. "Russian Telecommunications: A Monopoly in Transition." *Radio Free Europe/Radio Liberty Research Report* 36: 58-64.

Whitlock, E., and E. Nyevrikel. 1992. "The Evolution of Hungarian Telecommunications Policy." *Telecommunications Policy* 3: 249-58.

8

Post-Communist Competition Policy: Conclusions and Suggestions

Ben Slay

Competition policy in transitional economies is something of a novelty, as it had few institutional, policy, or ideological precursors in the old system. Nonetheless, competition agencies in much of what used to be called the "Eastern bloc" had by 1995 carved out important niches for themselves in the policy mosaic, and competition policy was acquiring an increasingly well-defined character. The first half of the 1990s thus constitutes a time period of duration sufficient to formulate some initial conclusions about post-communist competition policy, as well as advance some possible suggestions for improvement.

Tentative Conclusions

First, experience to date suggests that monopoly is not an important cause of inflation in post-communist economies. As the discussion in Chapter 1 shows, the "monopoly causes inflation" argument hinges on the assumption that the entire economy is monopolized, that is, the economy is one in which "monopolistic relations overwhelmingly predominate."[1] Otherwise, price increases in monopolistic sectors under conditions of relative macroeconomic stability can be expected to reduce effective demand in the relatively competitive sectors. Although output would presumably fall in competitive sectors, so would prices, which would serve as a deflationary counterweight to relative price increases in the monopolized sectors.[2] This argument thus assumes that competitive market forces are completely lacking at the start of the transition, and are unlikely to appear quickly once the transition begins–even if aggregate demand is stabilized.

Developments since 1990 have shown that, for relatively small, open economies like Hungary or Poland (and potentially, for most of the European post-communist economies), imports that provide competition for the producers of tradable goods can clearly constitute an important de-monopolizing force. The development of competitive markets can also be promoted by newly-created private firms, as well as by the smaller state enterprises that may appear via spontaneous deconcentration within the state sector. While import competition has not played such a large role in Russia (with its relatively closed economy), virtually all observers (including Starodubrovskaya herself) agree that market competition has developed significantly since 1992.[3]

De-monopolization in Russia has proceeded at a slower pace than in the Central European transitional economies, which has complicated macroeconomic stabilization efforts. Whether this slow pace is most appropriately ascribed to greater initial degrees of monopolization in Russia is another matter, however. Indeed, research by Brown, Ickes, and Ryterman may be interpreted as arguing that the structural potential for competitive markets in Russia is superior to that of most other transitional economies, due to the relatively large size of the Russian market and the large numbers of Russian firms.[4] Instead, the higher inflation and larger declines in output recorded in Russia during 1992-1995 may have had more to do with the greater difficulties Russian macroeconomic policy makers faced during that time. These macroeconomic problems can be most appropriately traced to two sources: (1) the more difficult initial conditions in which the Russian economic transition began (such as the greater macroeconomic and external imbalances prevailing in late 1991, or the shocks produced by the breakdown of inter-republican trade and the ruble zone); and (2) the structural imbalances inherited from the Soviet era, such as the value-subtracting activities associated with the military sector, or uneconomic production activities in Siberia or the Far North. All of this has little to do with monopoly. For these reasons, accepting the "monopoly causes inflation" argument on practical grounds would seem to be no easier than accepting it on theoretical grounds.

A second conclusion concerns the "privatization versus de-monopolization" debate of the early 1990s. Experience strongly suggests that this debate has in fact been resolved. It also indicates that this debate oversimplified decisions about organizational and ownership changes at the enterprise level.

To the extent that a victor in this debate can be declared, developments since 1990 clearly support the "privatize first" position: market competition has tended to develop independently–indeed, largely in the absence–of aggressive structural deconcentration campaigns. This is apparent in a number of respects. Competition agencies have generally avoided ambitious structural policies, mostly because, as the first President of the Polish Antimonopoly Office put it: "there is a major threat of making a mistake, since it is hard to define a proper balance between a more competitive structure and possible loss of advantages of economies of scale and scope."[5] This result is not surprising, since it is broadly consistent with Western competition-policy experience. Furthermore, many of the dissolutions and divestitures of state enterprises that have occurred have been instigated by state property agencies as part of the privatization process, either on their own initiative or in cooperation with competition offices. So even when dissolutions or divestitures have been executed, experience has shown that such divisions are best handled as part of the privatization process, and not performed solely by the competition agencies. Finally, the privatization of large firms has frequently become entangled with the controversies associated with dominant-firm regulation. Once a firm is classified as "dominant," its privatization often becomes much more complicated, if not impossible. The conceptual and policy controversies associated with dominant-firm regulation would seem to make this a particularly unfortunate basis upon which to realize in practice the "de-monopolize first" approach.

On the other hand, the "privatization versus de-monopolization" formulation has been shown by experience to be too stark and simplistic. The fact that many divisions of state enterprises have occurred within the framework of privatization itself shows that, in many cases, the relationship is more appropriately described as "privatization *and* de-monopolization."[6] Moreover, as Ádám Török points out in Chapter 2, the relationship between de-monopolization and privatization (especially where foreign investors are involved) is better understood as a triangle, of which trade liberalization constitutes the third side. Thus, if the sale of state enterprises to strategic foreign investors plays an important role in a country's privatization strategy (as is the case in Russia, Poland, and especially Hungary),[7] then the three goals of privatization, de-monopolization, and trade liberalization must inevitably be in conflict. This was apparent, for example, in Poland and Hungary during 1990-1991, when state enterprises' monopolistic positions were challenged by import competition. Here, the trade liberalization that promoted de-monopolization also reduced the sale values of many large firms slated for privatization. Alternatively, strategic foreign investors may demand increased protection of domestic markets–on which a significant share of the post-investment output produced in the host country is to be sold–as the price for investing in the host country's producing enterprises.[8] As

Török points out, in Hungary this even led to the sale of competing domestic firms to subsidiaries of the same foreign purchaser, which then lobbied for increased import protection on Hungarian markets. Here, the goals of de-monopolization and trade liberalization were sacrificed at the altar of privatization. Or, if imports are liberalized and foreign firms are permitted to acquire monopolistic positions in the host country's distribution channels, these positions can be used to foreclose market access for, and thus do grave damage to, rival domestic producers. In this case, the logic of competition policy is sacrificed for the goals of privatization and trade liberalization. Indeed, if the foreign firms' monopolistic distribution positions cause serious damage to rival domestic producers, and if these rivals are state enterprises undergoing privatization, the proceeds earned from the sale of the distribution networks will be offset by the damage inflicted upon the sale value of the rival producers by the foreign competitors' monopolistic practices. In this case, the goals of both competition policy and (to a lesser degree) privatization may be sacrificed for the benefit of trade liberalization. The "privatization versus de-monopolization" slogan hardly does justice to the complexities involved in trading off these costs and benefits.

A third conclusion suggested in this volume emphasizes the importance of post-communist competition agencies as advocates of pro-competitive, market-oriented policy solutions to economic problems. Although competition offices may have found numerous institutional allies in the initial cavalry charge of market liberalization, these allies generally tend to drop by the wayside with the passage of time. That is, while foreign trade ministries may have initially been strong proponents of import competition, over time they tend to be increasingly sensitive to the concerns of import-competing firms and sectors. Likewise, fiscal pressures increasingly push privatization ministers to sell monopolistic state enterprises to multinational corporations at a premium price, instead of breaking these firms up during the course of privatization. And the governments that champion market reform programs are frequently forced out of office after an initial period of "exceptional politics," to be replaced by cabinets with stronger ties to the old regime and lobbies, and very different attitudes towards market competition.[9] In effect, post-communist governments seem to be increasingly discovering what their predecessors already knew: "extraction of surplus provides the means of maintaining ...power,"[10] and that legalized monopoly is an excellent mechanism for extracting that surplus. It must not be forgotten that competition agencies are frequently the most important–if not the sole–line of defense against the (re)creation of such mechanisms. The fact that judicial systems are often unsympathetic to (and unfamiliar with) the logic of competition policy–and are all too often unable to execute those pro-competitive verdicts they do render–should also be kept in mind.

Suggestions for the Future

Technical Assistance

As William E. Kovacic and Robert S. Thorpe point out in Chapter 4, the provision of technical assistance by Western competition agencies and international donors comprises an important dimension of post-communist competition policy.[11] This study points to a number of areas where technical assistance should be more properly focused. These include the following:

Data Problems. Problems of obtaining comparable data for different countries over time present major difficulties in any comparison of market structures.[12] In the post-communist context, these problems are magnified by additional difficulties. Facilitating the development of comparable methodologies for defining markets and measuring structural concentration should therefore be an important goal in the provision of technical assistance in competition policy matters.

Assistance for Judicial Institutions. Although post-communist competition agencies generally possess administrative as well as executive authority, their decisions can generally be appealed to the courts. In many countries, prospects for judicial affirmation of even fairly innocuous competition-policy rulings are at best uncertain. The courts' significance in competition policy is further underscored by the fact that, once appealed, rulings by competition offices in some countries (e.g., Russia) are held in abeyance pending the completion of judicial review. Technical assistance programs should therefore be increasingly directed at judges, rather than at competition agencies *per se*. Helping to reform post-communist legal systems could also promote the broader goal of creating and strengthening the rule of law.

Promoting Inter-Agency Cooperation. Although the basic legal and policy frameworks in many post-communist economies are quite similar, communication and co-ordination between their competition agencies seems to have been rather sparse, especially outside of Central Europe. Moreover, serious problems with communication apparently exist between the territorial administrations of the State Committee for Antimonopoly Policy (SCAP) in Russia as well. The factors behind this lack of contact are many and varied, and not all of them are amenable to technical assistance. Still, increased efforts by Western and international agencies to promote the cross-fertilization of ideas and the sharing of information about "what works" would almost certainly be cost-effective and highly beneficial. In some cases, inter-agency communication could be dramatically improved by such relatively simple changes as the purchase, installation, and maintenance of telecommunications hardware and software. Subsidizing the production and dissemination of the bulletins and reports regularly issued now by most of the competition agencies could provide a large return for a relatively small investment. While these problems may not be burning concerns in the Central European competition agencies, they do seem to have a good deal of significance for the territorial SCAP administrations—a number of whom are responsible for regions greater (in area) than all of Central Europe combined.

Natural Monopoly Regulation. Problems of regulating natural monopolies in the post-communist context appear repeatedly in this book. Simply put, many of these countries are barely at the starting point in developing comprehensive frameworks for regulating natural monopolies. It is perhaps symbolic that Poland, the first post-communist economy to create a competition office (in 1987), had by mid-1995 not even been able to pass the legislation needed to create this framework. This state of affairs is the result of a number of factors, including: (1) the influential lobbies that represent many natural monopoly sectors (e.g., electric power generation, transportation, etc.); (2) the perception that antitrust (as opposed to regulatory) institutions and policies need to be developed first in the post-communist economies; and (3) the fact that monopoly regulation is itself undergoing something of a conceptual and policy revolution in the United States and other developed capitalist economies. Sectors like telecommunications and power generation that have traditionally been regarded as natural monopolies are now increasingly undergoing deregulation, and are being subjected to new sources of competition.

Since much of the "conventional wisdom" on natural monopoly seems to have evaporated in the past few years, technical assistance has been less able to offer easy answers to questions of post-communist natural monopoly regulation. While this reticence is understandable, it has had some unfortunate consequences. As described by Vladimir Capelik and Ben Slay in Chapter 3 (for the Russian case), the vacuum that results from the lack of well-defined policies towards natural monopolies has all too frequently been filled by clumsy systems of rate regulation that are more reminiscent of the old system than the new. There is therefore an urgent need for technical assistance programs that can pull together contemporary and appropriate descriptions of the regulatory (and deregulatory) trends in such sectors as telecommunications, rail and water transport, electric power generation and distribution, or municipal water and sewage treatment, in various developed (and developing) capitalist economies.

Dominant Firm Regulation

It is often argued (by Americans) that the emphasis on dominant firm regulation universally apparent in post-communist competition law is mistaken. According to this view, large firms should not be penalized for their size, which may be the result of current or past market successes. Furthermore, regulating the prices and profits of firms judged to be "dominant" may promote inefficiencies within these firms or lead to regulatory capture, reduce the probability of entry, and/or create unequal conditions between incumbent firms and entrants. While all this may (or may not) be true, dominant firm regulation does play an important role in Western European, as well as in Eastern European (and Mongolian) competition law and policy; it is not going to go away. Therefore, concerns about dominant firm regulation are perhaps best directed towards suggestions for appropriately adapting this framework to the problems facing post-communist competition agencies. One such suggestion is provided by Janusz A. Ordover, Russell W. Pittman, and Paul Clyde in Chapter 6: the competition laws' treatment of dominant firms could be used by competition agencies to initiate the more sophisticated regulation of natural monopolies. While this may not be the optimal approach to natural monopoly regulation, it would allow competition offices to circumnavigate some of the problems posed by the current lack of specialized natural-monopoly legislation and regulatory institutions.

Competition Advocacy and Coalition Building

As is described above, promoting market-friendly, pro-competitive economic policies has emerged as one of the post-communist competition agencies' most important tasks. However, the competition offices' allies in this battle–which were never numerous–have tended to dwindle over time. The resulting declines in political support can render competition policy partly or wholly ineffective. This places a premium on the competition offices' abilities to develop new political coalitions in support of pro-competitive economic policies. Potential alliances (or at least effective working relationships) with such pro-competitive actors as the news media, importers, consumer protection organizations, and progressive local governments constitute something of an untapped vein of political support. To be sure, the search for this support is not without risks, the most important of which is the possible politicization (or perception therein) of competition policy. Also, a political strategy emphasizing attracting public support for competition policy initiatives could push competition offices further in the direction of emphasizing price regulation, thereby reinforcing the popular perception that competition policy is really about keeping prices down. Still, the search for new sources of political support is almost certainly worth the effort. (This may be slightly less pressing for the Central European countries, for whom the likelihood of eventually joining the European Union means that they will eventually be subject to the strictures of the EU Competition Commission.)

Notes

1. Starodubrovskaya 1994:6.

2. If, on the other hand, price increases occur in the relatively competitive sectors as well as the monopolized sectors, this means that stabilization efforts are ineffective, and the root cause of the inflationary problem is unambiguously macroeconomic, not microeconomic.

3. See, for example, Starodubrovskaya (1994:9) for survey data showing increased importance of competitive market forces in Russia during 1992 and 1993.

4. Brown, Ickes, and Ryterman 1993. It should be emphasized that this is the author's interpretation of the work in question.

5. Fornalczyk 1993:37.

6. This can be viewed as an aspect of a more general argument, according to which the cause of de-monopolization is served every time property is removed from the control of that all-encompassing monopolist, the state. According to this view, "every act of privatization is simultaneously an act of de-monopolization" (Leitzel 1994:26).

7. This conflict would exist in the presence of domestic, as well as foreign, strategic investors. What is needed is a single actor (or a small, cohesive group of actors) interested in, and capable of, successfully lobbying for higher import protection as a *quid pro quo* for paying a higher price for the state enterprise(s) undergoing privatization. Since transitional economies do not generally possess large privately-owned domestic firms, these strategic investors are invariably multinational corporations.

8. This occurred in the Polish and Hungarian automobile industries, for example.

9. For a recent overview of the relationship between the economics and politics of the post-communist transition, see Bunce 1995.

10. Newbery and Kattuman 1992:319.

11. For more on technical assistance programs for post-communist economies provided by Western and international agencies, see Hardt and Kaufman 1995:Section II.

12. See Caves *et al.* 1992.

References

Brown, A.N., B.W. Ickes, and R. Ryterman. 1994. "The Myth of Monopoly: A New View of Industrial Structure in Russia." Policy Research Working Paper No. 1331. Washington D.C.: World Bank.

Bunce, V. 1995. "Sequencing of Political and Economic Reforms," in Hardt, J.P., and R.F. Kaufman, eds., *East-Central European Economies in Transition.* Pp. 49-63. Armonk, New York: M.E. Sharpe.

Caves, R.E., *et al.*, eds. 1992. *Industrial Efficiency in Six Nations.* Cambridge, Massachusetts: MIT Press.

Fornalczyk, A. 1993. "Competition Policy in the Polish Economy in Transition," in Estrin, S., and M. Cave, eds., *Competition and Competition Policy: A Comparative Analysis of Central and Eastern Europe.* Pp. 28-43. London: Pinter Publishers.

Hardt, J.P., and R.F. Kaufman, eds. 1995. *East-Central European Economies in Transition.* Armonk, New York: M.E. Sharpe.

Leitzel, J. 1994. "A Note on Monopoly and Russian Economic Reform." *Communist Economies and Economic Transition* 1: 45-53.

Newbery, D.M., and P. Kattuman. 1992. "Market Concentration and Competition in Eastern Europe." *The World Today* 2: 315-34.

Starodubrovskaya, I. 1994. "The Nature of Monopoly and Barriers to Entry in Russia." *Communist Economies and Economic Transition* 1: 3-18.

About the Contributors

Vladimir Capelik is Director of the Program on Natural Monopolies of the Ministry of the Economy in Moscow, and Leading Research Fellow at the Institute of the Economy in Transition. During 1993-1994 he worked as a Deputy Head of Department in the Russian government's Working Center of Economic Reform.

Paul Clyde is an economist in the Competition Policy Section of the Antitrust Division of the U.S. Department of Justice. He spent 1990 as a resident advisor in the Antimonopoly Offices of the Czech and Slovak Republics. He received his Ph.D. from UCLA in 1990.

William E. Kovacic is Professor of Law at the George Mason University School of Law in Arlington, Virginia, where his teaching responsibilities include antitrust, consumer protection, and unfair competition. Professor Kovacic has worked on technical assistance projects relating to antitrust and consumer protection in Mongolia, Morocco, Nepal, Russia, Ukraine, and Zimbabwe.

Janusz A. Ordover is Professor of Economics at New York University. He has also served as a Visiting Professor in the Yale University School of Organization and Management in 1989-90, and was Deputy Assistant Attorney General for Economics in the Antitrust Division of the U.S. Justice Department in 1991-92. He received his Ph.D. from Columbia University in 1973.

Russell W. Pittman is Chief of the Competition Policy Section in the Antitrust Division of the U.S. Department of Justice. He received his Ph.D. from the University of Wisconsin in 1979.

Ben Slay is Assistant Professor of Economics at Middlebury College in Middlebury, Vermont. He is author of a number of works on the post-communist economic transition, and is editor of *Russian and East European Finance and Trade*. He received his Ph.D. from Indiana University in 1989.

Robert S. Thorpe since January 1994 has been Director of the IRIS NIS-Market Environment Project in the Department of Economics at the University of Maryland at College Park. In 1991 he joined IRIS, whose Principal Investigator is Professor Mancur Olson, as Director of Field Programs, and it was in this capacity he went to Mongolia. Prior to coming to IRIS Mr. Thorpe practiced antitrust, telecommunications and trade regulation law as associate and partner at the Washington law firm of Arnold & Porter.

Ádám Török is Director of the Hungarian Academy of Science's Institute of Industrial Economics in Budapest, and Editor-in-Chief of the quarterly *Ipargazdasági Szemle* (Review of Industrial Economics). He is also a Professor of Industrial Economics at Janus Pannonius University in Pécs, and serves as the Hungarian co-ordinator of a World Bank project on enterprise behavior in transition economies. Dr. Török is currently an advisor to the Hungarian Ministry of Industry and Trade, and was the Chairman of the Hungarian National Bank Supervisory Board.

Erik Whitlock received his Ph.D. in Economics in 1993 while working as an economics analyst at Radio Free Europe/Radio Liberty's Research Institute. At the time of researching his chapter, he was deputy financial director at Vegyépszer Ltd. in Budapest. He is currently part the Moscow-based consulting team of the Program on Natural Monopolies sponsored by the Russian Federation's Ministry of Economy and financed by the United States Agency for International Development.

About the Book

Even in developed capitalist economies, markets function poorly without regulation by competitive forces. The countries that once were part of the Eastern bloc are introducing market forces into industries created according to the monopolistic logic of central planning, so that competition policy plays an important role in the transition to capitalism.

This interdisciplinary study examines how barriers to the development of competitive markets and competition policy are being overcome in Russia, Poland, Hungary, and Mongolia. A group of U.S., Russian, and East European specialists explores the institutions and programs of competition policy as well as its role in the overall post-Communist transition. Providing a complete, comparative picture of the development of competition policy in a broad cross section of formerly socialist countries, the contributors consider the extent of the post-Communist monopoly problem as well as progress in de-monopolization.

Index